Charting Your Path to Full

Charting Your Path to Full

A Guide for Women Associate Professors

Vicki L. Baker

Foreword by Pamela L. Eddy

Rutgers University Press

New Brunswick, Camden, and Newark, New Jersey, and London

Library of Congress Cataloging-in-Publication Data
Names: Baker, Vicki L., 1978– author.
Title: Charting your path to full : a guide for women associate professors / Vicki L. Baker.
Description: New Brunswick : Rutgers University Press, 2020. |
Includes bibliographical references and index.
Identifiers: LCCN 2019025790 | ISBN 9781978805934 (paperback) |
ISBN 9781978805941 (hardback) | ISBN 9781978805958 (epub) |
ISBN 9781978805965 (mobi) | ISBN 9781978805972 (pdf)
Subjects: LCSH: Women college teachers—Professional relationships. |
Women in higher education. | Mentoring in education.
Classification: LCC LB2332.3 .B254 2020 | DDC 378.1/2082—dc23
LC record available at https://lccn.loc.gov/2019025790

A British Cataloging-in-Publication record for this book is available from the British Library.

∞ The paper used in this publication meets the requirements of the American National Standard for
Information Sciences—Permanence of Paper for Printed Library Materials, ANSI Z39.48-1992.

www.rutgersuniversitypress.org

Manufactured in the United States of America.

To all the women academics managing multiple roles and taking care of everyone else first

Contents

Foreword by Pamela L. Eddy   ix

Note on the Text   xiii

Introduction   1

1   What Is Your Joy?   14

2   Organization, Organization, Organization   38

3   Let the Performance Speak for Itself   65

4   Take Control of Your Narrative   92

5   Smallest Publishable Unit   116

6   Mapping Your Mentoring Network   136
    Laura Gail Lunsford

7   Developing Your Persuasive Voice   162
    Karen Erlandson

8   Looking Ahead   188

Acknowledgments   217

References   219

Index   239

Foreword

This volume is a much-needed addition to help women understand the ongoing saga of faculty work and the complexity inherent in faculty career pathways. Vicki Baker provides a front-row seat into the life experiences of women on the road to full professorship. Her effortless and articulate narrative prose provides access to what is, in reality, a very complex topic. Midcareer and midlevel leadership are underresearched areas in higher education, and inclusion of a wider span of literature from business and management is necessary to locate best practices. Baker's disciplinary background and faculty work in management gives her a unique perspective to investigate this stage of the faculty pathway and borrows best practices from the human resources field.

Individual women experience career stages in ways that are unique to their own practice, yet commonalities and general markers of the pathway from associate professor to full professor exist. Baker adds the voices of others on the faculty pathway to her own in order to showcase a vivid picture of the lives of women and the juggling act required during this career stage. Men at the same stage professionally will relate to some of the arguments presented, but the gendered norms of faculty work in higher education present unique challenges for women in particular. Women more often take on childcare responsibilities (Hochschild and Machung 2012), not to mention the actual birthing process. Women are also measured against ideal worker norms (Acker 1990; Williams 2000) built on the premise that someone is at home taking care of the tasks to keep home life running smoothly. Once reaching tenure, many women do not prepare for or seek full professorship. Pointedly, women represent 45 percent of associate professors across all institutional types and only 32 percent of full professors (NCES 2017). Baker's work seeks to address the leaky pipeline for women on the way to full by providing a clearer road map and strategies for success. Perhaps most hopeful in this volume is the lack of judgment if women decide *not* to seek full professor but rather to find what brings them personal and professional fulfillment. This value of choice and the goal of identifying what gives a woman professor joy in her work is refreshing and begins to chip away at ideal worker norms that outline a particular and narrower type of work deemed most valued.

Midcareer faculty can thrive due to their own agency and when institutions remove barriers and institute supportive programming. At midcareer, "opportunities" for service and leadership abound (Neumann 2009, 94) and are often unevenly done by women faculty members. Yet, as Anna Neumann (2009) notes, not all opportunities are worthwhile to pursue. Choices must be made. This volume provides templates to identify just what brings passion to the work that midcareer women faculty engage in and to help prioritize the ultimate goals they identify to pursue. The symbiotic relationship between a thriving employee base and a thriving institution recognizes the importance of faculty growth to overall outcomes. In supporting a growth model for faculty work, KerryAnn O'Meara, Aimee LaPointe Terosky, and Anna Neumann (2008) outline four areas: learning, agency, professional relationships, and commitments. Baker's writing supports each of these components and furthers the work of faculty growth by providing specific tactics to address each area. Identifying what brings oneself joy starts the journey to building the type of career that is fulfilling. It also contributes to student learning and knowledge creation and provides real-life contributions. Knowing the rules of promotion and identifying what is valued at one's institution helps build the roadmap for how women move from midcareer to full professor.

The voices scattered throughout this book shape a counternarrative to what exactly constitutes a fulfilling career and work to chip away at ideal worker norms. For example, it is well documented that having children extracts a bigger cost for women faculty relative to men (Mason, Wolfinger, and Goulden 2013), but recognizing family as a priority and the need to integrate work and life (Lester 2015) recasts the discourse. Clearly, a toxic culture that is built around the concept of working at all cost results in the loss of talent, whereas an institutional culture that builds a thriving environment for employees provides both personal employee growth *and* better institutional outcomes (Pinder 2014). Providing templates and prompts for individual women to work through as they contemplate career planning allows individuals to envision how they can do the work necessary for advancement. This book empowers the reader to identify and achieve greater goals, both professionally and personally.

Readers will enjoy seeing a range of viable strategies to employ, as one can start immediately with planning and organizing work more intentionally by reading any single chapter. A focus on organization includes tips on managing overflowing email boxes, tracking important components for promotion dossiers, and building critical networks to advance one's work. Each chapter makes it feel like so much is possible. The handy to-do lists in the chapters help focus attention and apply ideas to practice immediately. Full professors and department chairs will glean ways to best support junior faculty but will also find ideas regarding how to think about their own career and work. The key is not assuming that faculty members know what is required for advancement. When full professors share their advice, future generations of faculty members benefit.

Woven throughout this volume is the way in which organizational structure and processes impede women and underrepresented faculty members. The challenge for department chairs and other college administrators is to take a close look at the barriers present for the advancement of women. Telling is the ways in which some of these barriers are not overt but rather insidiously located in microdiscourse that devalues or judges women poorly (Eddy and Ward 2017). Forms of second-generation bias (Sturm 2001) result in implicit bias that holds male norms as the gold standard and leaves women questioning their worth (Sandberg 2013). Baker's volume helps highlight how gender bias exists in student evaluations, the rigor of scholarship assessments, and the uneven distribution of service. Colleges and universities remain gendered organizations (Acker 1990), but by providing women and other underrepresented faculty members with tools to address inherent injustices, change can begin to occur. Peeking inside the black box of promotion and tenure increases pathway transparency and allows individuals to build their own road to a successful and satisfying career. Tricks, such as focusing on the smallest publishable unit and seeking out micromentoring opportunities, provide the bricks to build the pathway forward. The coverage of experiences of faculty working in community colleges, liberal arts colleges, comprehensive universities, and high-research universities reveals that the challenges facing women's advancement is found throughout the higher-education sector.

The central message of this book is that building a career pathway requires identifying priorities and making choices. Not making a choice is a choice, but this outcome is not always recognized by people in the trenches who are subsumed by the work of the day. Taking the time to read this volume gives the reader permission to reflect on how everyday choices contribute to long-term career outcomes. The groundbreaking work of Kelly Ward and her longtime collaborator Lisa Wolf-Wendel (2012) on academic motherhood reverberates throughout this volume, as Baker's new work pays homage to this prior foundation by extending strategies to the midcareer stage. Baker is a pracademic—a practitioner who is also an academic scholar (see chapter 6). This type of scholar is much needed today, as higher education is buffeted by so many challenges resulting in mounting pressure for faculty work. This book should be given to every woman upon promotion and tenure to associate professor to help plan for the future!

Pamela L. Eddy, Professor and Department Chair
The College of William & Mary

Note on the Text

In an effort to illustrate the institutional diversity represented by the women featured in this book, I share the Carnegie classification (http://carnegieclassifications.iu.edu) of educational institutions rather than specific institution names. Pseudonyms and divisions (e.g., social sciences), rather than discipline, are noted for the clients and research participants, in order to protect their identities.

Charting Your Path to Full

Introduction

I remember the moment painfully well. It was during the summer of 2014. As my spring sabbatical concluded, I was still working feverishly on writing projects—nine to be exact—that needed to be completed before starting on writing projects for the fall term. I decided to visit my family in Pennsylvania for a brief getaway while my husband worked his crazy "sun up until sun down" hours, seven days a week at the golf course of which he is now general manager. I had a fifteen-month-old daughter and a second child on the way. I was tired but determined to prove that my sabbatical was productive and that motherhood was not going to slow me down. Looking back, I am not sure whom I felt the need to prove that to. Nonetheless, I kept my eye on the full professor prize that was a mere two years away, with regard to both my eligibility and my intended goal.

I am fortunate, as a working mother, to have the flexibility that a career in the academy affords, as well as the means for child care. During my sabbatical and early months of motherhood, I worked in my upstairs bedroom with the door closed while the nanny cared for my daughter downstairs. I experienced the best of both worlds. I could focus on my sabbatical projects while being home to get lunch ready, give a hug if needed, or hold a hand while my daughter fell asleep for her nap. But what I perceived as balance was something completely different to my young daughter.

On one summer day, I sat on the back patio with my mother and daughter. My mother whispered that she would happily watch my daughter while I ran to the mall to go shopping. I craved alone time and needed to get some new clothes for the school year, so I jumped at the chance and enjoyed my two peaceful, yet guilt-ridden, hours away. I came home, however, to a story that rocked my world and made me reevaluate my approach to my career and motherhood.

At first, my daughter had not realized I had left because she was so engrossed in playing with her beloved nana. After some time, however, she noticed and became visibly upset. My mother tried to calm her and explain that I was gone, but my determined daughter searched the house anyway. She hobbled up the stairs, like a fifteen-month-old does, and arrived at my bedroom door. It was then and there that my daughter's perception of my so-called balanced arrangement became fully apparent. She turned to my mother, pointed to the closed door, and said "mama" while motioning as if she were typing on a laptop, confident I had to be in that room doing work.

It is the moment I will never forget, the moment my heart broke when my mother shared that story. My bedroom work sessions at our home in Michigan, with the door closed while I worked, clearly left quite an impression on my young daughter. This reaction from my daughter was an unfortunate but necessary assessment of my mis-guided strategy for managing motherhood and a career, with full pro-fessorship in sight. And it was not a good assessment. The truth was, I had no idea how to manage this phase of life and career while working toward the long-desired professional goal of full professorship. I had to make changes, to refocus my efforts to align with my realities, to be clear about whom I owed something to, and to enjoy what would be fleeting—being the mother of a beautiful fifteen-month-old daughter and, soon, a son too.

The Road to Charting Your Path to Full

Any mid-career professional will tell you that being left alone in a new organization is the last thing that they want or need.

—Athena Vongalis-Macrow (2011)

My scholarly agenda has aligned, and evolved, with my professional career stages. My dissertation research focused on understanding the doctoral-student experience in business. Specifically, I was eager to learn how not to be one of the 50 percent of doctoral students who became attrition statistics (Smallwood 2004). I wanted to learn about how they developed professional identities as future scholars and practitioners in relation to their social networks. The students I studied served as members of my own network and allowed me to gain some valuable lessons.

As I started my career as a tenure-track assistant professor at Albion College, I became very interested in early-career faculty socialization, particularly in the context of liberal arts colleges (LACs), given the very visible disconnects between how most doctoral students are trained at research-intensive universities and the realities of faculty life in LACs (Austin 2002; Baker, Lunsford, and Pifer 2017). I experienced this disconnect firsthand early in my career. My passion for studying the professoriate was influenced by this disconnect and, in part, inspired during faculty meetings. I took copious notes about the challenges we as faculty members discussed and the issues we felt compelled to focus on related to teaching and learning given our institutional mission. Scholarly and research expectations were also increasing, revealing an even greater divide between available resources and rising expectations (e.g., internal funding, a grants officer). Many of us struggled with how to manage a research or scholarly agenda with the demands of an LAC environment that tasked faculty to be effective teachers, mentors, advisers, and engaged community members. I felt confident that if we, at Albion College, were having these conversations, so too were faculty members at other institutions. These beginning years of observation and note-taking led me to embark on my scholarly agenda to date: understanding the faculty experience and aligning institutional goals and priorities with individuals' needs to create a more strategic, diversified portfolio of faculty-development supports (Baker, Lunsford, and Pifer 2017).

Midcareer: Depressing or Rejuvenating

Once I earned tenure, I experienced the common "what's next" moment. Clearing the tenure hurdle resulted in some freedom and flexibility, only to be slowed down by the realization that I had another, less clearly defined hurdle ahead: full professorship. What I found, however, was little to no support on how to manage this stage of my career (and life). As a management professor, I knew of other industries and the career-development supports that organizational leaders invested in to support their midcareer professionals. I began researching tips and strategies about how to manage this phase. What I found, particularly in higher-education literature, was depressing but relatable.

The midcareer stage has been described as evolving and, at times, is marred by conflicting roles and responsibilities (Clarke, Hyde, and Drennan 2013). A belief permeates the academy that once tenure is achieved, mentorship at the midcareer stage is no longer needed because the achievement of promotion and tenure means you are now an expert. Such a belief is misguided (Rockquemore 2011). Individuals need look no further than institutional policies and practices related to faculty-development supports to see, and experience, the implications of such a belief. More concerted efforts and programming are devoted to supporting early-career faculty, as compared to their mid- and late-career peers, in their pursuit of promotion and tenure (see, for example, Sorcinelli 2000).

Administrative and service expectations increase at the midcareer stage, particularly for women and other underrepresented populations, resulting in diminishing scholarly productivity (Misra and

Lundquist 2015a). Combine these rising work responsibilities with family, child-care, or elder-care responsibilities, and women associate professors often struggle to manage a successful career and home life that does not result in giving short shrift to either.

I have worked and interacted with many women associate professors who are either firmly in the midcareer stage or are new to the club. And yet the feelings shared by these women about the midcareer stage are consistent, regardless of discipline, institution type, or time in rank as associate professors. I share a few of the sentiments communicated to me here and ask you, the reader, if they sound familiar:

1 "I just hit this stage . . . so many concerns. This part feels more uncertain, for lack of a better word. Like, I can't just follow a certain formula to success. I know service will increase now but not sure how much is appropriate to say no to."

2 "More service and mentoring, more babies :). But same amount of teaching and time [hours] in the day! Hard to balance it all."

3 "I'm at associate level and am struggling not just with the work/life balance that has gotten more complicated since tenure. (I gave birth to my second kid one month after receiving my tenure notification.) The extra service burden/expectations, plus the additional graduate students I now support, make finding time for research and writing even more difficult than before. There's also the culture in my department of scrutinizing female faculty's work and encouraging them to delay personnel actions."

4 "I'm not willing to short shrift family time like I did to get tenure and I feel like a slacker. Early career opportunities abounded but midcareer opportunities seem scarcer (like sabbatical funding that doesn't require splitting up my family, since my spouse works full-time). And I still don't really know which service duties are both family friendly yet have a high return on time invested."

More recently, scholars and practitioners have revealed a deep desire and interest displayed by midcareer faculty to learn more, to seek developmental opportunities, and to have access to faculty-development supports that help hone formal and informal leadership skills (Baker, Lunsford, and Pifer 2017; Beaubouef, Erickson, and Thomas 2017; Strage and Merdinger 2015). Yet, when the realities of work and life intersect and developmental opportunities and expectations are either absent or unclear, the end result is midcareer faculty members "at a standstill" (Misra and Lundquist 2015b), with no plans or pathway toward full professorship. Researchers have revealed that women, in particular, either opt out or fall victim to the promotion process (Baker, Lunsford, and Pifer 2019b; Rommel and Bailey 2017; Wolfinger, Mason, and Goulden 2008). The scholars Kelly Ward and Lisa Wolf-Wendel share, "We were dismayed at the limited number of women who weren't preparing for promotion to full professor even though they were eligible (or nearly eligible) for advancement" (2012, 73).

Flipping the Script on Midcareer

Despite these challenges plaguing the midcareer stage, of which there are many, I also see the midcareer stage as an opportunity to re-envision the next phase of the faculty career, regardless of whether the aspiration is full professorship or otherwise. If approached from a different frame of mind, the midcareer stage can be used as an opportunity to take some professional risks; to reenvision oneself as a teacher, scholar, community contributor, and future administrator; and to be honest with oneself about what matters and why.

When my colleagues and I edited a volume geared specifically toward supporting midcareer faculty members, we offered insights into the unique and thoughtful ways in which institutions and their leaders develop their midcareer faculties. We reached out to scholars and practitioners across a range of institution types, domestic and abroad, to learn more about the ways in which midcareer faculty are supported on their respective campuses (Baker et al. 2019). We found and featured programming aimed at achieving a variety of goals, whether it be to support leadership development, scholarly pursuits, teaching and learning or to cultivate a network of support from similar others. What our volume does not address, however, is the nuts and bolts of how to manage this phase of the faculty career from an individual perspective in pursuit of advancement to full, continuing contract status, or other professional goals.

Based on 2015 National Center for Education Statistics data, of the 1.6 million faculty members in the United States, 52 percent are full-time and 48 percent part-time. These data reveal a total of 157,799 associate professors in the United States, 55 percent of whom were men and 45 percent women. There were a total of 173,031 assistant professors in the United States; 49 percent were men, 51 percent women. Faculty-rank-based data revealed a total of 182,204 full professors in the United States; 68 percent were men, 32 percent women. Of those full-time faculty members, 35 percent were white women, 4 percent were Asian / Pacific Islander women, 3 percent were Black women, and 2 percent were Hispanic women (NCES 2015).

On the basis of these data, there were more women assistant professors as compared to men in the United States. However, as we move through the ranks of associate and full professor, the proportion of women in the academy at these higher ranks drops significantly. Understanding the cause of this leaking pipeline is *important* (Baker, Lunsford, and Pifer 2019b; Wolfinger, Mason, and Goulden 2008); and supporting these women in their efforts to advance in the academy is *critical*. "Faculty need to stay vital at all stages for institutions to be functional" (Ward and Wolf-Wendel 2012, 76).

Owning and Informing My Perspective

Before sharing the goals and motivations for writing this book, I need to acknowledge a few key issues. First, I write this book as a management professor who studies the faculty experience in higher education. To accomplish this work, I draw from management, leadership, human resources, positive organizational psychology, and higher-education literatures to inform my thinking and career-management strategies offered across the chapters. The insights, recommendations, tools, tips, and strategies offered throughout this book are grounded and informed by literature, original research, consulting work, and the experiences and voices of the women associate professors I have the great fortune to work with. I also rely on and include data from two mixed-methods studies of midcareer faculty (Baker, Lunsford, and Pifer 2017; Baker, Lunsford, and Pifer 2019b). I also conducted a study focused solely on women from a range of institution types and disciplines who have already achieved full professorship or continuing contract status, to support the ideas and advice shared in chapter 8 of this book. In addition, I draw on case studies from my consulting work and the leadership, mentoring, and career-advancement workshops I conduct with faculty members. Many of the basic principles and recommendations offered in this book often transcend discipline and institution type, though examples of specific disciplines and institutions are shared to ensure that this book is a resource for women throughout the academy.

Second, I cannot stress enough the importance of cultivating your own network of individuals who are supportive, know your strengths and weaknesses, and hold you accountable for your professional and personal goals. Women faculty members have been instrumental throughout my career, with a few very important male mentors included. In particular, I worked closely with two women academics (coauthors and dear friends) who were at a similar career stage, who were equally motivated, and who shared similar work styles but who also offered complementary skill sets.

Lastly, I want to be clear that working toward full professorship, continuing contract status, administrative positions, or any professional goal, for that matter, takes effort. And I do not want to suggest that simply following what I and my associates have outlined will result in automatic success and the attainment of your career goals. Rather, such aspirations require a great deal of discipline, sacrifice, work, and personal agency, defined as strategic perspectives or actions toward goals that matter to the professor (Terosky, O'Meara and Campbell, 2014). The goal, however, is to make sure that the effort feels less like a never-ending obligation and more like a fulfilling journey.

The Reason for This Book

For the past decade, I have engaged deeply in research focused on the faculty experience and faculty development. This work has taken me to many campuses and afforded me the opportunity to connect with many bright, thoughtful women who have inspired me along my journey to full, including a group of women at the College of Wooster who inspired this book.

Two colleagues and I developed and delivered the Academic Leadership Institute for midcareer faculty in the Great Lakes Colleges Association (Baker, Lunsford, and Pifer 2019a). We worked with eighteen men and women at the associate professor rank seeking support in identifying, articulating, and achieving their career goals. Each participant was required to develop a leadership plan. Two of our participants proposed creating a faculty learning committee for women associate professors, which they planned to offer and cofacilitate on their campus upon their completion of the Academic Leadership Institute. I am proud to share that these women achieved the goals outlined as part of their leadership plans in the Academic Leadership Institute and earned a grant to host the faculty learning committee for women associate professors at the College of Wooster. As part of their efforts, they invited me to spend two days on their campus working with participants individually and in pairs and large groups. On the second day, my engagement with these women inspired me so much so that I emailed the editors I had worked with previously at Rutgers University Press to share the idea for this book. I discovered my joy— to help others achieve their goals—as I continue to reenvision the next phase of my academic career.

Goal for Charting Your Path to Full

The goal for writing this book is simple: to provide a resource for women associate professors as they work toward full professorship. I am a wife, a mother of two, and part of a dual-career couple, and I have primary financial and child-care responsibilities. I am employed in a very male-dominated academy, discipline, and department. I share this about myself to illustrate the myriad roles, identities, and responsibilities that define my life and mirror those of my women peer professors. Single parent, single woman, woman of color, queer woman faculty member, and primary caregiver also define women faculty members. These are the very identities that influence women's lived experiences in the academy.

Throughout this book, I offer a woman-focused perspective and insights into the challenges that we women still face in the academy. A resource developed featuring women's specific needs and challenges as they seek career advancement in the academy is long overdue. This is not to say that men cannot find this book a valuable resource; in fact, men at the associate level have also found great value in the framework I provide. However, I, along with my associates, take great care in sharing data, literature, vignettes, and lessons learned that highlight women-specific issues, and we tailor our message, action steps, and support accordingly.

I still practice the advice shared throughout this book regularly and think about how I can use these ideas to support my current and future efforts. Despite earning full professorship, I still have over two decades of my career ahead of me. It is depressing, to say the least, to think that I have achieved all that is possible in the academy from an incentive-based perspective. A motto I live by and communicate every semester to my students is, "Don't expect things of others that you are unwilling to do yourself." When I meet with clients, I walk them through this framework and demonstrate examples of how I enact it in the context of my discipline and institution. I live this framework in my day-to-day work, and it has helped me succeed professionally. Perhaps more important, however, is the freedom it has provided me to be selective about the projects I pursue, so that my family also knows and feels their value in my life.

How to Use This Book

Before I offer advice on how to use this book, I propose two essential recommendations. First, be clear about your professional goals. Do you seek to earn full professorship or continuing contract status? Do you aspire for administrative opportunities? I have worked with many associate professors who are interested in reenvisioning the next phase but have little desire to work toward full professorship as a result of burnout felt after going through multiple reviews or due to the lack of incentives to pursue full professorship at their respective institutions. Regardless of your end goal, this book can provide you with resources, tips, and strategies to work toward full professorship or continuing contract status or to help you craft an engaging career. Second, you need to be clear about what is expected of you by your institution to meet these goals, such as earning full professorship or continuing contract status, related to categories, time in rank, and process. For me, that meant referring to the faculty handbook at Albion College and reviewing the categories in which I had to exhibit "excellence," including value to students and my department, scholarly development, and campus-wide contributions.

Many associate professors I have worked with, individually or in groups, have been uncertain of what their institutional categories are, the process by which the evaluation occurs, the time frame in which someone is eligible for advancement, or even where to find this information. This reality is confirmed in research by others who are interested in understanding and supporting midcareer faculty (Ward and Wolf-Wendel 2012). In order to work toward a goal, clarity about the factors that contribute to that goal is critical.

Chapter Overview

The book has been written in such a way that the chapters can be read in sequence or can serve as stand-alone resources. If you are newly tenured and trying to get a jump on how to manage this phase of your career, I suggest reading the chapters in sequence, to start with the basics and build on them, given that each chapter provides the needed scaffolding to get started. Or you may be someone who is nearing the minimum time required at the associate rank before submitting your dossier for full professorship and are therefore needing help to organize your narrative and communicate your contributions with impact. If this is you, starting with targeted chapters may be most useful. Regardless of your personal goals and time in the midcareer stage, this book will provide you with support.

Chapter 1, "What Is Your Joy?," asks a simple yet powerful question to help you reframe and refocus your energies on the aspects of your career in which you find the most fulfillment. When one's job feels less like work, productivity and associated outcomes are likely to increase. The goal is to help you use joy, not institutional drivers and expectations, as the motivation behind your professional and personal decisions. Chapter 2, "Organization, Organization, Organization," is very action oriented and gives you guidance on how to develop a tailored organizational structure for success. Crafting a compelling and powerful narrative requires you to organize the evidence you must present as part of your dossier. Chapter 3, "Let the Performance Speak for Itself," is rooted in research and practice to illustrate the challenges women face in negotiating and advocating for themselves in the workplace. Strategies are shared to help you quantify contributions in the areas that matter to you and your institution and to show how you can use the voices of others as evidence to tell your story.

Chapter 4, "Take Control of Your Narrative," aims to help you define the categories important to earning full professorship or continuing contract status in the context of your joy and value added. Chapter 5, "Smallest Publishable Unit," introduces a framework situated in Ernest Boyer's (1990) forms of scholarship, in which you focus on an aspect of your work (often already on hand) in order to highlight key findings or takeaways in separate publishable pieces and to varied audiences. Chapter 6, "Mapping Your Mentoring Network," is a how-to guide in understanding your strengths and weaknesses and the needed areas of support. Guidance is offered to cultivate a network of mentors to support your path to full. Chapter 7, "Developing Your Persuasive Voice," addresses the reality of the new roles and responsibilities undertaken once promotion and tenure are achieved. Advocating for yourself and others becomes a necessary aspect of the midcareer stage. Chapter 8, "Looking Ahead: Advice from the Other Side," concludes the book with stories, lessons, and advice from those women who have earned full professorship. In each chapter, additional reading suggestions are offered to supplement the research, practice, tools, and strategies featured.

CHAPTER 1

What Is Your Joy?

---

joy *noun*
    1a: the emotion evoked by well-being, success, or good fortune or by the prospect of possessing what one desires
      1b: the expression or exhibition of such emotion
      2: a state of happiness or felicity
      3: a source or cause of delight

                                      —Merriam-Webster Online

---

We all prefer to spend the majority of our time in a "state of happiness," regardless of the roles and responsibilities with which we are tasked professionally or personally. The midcareer stage has been described as one of confusion, little clarity, and diminished supports and perhaps as more challenging than the early-career stage, given the diversification) accompanying the requisite tasks compared to our experiences as early-career colleagues (Baker, Pifer, and Lunsford 2018). So that you do not continue to be bogged down by the unknown that plagues this stage of the professoriate, my goal in this chapter is to help you to refocus toward your assets and your sources of strength and to view your current activities in a different way. Simply put, I want joy to be the driver of the activities you engage in; I want joy to be the source of where your energy is derived; I want joy to be the emotion, as opposed to guilt or obligation, that steers your day-to-day activities.

In this chapter, I provide a brief overview of the midcareer stage, followed by an introduction of one of the literatures that has informed my work, called positive organizational scholarship. I provide this research grounding to help situate the field of faculty development and the midcareer stage more broadly. That grounding supports my focus on joy as an important first step to managing the midcareer stage. In the second half of the chapter, I share three activities aimed to help you refocus your efforts on those that are joyful as a necessary step to achieving your path to full professorship or continuing contract status.

Faculty Development: The Midcareer Stage

I have a two-year window in which to go up for promotion, plus I just got back from maternity leave and haven't decided whether to pause my clock. So it's really a three-year window. I don't feel like I really know the pros and cons or whom to ask for advice about the timing of the decision.

—associate professor, school of law, special focus, four year

Scholars and practitioners have sought to refocus efforts to provide greater clarity on and supports for the midcareer stage, despite scholars calling attention to this need nearly forty years ago (Baker, Pifer, and Lunsford, 2018; Baldwin and Blackburn 1981). While more research and practice have been devoted to early-career faculty (see, for example, Sorcinelli 2000; Yun, Baldi, and Sorcinelli 2016), there have been efforts to comprehend the challenges and needs of midcareer faculty. However, one of the biggest hindrances to the study and practice of the midcareer stage is lack of clarity about how to define and understand the length of this stage. For example, Roger Baldwin,

Christina Lunceford, and Kim Vanderlinden (2005) characterize the midcareer stage as having no "visible hallmarks or boundaries" (98), while Baldwin and Deborah Chang (2006) describe the midcareer stage as "long and ill-defined" (28). For institutions in which a tenure system is present, the midcareer stage is said to begin once a faculty member earns promotion and tenure (typically a seven-year period; Austin 2010). As Ann Austin notes, "While the end of mid-career is not well defined, those categorized as mid-career faculty anticipate a number of years of work still ahead of them" (365). Throughout my research, I have relied on Kiernan Mathews's (2014) two categories of midcareer faculty, early midcareer and late midcareer, to acknowledge the length of time an individual can be in the midcareer stage. This classification system offers an essential acknowledgment: those faculty members who are newly tenured have different needs and goals as compared to their associate faculty peers who have been at the associate rank for six or more years.

More recently, the work of my colleagues and me reveals that administrators and faculty members agree that providing greater supports to midcareer faculty is a priority. Yet practice has failed to meet the demand and prioritization of adding a greater depth and breadth of midcareer supports to an existing portfolio of faculty-development programming (Baker, Pifer, and Lunsford 2016). On the basis of the clients and study participations I have worked with to date, this trend appears to permeate the academy regardless of institution type. This disconnect is unfortunate in that it signals a missed opportunity to add value at the institutional and individual levels. Missed opportunities and lack of supports can lead to the lost or unmotivated midcareer faculty member featured in research about the "midcareer malaise" (Monaghan 2017).

As I teach in my management courses, organizational leaders hate to see good employees leave (but remember, not all attrition is bad attrition). Despite the cost to the organization of losing good employees, I contend that leaders should be more concerned about the disengaged employee who stays, given the associated costs to morale, productivity, and overall atmosphere. And this same general philosophy holds true for the midcareer faculty member who is burned out and disengaged and who receives little to no faculty-development supports to get out of the rut. Think about the implications of this for midcareer faculty members and the institutions that employ them. What are the implications for student learning, faculty governance, and community engagement? What are the consequences of departmental colleagues who work with or are led by a disengaged colleague and for recruiting future generations of students and faculty? These faculty members are characterized as "terminal associate professors, . . . semi-scholars, found at every institution, who made it over the hurdle of tenure and then their careers simply stalled" (Dow 2014).

Full-time women faculty members appear to experience this stalled state to a higher degree as compared to male faculty members, evinced by the decreasing numbers of women faculty at higher ranks in the academy (NCES 2015). Data published by the Higher Education Research Institute (2014) reveal that 8.2 percent of women versus 7.5 percent of men with the rank of associate professor expect to retire within the next three years; 41 percent of women versus 39.6 percent of men considered leaving academe for another job during the previous two years; and 56 percent of women versus 58.9 percent of men considered leaving their current institution for another campus. Research specific to discipline and faculty population further confirms these findings as being the result of institutional barriers and challenges, as well as personal reasons (Croom 2017; Griffin, Bennett, and Harris 2013; Modern Language Association of America 2009; Sexton et al. 2012). I agree with Natasha Croom's (2017) observation: "There is no doubt that historical practices have led to the demographics seen in the professoriate today; however, the current trends and experiences require further examination in order to understand not only the experiences womyn of color, and Black womyn specifically, but also the policies and practices that continue to create inequitable and disparaging outcomes for minoritized faculty" (563).

There is burgeoning literature about midcareer faculty agency, particularly for women and other underrepresented associate professors. What we are learning from this line of work is that institutional structures, workload challenges, and issues of fit between personal values and institutional promotion criteria influence agency negatively, while institutional interventions and engagement in self-selected professional networks support feelings of and engagement in agentic behaviors (Terosky, O'Meara, and Campbell 2014). Given my perspective as a management professor, I draw from organizational studies and human resources fields to understand the tenets of career development and the implications of employee behavior at the individual, group/team, and organizational levels. Positive organizational scholarship, particularly the notion of thriving, provides a useful lens with which to give some guidance on how to build a stronger case for investing in midcareer faculty and focusing on joy as the driver for managing one's midcareer stage.

Positive Organizational Psychology

If you give your employees the chance to learn and grow, they'll thrive—and so will your organization.

—Gretchen Spreitzer and Christine Porath (2012, 3)

Colleagues at the Ross School of Business at University of Michigan initiated positive organizational scholarship and the associated movement, which focuses on understanding the factors contributing to sustained individual and organizational performance. The goal is "to inspire and enable leaders to build high-performing organizations that bring out the best in people. We are a catalyst for the creation and growth of positive organizations" (Center for Positive Organizations, n.d.). Rather than study the negative behaviors associated with the workplace (e.g., workplace deviance, turnover, absenteeism), positive organizational scholarship seeks to identify and understand the positive behaviors that employees display and the individual and organizational conditions that encourage such behaviors. Findings and lessons learned provide tools and strategies to employees and organizational leaders to implement in their workplaces.

A focus on positive workplace behaviors, and associated tools and strategies, resonates with me and aligns with the goals of this book on a deep level. The notion of thriving provides a counternarrative about employee behavior. It shifts the focus from reducing negative workplace behaviors to learning how to support individuals' prospering at work. Spreitzer and Porath (2012) identify a thriving workplace "as one in which employees are not just satisfied and productive but also engaged in creating the future—the company's and their own. Thriving employees have a bit of an edge – they are highly energized—but they know how to avoid burnout" (4).

Thriving is described as having two components: vitality and learning. Gretchen Spreitzer and Christine Porath (2012) describe vitality as the sense of feeling alive and being passionate and enthusiastic. These feelings are self-propelling but also contagious. Despite the fact that these behaviors are driven individually, organizational leaders can encourage such behaviors by helping employees realize and feel that their daily contribution matters to the success of the organization. Learning signifies the growth that accompanies developing knowledge and skill sets. "People who are developing their abilities are likely to believe in their potential for future growth" (Spreitzer and Porath 2012, 4). The caution, however, is that learning without passion can lead to burnout; vitality on its own, without opportunities to learn and grow, can be stifling.

When the idea of thriving is situated in the context of the academy and midcareer faculty members' lived experiences, we see the following parallels:

1 The significance of moving midcareer faculty research and practice beyond the study of personal experiences to instead "examine the specific processes these [associate professors] must endure if they wish to be promoted to the next rank" (Croom 2017, 557)

2 The need to reimagine the midcareer stage as one that provides opportunities for renewal and regrowth

3 The importance of passion, joy, and excitement as individual drivers that determine how, and in what ways, the midcareer professor invests in and allocates her time

4 The reminder that learning, specifically the desire to continually learn and develop, is an attribute of the professoriate that attracts future faculty to this career (see Baker, Terosky, and Martinez 2017; Neumann 2009) and that the desire for continued learning does not disappear once promotion and tenure are achieved

5 The awareness that an engaged, vital, and committed lifelong learner at the midcareer stage contributes positively to outcomes at the individual, departmental, and institutional levels

6 The need for a deeper examination of the ways in which institutional structures and policies (e.g., family leave) act as barriers to advancement for women and other minorities in the academy

7 The need to reenvision and modernize those institutional policies and practices to reflect the current face of the professoriate

The bottom line: creating institutional environments that tap into midcareer faculty members' joy, thus facilitating thriving, is a wise investment. In order to achieve this goal, institutions and the individuals who lead them must engage in an honest assessment of institutional culture, policies, and practice, particularly from the perspective of those who are advantaged *and* disadvantaged by these structures. Providing the tools and strategies to midcareer faculty members to support their own success, which is the goal of this book, is imperative, as the academy is slow to respond to a diversifying professoriate and antiquated structures that benefit the privileged.

Why Joy?

Many [associate] faculty members do important work other than scholarship (teaching comes to mind). Their problem is that the system does not reward the work that they do, and in fact often seeks to punish them.

—full professor, natural sciences, unknown institution type

I am often asked the question, "How do I prepare for full professorship?" This query is then followed with some combination of detail about the person's lack of clarity regarding the process or associated requirements on her campus. I immediately sense the fear, confusion, and feelings of being overwhelmed accompanying this question and observation. There are many factors, some within your control, that contribute to actively managing the process to full professorship for yourself.

Gaining as much clarity about the process as it applies to your institutional setting is important but less so as a first step. Rather, I begin my time with clients and study participants by asking, "What is your joy?" While this might seem strange, or perhaps overly simplified, I have found that individuals thrive when they are honest about what their joy is, leading me to believe that this is the foundation from which all efforts to reenvision or reimagine one's career (or life choices) should emanate. I have also found that focusing on the positive, whether it be joy, meaning, or passion, leads to positive outcomes when pursuing the path to full professorship or continuing contract status. With joy as the foundation, I help women associate professors outline a thoughtful and strategic approach to crafting short- and long-term plans. That joy results in outcomes beyond just publications, outcomes that are personally meaningful. I have found that most people, particularly women, do not ask this of themselves, for fear of feeling selfish or guilty. But taking the time to ask this question, reflect on it, and plan proactively is momentous. I often say that if posing the question gives you "permission" to focus on your joy as the driver of your efforts moving forward, I will happily take on that role.

My Joy and Its Role in Decision-Making

I have found a solid rhythm in my personal and professional life, but that rhythm has certainly been the result of many trials and tribulations, including both personal and professional failures. Further, my career trajectory has seen the addition of new identities, that of wife and mother, as well as the evolution of others, including teacher, scholar, mentor, administrator, committee member, and adviser. I am very aware that this rhythm can be thrown into a tailspin, however, at any given moment depending on what is happening at work or home. For me, the role and identity that has required the greatest effort to prioritize, balance, and reconcile has been motherhood in relation to my professional roles and identities.

The challenges of motherhood in the academy are many and have been well documented. Research by Mary Ann Mason, Nicholas Wolfinger, and Marc Goulden (2013) reveals that family formation negatively affects women's academic careers; the same does not hold true for their male professor peers. In fact, having children is a career advantage for men but is a career killer for women. Mason (2013) attributes these findings to the "rigid lockstep career track [in the academy] that does not allow for time out and puts the greatest pressure on its aspirants in the critical early years." These challenges are exacerbated for single academic mothers. Susan Murray (2011) has observed that her "tenure clock and biological clock have always been eerily and problematically matched as is the case for many women in academia." In her late thirties and without a partner, she became a single, soon-to-be-tenured mother who benefited from a family-friendly department, a low teaching load (given her employment in an R1 institution), and a generous maternity-leave policy. Unfortunately, not all academic mothers or caregivers have the same supports. We can draw on Murray's experiences as a guide for the types of institutional policies that can ease the challenges of motherhood and caregiving in the academy. I too have found "that motherhood and scholarship are not mutually exclusive or antagonistic" (Ward and Wolf-Wendel 2012, 1) if the right institutional policies are in place and if one takes advantage of career-development tools, tips, and strategies to manage caregiving and career advancement successfully and simultaneously.

I acknowledge that a focus on joy is considered a luxury, one that promotion and tenure afford. And that point is not lost on me. As an early-career faculty member, I felt more pressure to accept even the most soul-sucking work projects, committee requests, and publishing opportunities. I felt I did not have the comfort of being selective because every line on the curriculum vitae (CV) was crucial to jumping the promotion and tenure hurdle. But I felt some of the pressure dissipate once I earned promotion and tenure (and motherhood also played a role, though it brought different pressures). When clients or participants ask me in return what my joy is, I respond that my joy is helping people achieve their goals and advance their careers. I find this joy with the undergraduate students I advise and mentor; I find this joy with the online and graduate-student learners I support; I find this joy with the early-career colleagues I mentor and work alongside; I find this joy with my kids, whose dreams and evolving interests I encourage; I find this joy with the other women professors seeking to earn full professorship or continuing contract status with whom I interact. From my clients, I have heard that joy comes in the form of "developing future scientists," "providing for my children," "being an effective role model for my doctoral students when it comes to work-life balance," and "having time to read and think."

While the tension between motherhood/caregiving and successfully engaging in my professional role has been salient to my experience to date, another combination of roles that causes strain for women associate professors is being an administrator as well as a scholar and teacher (Baker, Lunsford, and Pifer 2019b, 2017; Misra et al. 2011; Ward and Wolf-Wendel 2012). Look no further than the midcareer faculty experience to realize that service and administrative responsibilities increase dramatically once promotion and tenure are earned, and this focus away from scholarship causes delays in or, worse yet, lack of achievement of full professorship or continuing contract status (Baker, Lunsford, and Pifer 2017; DeZure, Shaw, and Rojewski 2014; Grant-Vallone and Ensher 2017). Joya Misra and colleagues (2011) found that male associate professors spend a greater amount of time on research (37 percent) as compared to women associate professors (25 percent). Women, on the other hand, spend a greater amount of time on service (27 percent) as compared to their male associate peers (20 percent). Service and administrative work does not carry the same weight as research and scholarly pursuits in consideration of promotion to full or continuing contract status. Because of this, "women may hit a glass ceiling near the top of the ivory tower" (Misra et al. 2011, 2). This tension is particularly challenging for women of color and other minoritized women groups in the academy given the disproportionate amount of service they engage in, and not always by choice (Matthew 2016; Misra and Lundquist 2015a; Turner 2002).

Referring back to the story I shared at the beginning of this book, my daughter's perceptions of her reality rocked me to my core. I realized the pace at which I was working was unnecessary, unhealthy, and unbalanced. I needed to engage in a reflective self-assessment about my professional goals and aspirations; I needed to be clear about the type of mother I hoped to be and the role that identity would play in my daily life; and I needed to be much more deliberate about how I charted my path to full. I committed to accepting only a set number of projects and opportunities that could be mapped across a calendar year, and those had to be rooted in my joy. Once I met my cap for the year, I declined invitations or requested changed time lines to facilitate my participation, if possible. I, as well as those I have coached, have experienced that when joy is the driver of career decisions (at least the ones you can control), you are more likely to commit to those decisions and engage in the needed efforts to achieve the desired ends. Then the related work feels less like "work." I know what does and does not bring me joy. While I cannot remove the work tasks (or colleagues) that are unaligned with my joy, concentrating on those that are joyful makes the rest more digestible (and temporary), and I feel less stressed as a result.

Getting to Your Joy: Activities and Tools

One of the things I've been thinking about is the difference between disciplinary and institutional success. I've decided I would rather make my mark in the discipline and reach success through things like building speaking engagements and giving keynotes over becoming an administrator in my institution, which usually comes with a twelve-month contract and Monday–Friday hours. I feel like this is one way I can achieve success and achieve mobility/flexibility without getting locked into one institution.

—associate professor, humanities, doctoral university, higher research activity

In this section, I outline specific tools and activities to help guide your joy-seeking efforts. These are activities that I have worked through with study participants and clients and that I have used (and continue to use) myself. I also include activities that achieve similar goals but provide an alternate approach. As a classroom teacher of a variety of student populations, I know firsthand that all teaching styles and approaches are not created equal; neither do all approaches and styles resonate with all people at all times. Therefore, I offer diverse options to help get you started with the process of building a solid foundation of joy.

Activity 1: Discovering Your Joy

Pull out a pen and paper, and write an answer to the question, "What is your joy?" Some women answer this question within five minutes; others take a week to ruminate. On first blush, this question may appear a bit broad or perhaps overwhelming, and that is okay. I have found that most of us women do not take time to explore this question thoughtfully. And the answer can fluctuate based on personal and professional realities. The focus on joy has taken many forms across resources to support women, and I find them all so valuable (Barsh, Cranston, and Lewis 2009; Krawcheck 2017). The main premise is to let meaning be the motivation in life. "By deploying your greatest strengths in service of a meaningful purpose that transcends everyday goals, you open yourself up to long-lasting happiness" (Barsh, Cranston, and Lewis 2009, 22).

If a focus on joy is a bit too intimidating at the moment, consider the following questions to get you moving in the right direction:

1 Describe what you believe your goals are in and out of the classroom, for your scholarly endeavors or service to your department, campus, and community.

2 Upon reflecting on these goals and associated activities, describe what it is about these activities that gives you the most feelings of happiness and accomplishment (also known as joy).

3 Do you envision ways of engaging in these activities more regularly? In other words, what would a typical day, week, or month look like if you were spending the majority of your time engaged in these activities that bring you joy?

4 What efforts can you make today to infuse more joy in your routine?

I have found that women associate professors tend to struggle answering these questions initially because we immediately think in the context of expectations. In other words, what is expected of us across the roles and identities we manage seems to dominate our early thinking. Expectations include not only the ones we place on ourselves, which are immense, but also the expectations that others place on us. And those expectations can be enormous when you are one of a few or the only woman or member of a minoritized group in a department, college, or institution. The accompanying burdens and "emotional and mental work" are heavy. However, if given the chance to speak one-on-one with someone we trust (or who we know has our best interests at the forefront), we feel more empowered to think big, to think in ways that may not immediately align with expectations, and to imagine the possibilities.

To help illustrate this point, I am going to share the story of a client of mine. Sarah is an associate professor at a liberal arts college (LAC). Sarah is in the social sciences, and her work provides her the opportunity to engage with a community organization. She recently assumed the role of department chair, as the only woman in the department and with little to no support. She shared some emails from departmental colleagues with me, and to say that they were unprofessional and abusive would be an understatement. Sarah expressed concerns with her provost and the dean of faculty development on her campus and has been instructed to keep working through it, given "that's how they [her male colleagues] are." When Sarah and I met, she was quite discouraged and frustrated and considering resigning as department chair effective at the end of the year, despite having two years remaining on this appointment.

After listening to Sarah share her disappointments and dissatisfaction, we turned to her short-term goal of securing a sabbatical, which was competitive and would require an application process. She was afraid, however, that it would be denied due to a lack of scholarly productivity since she had earned promotion and tenure. I urged Sarah to set both her departmental culture issues and fears aside. Instead, I asked her to tell me what brings her joy related to her work and to think about where she believes she makes the most impact. She talked about her work with a community organization that provides a service for low-income, at-risk youth in the area. As part of this work, she is able to bring her advanced students with her to provide them with experiential learning opportunities. Sarah feels a great sense of pride about this community partnership because it offers a service that no one else in the community is equipped to provide; it strengthens the relationship between the college and the community; and her students get hands-on experience relevant to their career aspirations.

As part of our discussion, I asked her to summarize in three sentences or less the value of this partnership to her professional development, as well as on the development of her students and on the community. I told her that from this point on, she needed to have this statement hanging in her office and typed at the top of her sabbatical proposal. Sarah's entire demeanor changed when talking about this community work because of the great sense of pride she feels for her contribution. While she cannot change others' behaviors in her department, she can manage this community partnership and focus her energies in this way. We brainstormed ways she could build in more applied work with her students as part of her classes, using this community partnership as a vehicle. We also discussed building in four to six hours every week into her schedule to be on-site with the community organization. That time, I told her, was nonnegotiable.

Once Sarah became more energized and excited about reimagining her schedule to allow her to spend time where she finds joy and fulfillment, we started brainstorming ways to turn this work into deliverables. We talked through Ernest Boyer's forms of scholarship (see chapter 5 for more detail) and how she can document her work to share with others in the field. We discussed scholarship that focuses on fostering community partnerships as well as pedagogical scholarship based on the innovative curriculum she developed, which incorporates community-based learning. Sarah began to realize ways in which she can reengage in scholarship that is gratifying rather than burdensome. I told her our goal is to highlight her strengths and the areas that she feels very strongly about related to her field.

Activity 2: Job Crafting

Using three separate pieces of paper, title each with the following:

1 Task crafting
2 Relational crafting
3 Cognitive crafting

These three techniques are part of a process called "job crafting," in which employees engage in to redefine and reimagine their job design in personally meaningful ways (Berg, Dutton, and Wrzesniewski 2013; Wrzesniewski and Dutton 2001). Drawing from positive organizational scholarship, job crafting can be a valuable activity, particularly related to the midcareer faculty stage. Justin Berg and colleagues (2013) describe job crafting as a way to put employees "in the driver's seat in cultivating meaningfulness in their work" (81). The process of job crafting aligns with the notion of agency for women associate professors, which is becoming more prominent in the research and practice of the midcareer faculty stage (see, for example, Terosky, O'Meara, and Campbell 2014). Job crafting also supports an emphasis on joy as a driver in career choices.

Task crafting is the first technique in job crafting and involves adjusting the set of responsibilities prescribed by a given position. Adjustments include adding or removing tasks, altering the nature of tasks, or allocating time spent on a given task. When engaging in task crafting, ask yourself, "Am I finding joy in my daily or weekly tasks?" If not, in what ways can you alter your work responsibilities and associated tasks to have joy be a bigger driver?

Relational crafting involves shifting "how, when or with whom employees interact in the execution of their job" (Berg, Dutton, and Wrzesniewski 2013, 82). When engaging in relational crafting, ask yourself the following questions: "Which colleagues (or collaborators) do I find the most joy with when engaged in work? How can I ensure that my interactions with students and peers are driven by joy? How can I eliminate or minimize toxic relationships that detract from my personal and professional goals?"

Cognitive crafting involves employees' changing perceptions about the tasks and relationships that make up their job. Ask yourself, "How can I adjust my mind-set in relation to X aspect of my job and/or position? How can I recommit mentally so that my job is one of joy and is not burdensome?"

Job crafting is a process, not a one-time event, in which employees are continually evaluating and reimagining their job, the associated tasks, and organizational relationships. "Job crafting is a continuous process that is likely influenced by where employees are in their career trajectories" (Berg, Dutton, and Wrzesniewski 2013, 82). The process of job crafting empowers the employee to reenvision the next phase of her career and to do so with three critical components of what makes up a job and the organizational environment in which that job is situated. At its core, job crafting asks you to find meaning or joy in your work, and the three techniques provide the roadmap for engaging thoughtfully in this process.

Next, I situate the three techniques in the context of the midcareer stage and share stories from other women associate professors.

Task crafting. Institution type and mission will dictate the priority of these tasks, but the professoriate encapsulates the areas of scholarship, teaching, and service. These areas are still important for associate professors, but promotion and tenure provide an opportunity and the flexibility to rethink which tasks within these broad categories take priority. Perhaps an associate professor is interested in investing more in teaching or plans to pursue a new line of scholarly inquiry. Task crafting requires one to think about the primary areas in which one is expected to engage and to rethink how engagement in these areas can be realigned to find more meaning or joy. Let me share Maya's experience with task crafting.

Maya is an associate professor at a comprehensive university. While administrators at her institution talk about the equal importance of teaching and research, practice over the past decade at her institution illustrates a growing emphasis on research, despite resources failing to keep up with that evolution. As part of my work with Maya, she talked about her passion for teaching and wanted to refocus her energies there. However, she felt that a focus on teaching would not get her promoted to full professor. During our time together, we thought strategically about how she could turn that passion and love for teaching into publications. We focused a great deal of time on what she currently does in the classroom, debriefed on her teaching self-reflections and conversations with colleagues, and talked about the role of pedagogy in her field. We mapped out Maya's current teaching interests and compared those to campus, departmental, and student needs as well as to existing initiatives in her field (and professional conferences). This helped us identify areas of opportunity with regard to pedagogical development in her own classrooms, professional-development opportunities that would support her growth and expertise in these areas, and contributions to her field by way of teaching and learning advancements. Using the concept of smallest publishable unit (see chapter 5), Maya identified different streams from this mapping exercise that could form the basis of publications. In fact, she was able to identify three possible publications that would be targeted to outlets focused on the scholarship of teaching and learning as well as discipline-based pedagogy journals. This helped her center on her joy while also producing publications that she needed to advance to full professor.

Relational crafting. The technique of relational crafting supplies an opportunity to consider who, how, and when to engage with colleagues and collaborators. While a current department chair cannot altogether avoid challenging peers (and a faculty member cannot altogether avoid interactions with an abusive department chair), faculty members have a great deal of autonomy to decide with whom we want to engage, how often, and for what purpose. Oftentimes the women associate professors I work with have colleagues with whom they work that create either productive, positive environments or challenging and at times toxic or discriminatory environments. I guide them to think about the ways they engage with these colleagues to determine if the collaboration and interactions are joyous. If the answer is yes, I help women think about what outcomes are already in process as a result of this collaboration and how to turn those into deliverables that support their goal of full professorship or continuing contract status. If the collaboration is not one of joy, I help the women develop an exit strategy to finish out the collaboration and to abstain from any future work with those particular colleagues. If an exit strategy is not an option, it is still possible to engage in relational crafting to minimize a toxic situation.

Kim is an associate professor in the social sciences at a liberal arts college; she has over a decade of service at her current institution. Kim faced a toxic departmental situation with a verbally abusive department chair, resulting in a very challenging work environment. This department chair was a senior colleague in the department with a reputation across campus of being negative, offensive, and downright nasty to colleagues from departments (and disciplines) that he deemed less rigorous. Kim had a great deal of evidence that confirmed her beliefs and assertions about her discriminatory department chair and her fraught relationship with him. Over a period of several years, she had collected documentation that was confirmed by witnesses. She also communicated her concerns with the prior administration, the current administration, and human resources at her institution. Her beliefs about the toxic environment that her department chair created were affirmed by departmental and campus colleagues and by the current and previous administration, yet no action was ever taken.

Kim and I strategized how to manage this relationship because we both agreed that working in a nonabusive department was a reasonable expectation. On the basis of the egregious evidence she had compiled over the years, she had every right to hold the administration, particularly her provost, accountable for managing her department chair and this situation in a more formal way. Ultimately, Kim requested a meeting with the provost and her department chair to discuss a recent abusive situation. Prior to the meeting, Kim made clear to the provost that she would pursue further action, including legal action, should an acceptable solution not be presented. Corrective actions were taken to address the situation both in the short and long terms. Kim minimized interactions deliberately with her department chair to departmental business only. At the request of the provost, a senior colleague in the department agreed to support Kim in evaluative situations (e.g., performance review), as long as the current chair holds the position. Through relational crafting, Kim tempered the toxic departmental environment created by her department chair and sent a signal to the chair and her provost that such behavior was unacceptable and would no longer be tolerated.

I encourage all women to use Kim's example as a foundation from which to build. Kim was diligent in understanding procedural requirements as outlined by her faculty handbook. She sought counsel from members of her college's grievance committee and used that language to hold her provost and department chair accountable. I urge all women in this kind of situation to seek out their handbook and go to the appropriate places and people for support. Additionally, chapter 7 provides much-needed guidance to help develop a persuasive voice to manage this kind of toxic situation.

Cognitive crafting. The final job-crafting technique, cognitive crafting, can be the most challenging. This technique involves changing the way individuals perceive the tasks and relationships that make up their job. We all have some aspects of our jobs that we find less appealing or even downright awful. As Kim's story demonstrates, we are in control of the way we choose to view those individuals or tasks. Also, the ways in which we think about our own contribution and value added to students, departments, institutions, and communities (local and disciplinary) are also very much in our control. Many times, the women associate professors I work with are already engaged in fruitful collaborations and professional opportunities that they might not deem as fruitful, and I help them think through how to turn those work tasks into the needed deliverables to achieve promotion.

Liz, for example, had been working with humanities colleagues as part of a larger learning commission organized by a consortium of research universities focused on humanities initiatives. At first, she was frustrated by the task of representing her department and institution in this consortial effort because, as she put it, "this was just one more responsibility added to a growing service list post–[promotion and tenure]." However, I tasked Liz with engaging in cognitive crafting related to her engagement. The results were powerful. Through her participation, Liz connected with like-minded peers who kept in touch even after the learning commission's efforts had ended. Liz and her peers agreed that their work was quite value added both individually and disciplinarily. As a collective, they secured grant funds to sponsor a small-scale symposium in which humanities faculty and staff would share their scholarly and creative works and have the opportunity to network. I helped Liz think about how to turn the works shared across the several faculty and student contributions into an edited volume that both serves as a best-practice model of how to establish such disciplinary events and also features the great work being done at the faculty, student, and faculty-student-partnership levels. The secured grant funds, publications, and leadership effort will be invaluable to Liz's quest for full professorship at the research university in which she is employed. We also discussed how Liz could use cognitive crafting to identify future collaborators from this group with shared scholarly and teaching interests who could provide some much-needed motivation and professional accountability.

Activity 3: Career Mapping

Grab a piece of paper and a pen, colored pencils, or markers.

I was recently a panelist for a midcareer faculty workshop featured at the American Educational Research Association. I collaborated with a group of amazing women (Ann Austin, Pamela Eddy, Jaime Lester, Aimee LaPointe Terosky, and Kelly Ward) engaged in research and practice of midcareer faculty, many of whom focus on the experiences of women. Their research and practice contributions to the field of faculty development have been instrumental in contributing to our understanding of and support provided to women in the professoriate (see, for example, Austin 2010; Garza Mitchell and Eddy 2008; Lester 2008; Terosky, O'Meara, and Campbell 2014; Ward and Wolf-Wendel 2012).

Ann Austin, one of the leading scholars in the field of faculty development and the faculty experience, facilitated participants' engagement in a career-mapping exercise. She has also used such an exercise with graduate students and early-career faculty. She asked session attendees to reflect on daily work issues and their day-to-day experiences. To initiate the session, Ann simply asked, "Think about yourself at midcareer—what does that look like?" Upon reflecting on this question, session attendees were asked to answer by drawing a picture.

Session attendees shared those pictures with other attendees and were tasked with identifying common themes. Pictures illustrated the obstacles of midcareer as hills, brick walls, and heavy weights. However, session attendees also drew pictures of flowers and spring, signifying a sense of renewal that can accompany the midcareer stage. One picture was a fork in the road, which signified a dilemma. For this particular attendee, the dilemma was between continuing on the path toward full professorship or pursuing an administrative post.

As a collective, the group focused on the need to find the joyful components of their work and daily lives while firmly situated at midcareer, even when those are hard to find. To help facilitate that focus, Ann asked attendees to write down two joys and two challenges and to think about how they managed all four. This career-mapping activity is a valuable exercise because it requires you to be clear about where you currently are in your career and to understand the associated joys and challenges while thinking about how to move forward from that point.

TO DO

1 Ask myself, "What is my joy?"

2 Engage in job crafting (task, relational, cognitive)

3 Draw a picture of my midcareer accompanied by two joys and two challenges

Conclusion

Make no mistake, the midcareer stage has its challenges and can be rife with inconsistencies, contradictions, and the feeling of being pulled in every direction imaginable. However, the midcareer stage can also be one of renewal, characterized by an opportunity to chart a new course and to reenvision one's professional (and personal) identity. The midcareer stage is a marathon, not a sprint—one that requires strategizing, planning, and executing. A multifaceted approach is needed to be successful, and that approach needs to be broken down into more manageable components that build on each other. The goal of this chapter is to change your mind-set about your professional aspirations, particularly the path to full professorship or continuing contract status. Participating in thought-provoking activities like job crafting and career mapping will allow you to refocus your energies on what is joyful, rather than burdensome, in order to be more thoughtful about what the midcareer stage can (and should) look like for you. In chapter 2, I concentrate on strategies to achieve a laser-like organization in order to put you in a position of success during this long-distance race we call the midcareer stage.

Additional Resources

For readers interested in more resources and understanding related to faculty development, I highly recommend the following resources:

Austin, Ann. E., and Mary Deane Sorcinelli. 2013. "The Future of Faculty Development: Where Are We Going?" *New Directions for Teaching and Learning* 133:85–97.

Beach, Andrea L., Mary Deane Sorcinelli, Ann E. Austin, and Jaclyn K. Rivard. 2016. *Faculty Development in the Age of Evidence: Current Practices, Future Imperatives.* Sterling, VA: Stylus.

Ouellett, Matthew. 2010. "Overview of Faculty Development: History and Choices." In *A Guide to Faculty Development*, edited by Kay J. Gillespie and Douglas L. Robertson, 3–20. San Francisco: Jossey-Bass.

Sorcinelli, Mary Deane, Ann E. Austin, Pamela L. Eddy, and Andrea L. Beach. 2006. *Creating the Future of Faculty Development: Learning from the Past: Understanding the Present*. Bolton, MA: Anker.

For readers interested in other midcareer supports, see the following:

Mathews, Kiernan R. 2014. "Perspectives on Mid-career Faculty and Advice for Supporting Them." White paper, COACHE, Harvard Graduate School of Education, Cambridge, MA.

Rockquemore, Kerry Ann. 2017. "Posttenure Planning." *Inside Higher Ed*, November 2. www.insidehighered.com/advice/2017/11/01/ongoing -planning-life-after-tenure-essay.

CHAPTER 2

Organization, Organization, Organization

We've all heard the famous saying, "There are three things that matter in real estate: location, location, location." A great location can, at times, outweigh other shortcomings in a given property. Similarly, there are three things that matter in managing career advancement: organization, organization, organization. In this chapter, I offer an overview of practical guides and resources from the business and human resources fields that will help support the achievement of career goals. Next, I share targeted activities and exercises that I use both professionally and as I work with clients to assess current and future career goals and aspirations. I conclude the chapter by sharing some simple hacks that help you to "reclaim your time" (thank you, Maxine Waters).

What Are Your Goals?

If you know what you want, you can have it.

—Henriette Anne Klauser (2001, 16)

As a woman in the academy, I have certainly faced challenging environments, and I know my women peers, particularly those from underrepresented and underresourced populations, have even steeper hills to climb to achieve equality in the academy. I am also keenly aware that despite hard work and an organizational focus, the obstacles can appear insurmountable. My aim in this chapter, however, is to provide the needed grounding and tools that can support women's efforts in the academy while also acknowledging the inequality we face regularly.

Before you can develop plans, strategies, and a toolkit to achieve your professional or personal goals, you must be clear to define your goals. In the academy, that can include the attainment of promotion, administrative aspirations, or greater balance. I recall a funny, albeit somewhat depressing, story that my minor adviser shared in one of our colloquium sessions in graduate school. He had just received what he called "the shit sandwich," which was a peer review of his research paper. It started as a glowing review and even ended on a positive note, but everything in between basically described him and his research as terrible. After telling our class about this review, he then proceeded to describe the academic career as follows: You sacrifice and work hard as a second-class citizen to get through graduate school to set yourself up to earn a tenure-track appointment. Once in that tenure-track appointment, you continue to make personal sacrifices while occupying only a marginally elevated citizenship in your new department. Then finally, it happens. You earn promotion and tenure to realize that the work, sacrifice, and never-ending barrage of negativity must continue should you choose to work toward full professorship or continuing contract status. If you have the fortitude (and interest) to continue on this path of impression management, working at a nonsustainable pace and asking for forgiveness regularly from friends and family who have been patient and understanding, you keep producing until you finally achieve full professorship. Then, "you die."

We all laughed at his abbreviated description of the academic career. And while he was clear about the many wonderful things that happen along the way, at times, the academy and the professional milestones can be draining, to say the least. This is why I think it is so important to be clear about your goals, professional and personal, and to ruminate about how these goals intersect (or not) and what it takes to achieve them.

Throughout my work, and as evinced in the literature, I have met many associate professors who have no desire to pursue full professorship (see, for example, Baker, Lunsford, and Pifer 2018; Ward and Wolf-Wendel 2012). For some, this next milestone is simply not worth it and may irreparably damage already-tenuous relationships or one's health. In the context of their institutions, full professorship or continuing contract status does not result in higher pay or other privileges except for perhaps entree to a select few administrative positions on their respective campuses that require the occupant to have achieved this status. Given that most of these individuals have fifteen years or more remaining until retirement, I still push them to think about other professional goals in order to stay motivated and engaged. I write this book guided by the assumption that you are reading it because you seek promotion. However, for those of you reading this with no aspiration toward promotion, I assume you want to continue to make contributions to your field, discipline, and institution. Therefore, regardless of your goals, the tools and strategies shared throughout this book will be of value.

Full Professorship at Your Institution: Getting Started

For those who do aspire to full professorship or continuing contract status, being clear on this goal and what it takes to get there in the context of institutional expectations and standards is critical. Therefore, I encourage you to find out two important points from either your faculty handbook or some other institutional documentation:

1 Criteria to earn full professorship or continuing contract status

2 The process by which promotion is awarded

These two items of information become critical opportunities to develop short- and long-term strategies to achieve those goals.

By criteria, as noted in point 1, I am referring to the categories in which "excellence" is determined across the triumvirate in the academy: teaching, research, and service. The relative weight attributed to these areas will be dependent on institution type and mission. For example, in a research university setting, research dominates promotion and tenure decisions, followed distantly by teaching and service (Fairweather 2005). Comprehensive college and university faculty are seeing growing institutional expectations related to research as important for career advancement, followed closely by teaching and regional outreach (Baker, Terosky, and Martinez 2017). In LACs, teaching is the primary category by which promotion and tenure decisions are made. However, research expectations are on the rise, particularly in the more selective LACs, placing scholarly productivity at a close second to or holding the same weight as teaching in promotion and tenure decisions, followed by service (Baker, Lunsford, and Pifer 2017). Teaching and supporting students is the dominant focus and consideration for promotion and tenure decisions in community colleges. However, research has revealed that community college faculty are engaging to a greater degree in research both as scholars and as mentors in undergraduate research experiences, in response to evolving institutional expectations (Cejda and Hensel 2009; Levin, Kater, and Wagoner 2006).

Throughout my work, I have found very few institutions that communicate explicit metrics across these categories (e.g., we expect seven publications to earn tenure; we expect average teaching evaluations of 2.0 or better on a scale of 1 to 5, with 1 being a perfect score, etc.). Rather, these categories are broad to account for disciplinary and institutional nuances. With this broadness also comes instances of inconsistency across candidate reviews, given that committee membership is cyclical. This lack of clarity and consistency is frustrating, with women and faculty of color suffering most from this vagueness (Turner 2002). It also presents an opportunity to craft your narrative according to your strengths (see chapter 4 for more detail).

When you collect the criteria for promotion (in the second half of this chapter, I walk you through a strengths, weaknesses, opportunities, and threats (SWOT) analysis taking this information into account), determine the categories and the definitions or descriptions of how these categories are communicated. I strongly recommend reaching out to individuals who have been successful in their bid for full professorship *within* your disciplinary/divisional domain. Ask to see a copy of their narrative as a guide. I suggest asking someone within your disciplinary/divisional area, given that there are differences in how scholarship is defined, what constitutes good teaching, and the kinds of service at the institution or within professional associations that are value added. Gaining disciplinary insights and perspectives is a strategic move.

I also recommend seeking copies of personnel files or narratives from individuals *outside* your disciplinary area to see how others organize their materials. Find a trusted colleague to share his or her narrative but also to serve as a friendly review. Note that you want friendly reviews within and outside your disciplinary area. The outside reader serves as your educated yet uniformed reader, while the reader within your disciplinary area can be a second set of expert eyes on your work. Personnel committees are made up of faculty and administrators spanning all divisional areas, so your narrative must be written for the educated yet uniformed reader.

Contact current and previous members of the personnel committee on your campus. Ask them to share insights about their experience on the committee, what they found frustrating, and what they found particularly helpful when reviewing dossiers. While current and former committee members cannot provide explicit details about individual cases, they can share trends and advice based on their review experiences. In my bid for promotion and tenure, as well as full professorship, I engaged in every one of these steps and benefited greatly from colleagues who were willing to share their narratives and copies of files. One colleague also shared his interim and tenure letters so I could see how they were organized and what the committee focused on as part of his review. I always make my files and letters available to colleagues within and outside the department and also share with my clients.

There are a few key considerations when considering point 2, the process by which full professorship or continuing contract status is awarded. First, determine how long you must be at the associate rank before you are eligible for promotion. I have seen time frames ranging from four years up to eight years. Second, identify if promotion is an application process or if it is simply awarded after a certain amount of time spent at the associate rank. While all the clients I work with fall under the prior category, I have found through my research that the latter exists. Third, for those individuals who are in an application-process system, clarify what documents need to be included in your dossier. Such documents can include the following: a personal narrative, copies of teaching evaluations and summary scores, copies of publications, metrics on publications (e.g., impact factors, citation counts), letters of support (e.g., from departmental colleagues, campus colleagues), and an external reviewer list (if your institution engages in external review as part of this process). Some institutions, particularly research institutions, require details about the level of your contribution on publications or grants. For example, if you are lead author with one coauthor on a publication, your contribution might have been 60 percent, while your coauthor contributed 40 percent of the work required to complete that research. Or you may have two coauthors, and you all contributed equally to a monograph, in which case you will note your contribution at 33 percent (and each of your colleagues at 33 percent).

The process of earning full professorship or continuing contract status is truly a marathon that becomes nearly impossible to complete without a basic understanding of these two main points. Knowing what you have ahead of you, what is expected of you, and the process by which the review occurs is vital to your success. In the next section, I offer a review of business and human resources tools and insights that help support the development of short- and long-term goals.

TO DO

1   Obtain/review criteria for promotion

2   Understand the promotion process

3   Review others' dossiers

4   Seek friendly reviews in and out of your disciplinary area

5   Talk to current and former members of the personnel committee

Where to Begin

My motivation to go up for full for another modest pay bump is . . .
minimal. I'd rather take my time charting a research agenda that's
meaningful to me. But also, I'd like to save for retirement and my kid's
college education, you know?

—associate professor, humanities, doctoral university,
highest research activity

Now that you have the basic building blocks, knowledge, and understanding about what you are about to embark on at your institution, you need to start developing short- and long-term plans to get you moving toward promotion. I am a big fan of writing down goals, keeping to-do lists (with time frames attached), and working with other motivated, organized individuals who support accountability. I am *that* person who loves buying school and organizational supplies, and I make to-do lists about my to-do lists (it is a sickness, but it works).

Write It Down, Make It Happen

There's power in conceiving goals, followed by the act of writing them down as a visual record. To help guide you in doing this effectively, I highly recommend reading the book *Write It Down, Make It Happen* by Henriette Anne Klauser (2001). She recites the famous line from the movie *Field of Dreams*, "If you build it, they will come." She compares the line with the act of writing down one's goals: "Building it before he gets there is stepping out in faith, just as writing it down says you believe that it's attainable" (Klauser 2001, 19).

If the goal is to attain full professorship or continuing contract status, write it down. If the goal is to pursue an administrative career, write it down. If the goal is to substantially revise your courses, write it down. As Klauser asserts, visualization directs your brain toward your dreamed-of destination. But she argues that the goals need to be specific and that you need to refer to them often. Additionally, Klauser discusses how to rely on your reticular activating system to your benefit, which refers to a brain filter that helps you focus on important tasks or ideas while ignoring those that are not moving you toward your goals.

Situating this notion in the academy, it can be easy to focus on everything other than what is needed to help us achieve our goals. Never-ending tasks like administrative work or grading keeps us from writing, which is often the biggest issue that my clients struggle with as they think about the most pronounced barrier to achieving promotion. A woman associate professor in the sciences from an LAC notes, "So there's no external incentive [to go up for full]. It's more just about the prestige of having it. For a long time, I just didn't care about it, because I didn't think it was something that I'd be able to do. My focus has been more administrative than it has been on research for a while. I'd say, in the last year, when I got reengaged with my research, I've started to think about that [going up for full] as a possibility again."

While we cannot ignore those work tasks that are necessary, we need to realize that they interfere with the achievement of goals (refer to task crafting from chapter 1 to help minimize some of the nonurgent or unnecessary ones from your to-do list). We can be more focused on saying yes to those activities that will propel us toward our goals. Being specific and focusing on our outlined short- and long-term goals and action steps allows us to train our brains to filter things that are distracting from attaining the dreamed-of destination.

Throughout Klauser's book, she offers suggestions aimed at helping the reader focus on developing specific goals, moving past the fears and hurdles that can become debilitating, and the importance of peer (and personal) accountability. The framework offered helps individuals think thoughtfully and strategically about how to make that first step in being clear about goals and associated intentions, writing down goals and referring to them often, and creating the space in which you and others respect those goals and support efforts to achieve them.

The Seven Habits

I think we have all heard of, and perhaps utilized, advice and tools from Steven Covey's work over the years. I was fortunate to take a course of his while working in executive education at Harvard Business School, and I require Covey's book *The 7 Habits of Highly Effective People* (2013) as part of my "First Year Experience" course at Albion College.

From being proactive (habit 1) to keeping the end in mind (habit 2), Covey, much like Klauser (2001), focuses on the importance of taking ownership of our experiences and focusing on the end goal. Taking personal ownership aligns with the notion of employing personal agency to combat institutional barriers and outdated policies as faculty members navigate their academic careers and support their professional and personal development (O'Meara, Terosky, and Neumann 2008). Even better is when personal agency improves the experiences of and opens the path for others.

Take Tara's efforts for example. Shortly after earning tenure, she became the chair of her department's personnel committee. She shared the following agentic behaviors: "I became the chair of our departmental personnel committee immediately after tenure, so I decided to be proactive and insisted our P&T [promotion and tenure] guidelines be rewritten to be more transparent and provide some guidance and minimum benchmarks. . . . After I analyzed the [collected] data, we convened a committee with a rep from each program and are creating standards within teaching, scholarship, and service. This will take a load off from anticipating expectations."

I think many women professors, regardless of rank, struggle with habit 3 (put first things first). But the new roles and responsibilities that become part and parcel of the midcareer stage make this habit particularly challenging at this career stage. Hence, keeping the end in mind is an important reminder.

Covey's habit 4, win-win, encourages a life view in which cooperation, rather than competition prevails. The goal is to seek mutual benefit for all human interactions, which is particularly important as women in the academy seek to support other women along their journey. Covey's habit 6, synergize, recognizes that "two heads are better than one." Human nature often causes us to seek like-minded individuals, but we should strive to seek to innovate and problem solve with a diversity of individuals who bring their own experiences and knowledge to the table. Habits 4 and 6 are particularly vital for women professors seeking to advance in our careers while managing the myriad roles, responsibilities, needs, and challenges that we face daily. They speak to the power of collaboration and building support systems (see chapter 6) but also to being a support to others along the journey. The importance of mentorship for women faculty who aspire to full, particularly for women of color, is well documented in the literature (Croom 2017; Croom and Patton 2012). Institutional efforts are under way to address this need. A woman associate professor in education (master's colleges and universities: larger programs) shared, "Our campus has implemented a mentoring program for women interested in navigating associate to full. There are several components, and it is in response to the gender gap documented at our institution." Other national efforts such as the National Science Foundation's ADVANCE program target specific disciplines, in this case women in STEM fields. We can draw examples and strategies from programs like these and others to support individual and institutional efforts as we seek to support women's advancement in the academy.

If your institution does not have a formal mentoring program, I encourage you to ask your department chair, provost/dean, or the person tasked with professional-development responsibilities on your campus to help you find an appropriate mentor. If this effort falls short, then seek mentors from your disciplinary or professional associations. Refer to the "Additional Reading" section at the end of this chapter for a link to a "Quick Start Guide" that can help you start the conversation with a potential mentor (and to be clear about your own mentoring needs).

"Seek first to understand, then be understood" (Covey's habit 5) can be challenging for many of us, and I am no exception. Our own insecurities, exhaustion, and guilt, not to mention long-standing institutional biases in the academy (Bingham and Nix 2010), put us in a position where we feel the need not only to always have a response but to have the "right" response in our quest to command the respect we have worked so hard to earn. And, if you are anything like me, you will replay that response over and over again in your mind and think about all the ways in which it could have been different if "I had only said . . ." Sound familiar? To earn promotion, it's imperative to be a good listener and effective communicator. My grandfather, someone I regarded as a professional mentor of mine, gave me some good advice when it came to deciphering what was and was not important feedback that required action. He said, "Do you respect the source of the feedback? If yes, then think about the feedback and how you need to act on it. If you don't respect the source, don't waste another second thinking about the feedback or the person who provided it."

Finally, habit 7, sharpen the saw, can be the hardest for women to act on (Dempsey 2017). Habit 7 is an all-important reminder to see continuous improvement and engage in self-care that supports personal and professional renewal. Our greatest asset is ourselves, and that asset requires nurturing and self-renewal across four key areas: physical, social/emotional, mental, and spiritual. We so freely (and often) give to others to the detriment of ourselves. Research by Kimberly Griffin and colleagues (2013) noted that the Black women in their study described the "emotional and physical exhaustion" they felt when they engaged in nonresearch activities that directed their efforts away from those activities (e.g., research) that would support their career advancement. The full professor journey requires stamina. It is a journey that cannot be traversed successfully if we are in poor health, whether it be mental, physical, emotional, or spiritual health. A gentle reminder to take care of ourselves so we can be at our best for those who need us most, including ourselves, is always welcome.

My Go-To Strategies

I feel like there are a hundred different ways I could go, but I have little direction or mentorship. So I feel like I have to do all one hundred things, and it is overwhelming.

—associate professor, social sciences, master's college or university, larger program

---

In this section, I share examples of tried-and-true strategies, tips, and tools to support motivation, engagement, and a focus on joy. The tools and tips shared are grounded in human resources and career-development literatures and practice. They are some of my go-to activities and resources that I share in workshops and with consulting clients to great success.

"Atta Girl" Folder

I am sure we have all experienced a time when we were preparing a yearly review or some evaluative narrative and we were sure that we received an email from someone noting the importance and quality of our work. Yet that email appears to have vanished. To combat this, I strongly encourage you to create an "Atta Girl" folder in your email and/or on your computer desktop. In fact, take two minutes and create one right now—you will be glad that you did.

I swear by this simple organizational tool to keep all the correspondence I receive from students, parents, peers, colleagues, alumni, and anyone else who can speak to my value-added contribution across the many contexts in which I engage. If you opened my email inbox right now, you would see a long list of email folders that I create per project, task, or course. I delete the folders after they are inactive for two years (except for course-specific folders). If you look in my alphabetized email folder list, for example, you will see the following:

Aspiration Paper

Assessment

Associate Director Candidate

Athletic Advisory Council

Atta Girl Post-Full

Atta Girl Post-Tenure

Atta Girl Pre-Tenure

AUP Materials

Every correspondence in which I receive feedback that speaks to my contribution in the classroom, in research, in consulting, to the life of the campus, and so goes in one of these folders. And you will note that I have created new folders that align with the career stage I was or am in to keep better track chronologically of such correspondence. For example, one email from a student in my "Atta Girl Post-Full" folder reads, "Hi Vicki, I just wanted to say thank you for always providing feedback on our assignments and papers in a timely matter. I have definitely had my fair share of professors who lack this ability and really appreciate you taking the time to offer individual feedback. Thanks again!"

For the purposes of a narrative to be used for promotion and tenure, I might include this email to illustrate my "excellence" in teaching. While I assume all of my peers provide feedback and do so in a timely manner, my assumption was clearly incorrect, on the basis of this message. To have the words of a student who speaks on my behalf about the quality and timeliness of my feedback and review is more powerful than my simply communicating as much in an evaluative document that I prepare on my own behalf. Faculty peers might view the timely feedback I provide as expected; when communicated by a student, it signals a potentially higher, more thoughtful quality of feedback that goes above and beyond what is expected and clearly executed by some of my peers.

In addition to including email correspondence in these folders, I also include other documents such as features in the press; featured stories at Albion College in which my teaching, research, or service are noted; or when my name is included in professional association newsletters or other correspondence. Once it's time to create my narrative for merit, bonus, promotion, or other professional purposes, I rely on these words and comments to illustrate my contribution and successes (read more about this in chapter 3).

Saved Atta Girl emails also serve a second, significant purpose. On those days when you find it especially challenging in the classroom or when data analysis is not going the way you had hoped, reading others' encouraging or complimentary words helps to assuage the disappointment. Atta Girl emails are a good reminder that you have made a difference in the life of a person and your institution. Read them often.

Project Tracking Sheet (or Program/Application)

Today, there are many application-based organizational tools available such as Trello, Wrike, and Gantt. I have worked with Gantt on consulting projects, and it has worked well for providing a visual of the work, percentage of completion updates, and details about my team members' progress and assigned responsibilities (including my own). I prefer to track my projects via an Excel file that I now turn into a Google Doc so collaborators can make edits and updates as well.

Regardless of what you find most useful and stress-free (because no one wants an organizational tool that causes more stress and anxiety as opposed to less), a project tracking sheet serves as a visual accounting of research or other work-related tasks that include short-term goals and associated tasks, as well as the end goal with a projected completion date. This visual accounting and level of detail goes back to the guidance of Klauser, in which you write it down to make it happen.

In the vault of great advice from my minor adviser in graduate school is his visual accounting of research-related projects in the form of a color-coded Gantt chart consisting of several projects at different stages. He illustrated projects that were spanning the conception stage to those that were in progress (data collection, data analysis) and those that were near completion and were in the dissemination and publication-preparation phase. This allowed him to have a research pipeline and a multitude of projects that would help him achieve the "research excellence" criteria that accompany being a business professor in a top research university.

Accepting different roles across research or teaching serves a purpose as well. Diversifying your roles solves the time dilemma, as it is impossible to lead every project, produce at the levels expected by your institution, and still be sane when all is said and done. In the context of research, for example, my minor adviser urged the importance of illustrating my ability to lead a collaboration (e.g., principal investigator [PI] on a research grant, lead author with one or more collaborators), to be a strong collaborator (e.g., co-PI on a research grant, second or third author on a publication), and to be self-directed, as evinced through sole authorship. I have been deliberate in assuming these roles at various points throughout my career.

As Covey notes and as explained further in chapter 6, collaboration is instrumental. Over the span of the majority of my career, I have been fortunate to have two amazing colleagues, Meghan J. Pifer and Laura Gail Lunsford, who are also my coauthors. In fact, Meghan and I have been collaborating since graduate school. We maintained what we called the "Baker-Pifer Research and Publication Plan" to track our research-related projects. This project plan got me through promotion and tenure and was an essential organizational tool for both of us. As you can see from the 2014 version of the plan (figure 2.1), we tracked all aspects of a given project. We have since published every paper

Manuscript	Project	Type	Conference	Authorship	Next deadline	Publication	Submit goal	Submit date
1. Professional / Relational / Personal Framework	Doc Ed / Pifer Dissertation	data analysis	ASHE 2010	Pifer/ Baker		*Teachers College Record*	—	6.13.14
2. Challenges and Opportunities of the Doctoral Education Process: Insights for Students, Faculty Members, and Administrators	Stage 2 / Stage 3	data analysis	ASHE 2009	Pifer/ Baker		*Change*	Dec. 2014	
3. Identity & The Academy	Identity & Professoriate	data analysis	ASHE 2012	Pifer/ Baker		*Handbook of Higher Education*	Fall 2014	
4. Conceptual Model of Doctoral Education	Doctoral Education	lit review / theoretical		Baker/ Pifer		*Review of Higher Education*	Spring 2015	

Figure 2.1 Sample worksheet from the Baker-Pifer Research and Publication Plan

idea that appears. Our main headings included shortened manuscript title, project focus, type of research, conference, authorship order, targeted publication, submission goal, submission date, and so on. We (1) tracked which publications were under review, accepted, and in development (this categorization aligns with the advice that my minor adviser gave about having multiple projects across various stages), (2) noted published manuscripts, and (3) labeled timeline goals by month.

This tool helped us both stay accountable to each other and the research we committed to and was an excellent visual reminder of our goals and the short- and long-term tasks we needed to tackle to accomplish these goals. We would schedule check-in phone calls to update the project plan and to act as a good gut check to see if we were on target or getting behind. If we were fortunate enough to meet in person at a conference or data-collection site, we always spent time with this file pulled up on our laptops to review together and make sure these were the right publications in the right order. At times, we realized based on the direction of our field that we needed to move a project to a higher priority to make sure our work was visible and timely. We used this project plan as a strong accountability tool but allowed ourselves to adjust when needed.

Also, of importance is the inclusion of targeted conferences on the research plan tracking sheet. We would target a conference, submit a proposal, and use the conference as a milestone to present our research but also to ensure that we had a complete draft of the paper required by the conference. We would then treat feedback from our conference-session discussant as an "outside friendly review" and revise our paper as necessary before submitting for publication. As part of our team check-ins, we would review our conference presentations to make sure we had a plan for turning them into an "in-process publication." We were both mentored not to allow conference presentations to build up without turning them into publications, which can happen easily over time. This is a lesson that both Meghan and I have kept on the forefront of our professional goals. The aim is to maintain balance between presentations and publications.

My intention for including a section on organizational applications and tools is to get you thinking about the ways in which you can better organize your short- and long-term goals (and corresponding outputs), which can include collaborations with colleagues, as you seek to have a clearer path toward promotion. The project plan headings and mechanisms I have used (and continue to use) may not align with your institutional expectations or disciplinary norms. But you can take these templates and ideas and think about how they can be adapted and adopted to meet your personal needs and expectations as well as those that are predetermined for you professionally.

TO DO

1   Create your "Atta Girl" folder

2   Develop (and use) a project tracking system

Get Your Pen Ready

I'm drowning in service/administrative work and taking on tasks to protect junior colleagues. I'm figuring out research directions/priorities while making a five-year or n-year plan—and still working to find time for family/self-care and avoiding burnout.

—associate professor, STEM, baccalaureate college, arts and sciences focus

In this section, I walk you through three hands-on activities that I use with clients and as part of leadership development workshops I deliver for organizational and institutional clients. I have found them to be particularly useful for midcareer faculty members as they seek to reenvision the next phase and understand where they currently are in achieving your goals.

SWOT Analysis

The business field offers some great tools and resources that can be adopted and adapted for use in higher education. One such tool is a SWOT analysis. This analytical tool can be used for project-planning purposes as well as an individual career-development tool (Osita, Onyebuchi, and Justina 2014). *Strengths* focuses on the characteristics, skill sets, or knowledge that give you an advantage or serve as a differentiator. *Weaknesses* are those aspects, characteristics, or realities you must manage that put you at a disadvantage in relation to your professional or personal goals and expectations. *Opportunities* are those elements in the environment, whether institutional, disciplinary, or professional, that you can utilize to your advantage. Finally, *threats* are those contextual factors that could impede progress toward goals and expectations. Now that you know what these categories are and how they are defined, get a pen, a piece of paper, and a copy of your institutional promotion-to-full criteria in front of you (e.g., categories and any associated descriptions/definitions).

Step 1: Re-create the matrix in figure 2.2.

Step 2: Take no more than five minutes per category to complete the following: for each evaluation category found in your institutional promotion criteria, complete a mini SWOT analysis. For example, for the teaching category, ask yourself:

1 What strengths do I offer in teaching?

2 What are my primary weaknesses in teaching?

3 What opportunities can I capitalize on related to my teaching?

4 What threats do I need to be aware of or better manage related to my teaching?

Repeat this analysis for research, service, and any other evaluation category.

Step 3: Ask yourself, "What do these SWOT analyses tell me about where I currently stand in relation to promotion criteria? What do these SWOT analyses tell me about short- and long-term directions I need to take to achieve my goals?"

I first have clients stick strictly to the five-minute-per-category time frame so as to avoid getting too bogged down by overthinking. The aim is to jot down the ideas that first come to mind, which serves as an excellent starting point. Further, completing a mini SWOT analysis for all promotion categories forces you to engage in an honest assessment of where you are and where you need to be, rather than merely focusing on those categories that seem insurmountable (which is demotivating and self-defeating) or those categories in which you excel (which may give you an unrealistic or skewed assessment of where you are in relation to successfully earning promotion).

I have a handful of full professor peers who were denied promotion to full one or more times, and all expressed a level of surprise at that outcome, which resulted in resentment and feelings of bitterness

Strengths	Weaknesses
Opportunities	**Threats**

Figure 2.2 SWOT analysis template

toward the institution and their colleagues who served on the committee at the time of their review. As a professor of human resources, I am a big advocate for realistic job previews and timely, developmental feedback. If someone is going to be dismissed or fail to earn an expected promotion, that news should not be a shock to the person on the receiving end. However, as individuals, we have agency over how we prepare and organize our materials so as to minimize the uncertainty that is within our power to control.

Once you have your mini SWOT analyses completed, then ask yourself these three questions:

1 Are there clear areas in which I need to develop?
2 Are there areas in which I am unclear of "what counts" in relation to the promotion criteria?

3   Do I have mentors who can support my identified areas of development (see chapter 6)?

At a later time, you can spend more time populating these areas when mapping out short- and long-term goals, but your responses (and assessments) to these three questions, along with the results from your SWOT analyses, will give you a starting point from which to build.

Before you begin, there are two notes of caution. First, populating this matrix comprehensively at the outset can be overwhelming. You could literally spend hours on populating these areas. Do not allow this activity to become unproductive time when it should be the foundation from which you can build toward productivity. Second, focus on no more than one to two matrixes at a time for short-term planning. The goal is to break this process (and earning promotion) into smaller, more manageable pieces. If you look at the whole, you can once again become easily overwhelmed and opt out. When I trained for (and ran) marathons, I never began my training or the race focusing on the 26.2-mile target—talk about panic! Instead, I broke down the race into five-mile increments, knowing I could easily (and often) run five miles. This made the race less mentally defeating. The same principle applies for long-term career-development processes.

My goal in offering the SWOT analysis as a tool is to help minimize the feeling of being overwhelmed. Instead, I want you to be clear about what your value added is and where your developmental opportunities are. I also want you to see, which my clients often realize, that a great deal of work is already in process from which you can build. You just need to develop a plan to turn that work into deliverables, and the tools, strategies, and recommendations throughout this book should assist you with that effort. Less than 5 percent of my clients actually need to start new projects to begin their path to promotion. Rather, they apply the smallest publishable unit (SPU) concept (see chapter 5) to build on existing work. It is all about the power of small wins to get moving in the right direction.

Criteria Catalog

The criteria by which promotion and tenure are earned at Albion College are as follows: value to students, scholarly development, value to department, and campus-wide contributions. This means that I had to present evidence across these four areas in order to receive tenure and to advance to associate and full professor. I still present evidence across these areas for my yearly evaluation. Note that I used the word *evidence*. As part of my narrative, I summarize my achievements across these areas and include evidence either as supplemental files or as links that will take the reader directly to the evidence (e.g., a hyperlink to an article in which my research or teaching is quoted).

To keep track of the evidence, I maintain what I call a *criteria catalog*. I compile evidence of my contribution in each of these categories, which saves time, helps me draft the narrative, and serves as the actual evidence. At first, these criteria catalogs were manila folders in my work office because I printed copies of everything that related to these four categories at Albion, then organized them per binder using label tabs (those label tabs have evolved into headings in my narrative; see chapter 4 for more detail). Now, I have electronic folders saved as subfiles for each category under the "personnel folder" on my computer desktop and backed up in Dropbox. Duplication of some items in an Atta Girl folder and one of the subfolders is okay.

The purpose is, in real time, to place items in these folders and leave them there. Do not view this as one more file to manage continually. Rather, place items as they become available in these folders and let them sit until it is time to organize them more formally. I set a date at the beginning of each semester that I prepopulate on my calendar for the end of each semester, on which I set aside a maximum of two hours to review the contents in the subfolders and organize accordingly. I then prepare a brief end-of-semester write-up in a running Word document under semester headings (e.g., "fall 2018 evidence") that briefly summarizes each semester's successes across these areas. I also include a "what's ahead" paragraph that keeps me on task based on what is included in these subfolders. The summary, with refinement, can be used at a later time for promotion and yearly evaluation narrative materials, but it is also a good cross-check against the short- and long-term goals you set for yourself. Ask yourself, "Am I on track? Am I behind? Do I see opportunities to address certain categories? Am I need of some collaborators to support my efforts?"

Urgent/Important

Throughout my consulting work and research, time is the number-one challenge that prevents faculty members from meeting goals, viewing advancement to full or continuing contract status as a reality, engaging in professional development, or managing work tasks appropriately (Baker, Lunsford, and Pifer 2017). And although I cannot add more hours to the day, I can help you think about how to more wisely and effectively use time to your advantage.

As part of the Academic Leadership Institute (Baker, Lunsford, and Pifer 2019a), my colleague (and author of chapter 6) Laura Lunsford walked participants through an urgent-versus-important exercise. And I have since used this exercise in my work with leaders who struggle with time management and prioritization for themselves and their team members. In this section, I walk you through a brief but important exercise to gain a better grasp on where you are spending your time, to determine if that time spent is value added and to identify work tasks or other commitments that are candidates for removal.

First, look at your schedule either on a biweekly or monthly basis. Where are you spending your time? This includes the times you are teaching, office hours, long-standing research or project meetings, departmental meetings, and any other events that appear on your schedule. Review these events to determine under which of the categories from figure 2.3 the event falls. For example, the provost may have scheduled a last-minute mandatory meeting for all members of the curriculum and resource committee. I would label such an event as urgent (and hopefully important). A long-standing meeting with a research collaborator may fall under the category of important but

Urgent and Important	**Urgent but Not Important**
Not Urgent but Important	**Not Urgent and Not Important**

Figure 2.3 Urgent versus important

not urgent, given that it is a weekly check-in to ensure the work tasks are on schedule.

The first candidates for removal from your schedule are any events or activities that are not urgent or important. There is no reason to engage in activities that fall under this category, and any future invites for projects, meetings, or work tasks that fall under this category should be declined as much as possible. The next area in which activities should be closely evaluated is the urgent but not important category. At times, we are requested by a department or committee chair or a campus administrator to provide needed information, and that request is accompanied by a short time table. Although we cannot decline or remove all of the activities that fall under this category, we can be extra diligent in limiting how many of these we take on. We can also make sure we are not the requestor asking others to give up their precious time on urgent but not important requests that do not have a value added to the person to whom we made the request.

Ideally, you are viewing your calendar and labeling most of your blocked-off work time as not urgent but important. This is the space you want to be spending the majority of your time because you can see the value added of your efforts and you can see the degree to which these tasks are associated with key responsibilities of your current position or that the time spent directly aligns with your short- and long-term goals (including the goal of balance achieved by spending more time with family). And you aren't engaging in associated work tasks feeling a great deal of pressure to meet an unrealistic deadline. The tasks that appear on your calendar should be those that are most joyful and value added to your efforts, that do not evoke feelings of anxiety and panic.

The last category is urgent and important. While these events and activities can and do find their way onto our calendars, the majority of them should not be labeled as such. If they are, I suggest you add the goal of time management to your list of short-term goals.

Reclaiming Your Time: Time Hacks

I've just been asked to submit my package to be considered for full. I feel like I knew it was coming but have been so busy with three- and four-and-a-half-year-old kids / single mom / begging for funding (that's all dried up anyway) that I haven't really thought about what my "whole package" looks like. So I have four days to pull my shit together. . . . Fun!

—associate professor, STEM, doctoral university, highest research activity

---

The main aim of the urgent-versus-important exercise is to gain some control and a total sense of awareness over your time and to use the time you do have in the most efficient, productive manner possible. This also means saying yes to those efforts that do advance your goals and saying no to those that do not as you seek to reclaim your time.

Some techniques you might employ to better manage your calendar include asking for clarity when you are invited to a meeting. Understanding why you have been invited, what is expected of you, and the associated time commitment helps you better manage your calendar and your time and to feel confident in declining a request.

My colleague Laura does not schedule or participate in meetings that are longer than thirty minutes. Her approach is that if the meeting is managed efficiently and has a clear agenda, most work can be accomplished in thirty minutes. If she is invited to a meeting that is scheduled for longer than thirty minutes, she requests an agenda to determine which part of the meeting is relevant to her. While she cannot decline all invites, she uses the thirty-minute rule as a guideline to help manage requests that are made of her, and she applies this same rule when scheduling meetings with others to illustrate the respect she has for her peers' time.

I employ the twenty-four-hour rule when it comes to accepting invites for work tasks or projects that will extend beyond one or two meetings. I will not say yes on the spot to any invite, no matter how wonderful that possible project is. Early in my career, I had the tendency to take on lots of projects, which sometimes meant that the work I contributed was average, given that those efforts were spread across five initiatives, for example. Instead, I realized that it was better to take twenty-four hours to think about the project and its relation to my professional (and personal goals) and to look at my calendar honestly to see both present and future obligations and to determine if I do in fact have the time to contribute in a meaningful, highly value-added way. I communicate my twenty-four-hour rule to the person who is requesting my engagement by saying something like, "That sounds like a great project, but give me twenty-four hours to think about it and check my calendar, and I will get back to you." This sets expectations for myself and those who are waiting on a response. I find that I am able to accept the invitation and can contribute immediately; or I can accept but not for some specified period of time (e.g., six months), which may or may not be acceptable to the person who extended the invitation; or I need to decline because I do not envision an opportunity to engage at the level I expect of myself.

Conclusion

My training and experiences in higher education and business have allowed me to employ an interdisciplinary approach to my career and have been a benefit, I believe, to my students, colleagues, collaborators, and institution. That interdisciplinarity has also allowed me to be strategic, taking research, practice, tools, and resources from these two disciplinary areas to inform my own career management and my support of others' career-management journey. Organization is a key building block needed to assemble the necessary foundation of success.

Additional Resources

I briefly mentioned a concept referred to as the power (or psychology) of small wins. There is a great deal of research and practice focused on this idea. It's well worth the read. Here are a couple of suggestions.

Amabile, Teresa M., and Steven Kramer. 2011. "The Power of Small Wins." *Harvard Business Review* 89 (5): 70–80.
Amabile, Teresa M., and Steven Kramer. 2011. *The Progress Principle: Using Small Wins to Ignite Joy, Engagement, and Creativity at Work.* Boston: Harvard Business Review Press.

Earlier in the chapter, I mentioned a "Quick Start Guide" to help you initiate conversations and set expectations with a prospective mentor. I include that reference here. Despite the focus on PhD advisers, the suggestions and outlined steps will be of value.

Baker, Vicki, L., and Laura G. Lunsford. 2016. "Mentor Well: Quick Start Guide for PhD Advisors." Lead Mentor Develop, LLC. https://static1
.squarespace.com/static/57a36878440243b50f0cb1db/t/57c741f0f7e0aba
57ab14810/1472676338947/LMD+Flyer+for+Faculty+Mentors+Jan+28
.pdf.

CHAPTER 3

Let the Performance Speak for Itself

Women have a hard time advocating for themselves or feeling confident talking about accomplishments (Case 2015; Siegel 2016). And, even when it is completely justified to talk about successes, others may deem that communication to be inappropriate or arrogant. Since my days as a doctoral student at Penn State, I have subscribed to the motto, "Let the performance speak for itself."

This chapter focuses on quantifying accomplishments in the areas in which you find joy and that align with the expectations of your discipline and institution. More specifically, the aim is to provide you with examples and tools to help you articulate your accomplishments related to two defining criteria: purpose and scope. Focusing on "let the performance speak for itself" will minimize feelings of uneasiness when communicating accomplishments. Instead, let the facts and corresponding evidence be the "voice" that shares your professional story.

Women in the Workforce

What this meant for women faculty at the mid-career stage was an attention to how to manage family responsibilities while thinking about the myriad of opportunities available to established faculty members, including administration, promotion to full professor, and changes in responsibilities.

—Kelly Ward and Lisa Wolf-Wendel (2012, 71)

We must be deliberate in our approach to managing the mental, emotional, and physical work that accompanies managing career and personal responsibilities, including the many identities that define who we are. While women's role in the workforce has evolved for the better, we as a society have a long way to go to achieve a discrimination- and harassment-free, equitable workplace (and home life) as evinced through accounts shared via the #MeToo movement (https://metoomvmt.org/).

Women are more likely than men to earn a bachelor's degree by the time they are twenty-nine years of age. In fact, the percentage of women holding college degrees in the workforce has quadrupled since 1970. Based on US Department of Labor Statistics, nearly 47 percent of US workers are women, and they own nearly ten million businesses, "accounting for $1.4 trillion in receipts" (DeWolf 2017). Despite impressive strides in the workforce since World War II, gender imbalances and inequities still exist.

Researchers reveal different experiences for women depending on the type of work environment in which they are employed. For example, in Kim Parker's (2018) research on the experiences of women in men-dominated workplaces, she found that "women who report that their workplace has more men than women have a very different set of experiences than their counterparts in work settings that are mostly female or have an even mix of men and women." Gender was a dominant factor in inhibiting advancement for women in their careers and resulted in less equitable treatment in the workplace. Further, women in workplaces where the majority of employees are men experience gender discrimination at significantly higher rates. On the basis of research data, the academy is still very much a men-dominated workplace (Curtis 2011)

The environments in which women work continue to be rife with institutional and industry-driven biases. As reported in *The Simple Truth about the Gender Pay Gap* (AAUW 2018), women are paid 80 percent of what men are paid. Pay equity is not predicted to be achieved until 2059. Also, where you live matters; data published by the American Community Survey found that the pay gap is the smallest in New York (89 percent) and the largest in Louisiana (70 percent) (US Census Bureau 2018).

Demographic factors also contribute to the gender pay gap (AAUW 2018). Asian women, for example, show the smallest gender pay gap compared to white male peers, at 85 percent, whereas the largest gap is found for Hispanic women, at 54 percent. Age also factors into the gender pay gap. For instance, for full-time workers ages twenty to twenty-four, women were paid 96 percent of what men were paid on a weekly basis. However, this gap widens with age. Women are paid only 74 percent of what men are paid by the time workers reach fifty-five to sixty-four years old. A variety of factors may contribute to this result, such as time out of the workforce to manage family responsibilities.

Women in Higher Education

Pay inequities are also present in the academy. According to a report published by the American Council on Education, women faculty members were paid, on average, $15,408 less than male faculty members annually. Research findings further revealed, "No matter the academic rank, men make more than women and are more likely to hold a tenure track position" (H. Johnson 2017, 8). Despite the strides women are making in higher education at the student level, professional and academic women face barriers and a chilly climate in the academy

(Britton 2017). John Curtis (2011), director of research and public policy at the American Association of University Professors (AAUP), notes that "by and large . . . progress for women into the most prestigious and well-paid positions in academia has lagged far behind the advances experienced by women students" (1). The phrase "the higher, the fewer" is perhaps the most apt description of the trends identified by Curtis (2011) and later by Heather Johnson (2017) with regard to women faculty representation in the academy. Despite the fact that women have achieved higher education-attainment levels compared to men, this success is not reflected in the number of women in positions of high faculty rank, salary, or accompanying prestige.

These trends capture the experiences of women faculty in the United States and globally. In Australia, for example, women hold fewer academic positions compared to their male peers at the senior lecturer level (44.7 percent) and higher (31.7 percent) (Strachan 2016). In Canada, women occupied 40.2 percent of full-time academic teaching-staff positions from 2016 to 2017, up from 37.6 percent five years earlier. Trending in a promising direction, the gains were found at the higher-ranking positions of full and associate professor. Yet men still held the majority of these ranks in Canada (Statistics Canada 2017). Women are also in the minority among senior academics (classified as Grade A positions) in many European countries including Belgium, Germany, the United Kingdom, France, Switzerland, and Sweden. This minority position also carries over into executive leadership positions in higher education, with women occupying a mere 20.1 percent of heads of higher-education institutions (European Commission 2017). These same trends characterize India, with only 25.8 percent of Indian women occupying full professor status (Government of India 2017), and Japan, with only 23.7 percent of women occupying full-time university teaching positions (Government of Japan 2017). These findings reveal an opportunity within the academy globally to examine institutional biases and to provide greater supports beyond early career to support women's advancement through all stages of the professoriate.

Women's Experiences in the Academy

In an environment that lacks representation and has a wage gap, the women who do earn senior positions in the academy experience difficulty in this environment. "Within academia, women must mask (disguise) or compartmentalize (hide) identities (e.g., identities related to sexual orientation, motherhood, religion, communities), thus negotiating which identities to reveal or hide to aid in career maintenance or progress, depending on context" (Reinert and Yakaboski 2017, 321). Many face discrimination, harassment, and a "chilly climate," particularly women in the STEM fields, women of color, and queer faculty (Serra Hagedorn and Vigil Laden 2002; Sallee, Ward, and Wolf-Wendel 2016; Settles et al. 2006; Turner 2002). Lesbian, gay, bisexual, and transgender (LGBT) faculty have the burden of heterosexism and the feeling that they must conceal their sexuality as key obstacles to equity and inclusion (Reinert and Yakaboski 2017). Further, women faculty members who aspire to have a family and a career feel compelled to keep plans for family private out of fear of negative implications on career advancement (Armenti 2004). Once child-care or elder-care responsibilities become a reality for women faculty, certain professional opportunities become challenging (e.g., membership on faculty-elected committees that meet after work hours) and must be minimized or declined. This, in turn, limits campus visibility and interactions with senior colleagues, thus negatively affecting career advancement (Baker, Lunsford, and Pifer 2017; Reinert and Yakaboski 2017).

In sum, women in the academy have different experiences than men do, and those differences are often obstacles that create challenges for women's advancement along the path to the professoriate. However, women faculty are not a monolithic group. As the literature illustrates, women of color, academic mothers, LGBT faculty, single mothers, and those with or without partners all experience the academy differently, which may further complicate the path from associate to full professorship or continuing contract status.

Academic Leadership

Academic leadership is also an area in which there is room for improvement. Data from a 2006 study revealed that women's representation among college and university presidential positions doubled over the preceding two decades and was sitting at 23 percent in 2011 (Curtis 2011). By 2017, that percentage rose to 30 percent (Samsel 2017). And while women occupy other senior leadership positions to a greater extent as compared to presidential positions (Curtis 2011), leaking leadership pipeline issues (Baker, Lunsford, and Pifer 2019b), lack of career-advancement opportunities (Parker 2018), significantly higher service expectations and engagement (Guarino and Borden 2017), and poor career guidance delivered to women from their male counterparts (Tickle 2017) push women into roles that are not traditionally perceived to be pathways to executive leadership positions. Women occupy administrative positions that are in supporting roles (e.g., student services), whereas their male counterparts occupy leadership roles tied to budgets and strategy (e.g., business and administration) (Tickle 2017).

While women are making advances in the workplace in both industry and higher education, men and women can and must do better. In higher education, we draw attention to and research inequities, and the associated outcomes and needed interventions, to remedy these inequities at the student levels. Yet we are inexcusably lagging behind when it comes to supporting women professionals in the academy and their career advancement along the path to the professoriate.

Lesson Learned

Women get evaluated on their performance; men get evaluated on their potential.

—Douglas McCracken (2000, 164)

During my third year as an early-career faculty member at Albion College, a peer institution in the Great Lakes Colleges Association (GLCA) courted me. I was not looking for another faculty post but appreciated the interest. Plus, as a single, early-career woman, the position would have placed me much closer to family and would have allowed me, much like at Albion, to create a management-based curriculum from nearly scratch. I participated in the early part of the process before pulling my name from consideration because I truly enjoyed my position at Albion. During this time, however, the provost and my department chair were made aware of this situation. To my department chair's credit, he approached me and asked, "What do we need to do to keep you?" This all occurred during the recession around 2008–10, so additional salary was not an option; and quite frankly, a financial boost alone was not an immediate interest to me. Rather, I wanted to go up early for promotion and tenure. My department chair acquiesced, pending the results of my interim review, since I came in on the seven-year clock.

At Albion, the interim review process results in either a "satisfactory" or "unsatisfactory" rating. However, whispers communicated that it also included informal letter-based results—A, B, or C. A letters are rare, signifying exceptional performance with no areas for improvement. B letters were standard and developmental in nature, noting strengths but also areas for improvement. C letters are not necessarily a ticket to an automatic dismissal, but they do signal the need for significant improvement during the remainder of the promotion and tenure process. B letters are the standard.

Following my interim review, I weighed my option of going up early for promotion and tenure. I shared the review results with my department chair, who said it was one of the most positive ones he had seen in his over twenty years at the institution. When I shared with my peers, several labeled it an A letter and encouraged me to go up early. As a result, my department chair and I agreed that we would approach the provost about going up early for tenure at some point in my fourth year. The provost agreed to support the decision with the caveat that if I were denied tenure, I would not be able to return to my original tenure clock and would not have another opportunity to go up for promotion and tenure at Albion College.

This decision, however, was not met with positivity from all of my departmental colleagues. I was going up at the same time as a male colleague who was hired before me and happened to be one of my favorite colleagues. While Albion does not subscribe to the approach that only a certain number of individuals can earn tenure in a given department at a given time, I received implicit and explicit messages that some of my departmental colleagues did not want the two of us to be compared by the committee at the same time. While my peer's scholarship was lacking, he was an excellent teacher and students loved him.

My department chair held a meeting with the senior colleagues in the department, who happened to be all men, to seek input regarding my early bid for tenure. This meeting was peculiar, as I had the support of both my department chair and provost. From what I was told, this meeting got pretty contentious, with one member in particular noting that he would write a letter of nonsupport if I chose to go up early. A few days later, a different departmental colleague informed me of the combative tone displayed by a senior colleague in the department and then proceeded to say, "While I think you are making a political mistake going up early, given [the colleague's] lack of support, I will write you a positive letter because the performance is what it is." Two ideas immediately came to mind: (1) this friendly colleague is overestimating the political clout that the senior colleague has, and (2) my approach to managing my career was paying off—let the performance speak for itself. It did, in fact, speak for itself, and I was awarded promotion and tenure early and have continued to focus on quantifying my performance in every way possible.

In sum, there are a few lessons I hope you take away from my experience. First, you and you alone are in control of your career advancement and managing your career. I was resolute in my abilities and accomplishments and was willing to stand behind my performance. Second, the "good old boy" network of the academy is very much intact. While I do believe my department chair was advocating for me, the meeting with senior departmental colleagues was less about supporting my advancement or talking through what was in my best interest and more about talking through how it might affect my departmental peer's bid for tenure. Third, colleagues will offer good and bad advice, and it is our job to filter through that advice to do what is in our best interest. Lastly, we cannot control all of the "noise" in the workplace. Thus, it is imperative to build a solid case in which work and community contributions are quantified, thereby making it impossible for a committee of educated yet uninformed peers to misinterpret or misunderstand the value you bring to your students, department, institution, and local and professional communities.

Purpose and Scope

I was tenured in 2012, and my mantra has been "full before forty-five." So the plan is to submit by 2020. Our tenure and promotion guidelines in the department are super vague and confusing—even less guidance at the university level.

—associate professor, social sciences, doctoral university,
moderate research activity

I spend a great deal of time reviewing resumes and CVs. Inevitably, I push the resume or CV writer to focus on clarity around two key factors: purpose and scope. If you leave it to the reader to make sense of what is there, the corresponding interpretation will not be in your favor the majority of the time (see chapter 4). "Purpose" refers to the reason behind engaging in a given activity and the associated goal of that activity. "Scope" refers to the depth and breadth that a given effort spans, including details about the beneficiary. A focus on these factors supports the quantification of key contributions in the areas that bring you joy and that are valued by your institution.

The remainder of this chapter is organized by the three broad evaluation categories found across all institution types: scholarship, teaching, and service. I also include a fourth category, administration, given that this is a role many women associate professors assume once tenure and promotion are earned. Within each category, examples spanning institution type and divisional areas demonstrate how to communicate purpose and scope, focusing on ways to quantify evidence to illustrate excellence in these areas.

Evaluation Criteria and Promotion Processes

I must stress that the goal in sharing the examples throughout this chapter is to provide you with a diversity of ways in which to organize your materials. This is not meant to set some artificial standard of productivity that becomes demoralizing for you if you do not have the same number of publications or teaching performance as the women whose examples are offered here. Do not compare yourself to others and use that comparison as a reason not to pursue your career goals. Focus on *your* strengths and performance as the only metrics that matter.

The areas of scholarship, teaching, and service permeate the academy. Read a faculty job description and you will find mention of these categories to varying degrees. Given the mission of knowledge creation and dissemination, research universities prioritize research the highest. Research has been described as the "yardstick that plays a role in reputation, recruitment, and retention of top professors" (Bugeja 2009), but teaching and service also play a role. For a LAC, based on my experience as a faculty member, researcher, and external reviewer of personnel files, teaching is the predominant focus given the institutional mission. However, scholarly productivity is increasing in importance in LACs (Baker, Lunsford, and Pifer 2017), and in some instances, the expected productivity is comparable to that of research universities (Hughes 2014). For selective LACs, strong teaching alone will not result in a successful bid for promotion and tenure and certainly not for full professorship. Scholarly expectations are on the rise across all institution types (Baker, Terosky, and Martinez 2017; Ward and Wolf-Wendel 2012). Despite the notion of service being present across all institution types, an overabundance of service will not secure promotion and tenure (or advancement) in the absence of strong scholarship and teaching, nor will it be the cause of a failed bid if scholarship and teaching excellence are present. As the scholars Ann Ortiz, Don Haviland, and Laura Henriques (2017) note, "If it is a choice between getting an article or grant submitted and serving on a time-consuming committee, the scholarly work is probably a better choice."

Scholarship/Research

Regardless of institution type, scholarship, research, and creative activity factor into career-advancement decisions and outcomes. In keeping consistent with my focus on organization from chapter 2, I recommend the use of headings as guideposts to walk the reader of your resume or CV through your accomplishments with quantifiable details that correspond with each heading. These should align with the categories you are expected to address as part of a narrative and any supplemental materials you attach to your narrative.

At the beginning of any narrative, I recommend including a snapshot of highlights to summarize the main contributions across the categories addressed in the dossier or application. Highlights can appear at the beginning of the entire narrative (including highlights of the other key categories) or as part of each specific category (e.g., teaching, research, service). Just as we are sure that our students do not read every word they are assigned, we can assume our colleagues do not read every word of a submitted narrative. These highlights allow the reader to get a solid understanding of what is addressed in the narrative in a very quantitative way. For example, in 2017, I submitted the award application shown in figure 3.1, which uses this highlights model.

For me, the "highlights" mostly focus on recent accomplishments (e.g., the year in which I submitted the award application) but also incorporate metrics that span my body of work. To provide evidence

Teaching Excellence:
- Instructor effectiveness rating average across courses: 1.19 (1 = highest rating; old system)
- Instructor effectiveness rating average across courses: 4.70 (5 = highest rating; new system)
- 46 formal academic advisees (most in E&M Department; most on campus)
- Developed/delivered 6 new courses since arriving at Albion; substantially revised 2 existing courses (8 unique courses, in total)
- Students' Choice Professor of the Year
- Arthur Anderson New Faculty Teaching Award

Scholarly Excellence:
- 55 publications (30 total peer-reviewed journal articles; 14 peer-reviewed journal articles in impact-factor journals)
- $1.8M National Science Foundation Grant (Project Title: Using Networks to Scale Improvement of STEM Undergraduate Education: A Comparative Study of Network Goals, Processes, and Strategies to Advance Organizational Change; Michigan State University. Role: Senior Scholar Timeframe: August 2017–August 2021)
- Two books in 2017:
  - Baker, V. L., Lunsford, L. G., and Pifer, M. J. (2017). Developing Faculty in Liberal Arts Colleges: Aligning Individual Needs and Organizational Goals. Rutgers University Press
  - Baker, V. L., Lunsford, L. G., Neisler, G., Pifer, M. J., & Terosky, A.L.P. (Eds). Success after Tenure: Supporting Mid-Career Faculty. Stylus Publishing, LLC (full volume draft submitted to editor—Nov. 2017).
- Two monographs in 2017:
  - Baker, V. L., Terosky, A.L.P, and Martinez, E. (2017) "Faculty members' scholarly learning across institutional types." Jossey-Bass ASHE Higher Education Report Series (AEHE).
  - Crisp, G., Baker, V. L., Griffin, K. A., Lunsford, L. G., and Pifer, M. J. (2017). Mentoring Undergraduate Students. Jossey-Bass ASHE Higher Education Report Series (AEHE).
- Phi Beta Kappa Scholar of the Year

I believe my body of work to date, as summarized above and throughout this application, embodies the spirit and intent of endowed professorships, as noted in the Faculty Handbook, "to recognize and support truly distinguished teaching and research." I am proud I have been able to consistently maintain high levels of success in and out of the classroom.

Figure 3.1 Application highlights

of scholarly excellence, highlighting accomplishments in key areas such as publications or other creative works and exhibitions is a must. Also grants, presentations, scholarly awards, and disciplinary or field recognition are all examples of "scholarly excellence" that should be quantified and discussed.

Publication and creative works. Providing numbers of publications, types of publications, and associated details about those publications (e.g., journal impact factor) is important. My minor adviser once told me, "In order to get tenure and promotion, you need to publish. In order to get promoted to full professor, you need to illustrate your contribution to the field." To illustrate "contribution to the field," I recommend organizing publication-related details in a table including the year of publication, title, journal, and citation count. Lead authorship should be indicated in some way (I use a double asterisk symbol; see figure 3.2). For our purposes here, I include only the beginning portion of what I use in my materials, but my complete table includes all peer-reviewed publications to date in chronological order.

Another way to communicate similar information is through bullet-point form. The following is an excerpt from a section of a narrative called "research contributions," shared by a full professor in the social sciences (doctoral university, highest research activity).

- To date, I have authored over 40 publications (23 post-tenure), including a monograph and edited book.
- 50 percent of my journal articles appear in top tier, high impact education journals.
- To deepen the reach of my work, I have also contributed to 14 book chapters including the SAGE Handbook of [disciplinary field], a highly regarded international publication.
- According to Google Scholar, my scholarship has been cited in over 2,400 publications (H-index=22).

The same professor included the following publication-specific detail in her dossier materials related to journal quality:

- Tier 1 Journal, SJR Ranking 1.724, H-index 57
- Tier 2 Journal, SJR Ranking .344, H-index 6

Some institutions have prepopulated forms in which the headings are determined by discipline or division. One example, from a full

Year	Title	Journal	Citations
2006	Beyond Being Proactive: What (Else) Matters for Career Self-Management Behaviors?" Research Note	*Career Development International*	116
2007	Extra-Role Behaviors Challenging the Status Quo: Validity and Antecedents of Taking Charge Behaviors	*Journal of Managerial Psychology*	74
2008	Moral Disengagement in Ethical Decision Making: A Study of Antecedents and Outcomes	*Journal of Applied Psychology*	694
2009	**Towards a Theory of Doctoral Student Professional Identity Development: A Developmental Networks Approach	*Journal of Higher Education*	244
2010	**Developmental Networks and Learning: An Interdisciplinary Perspective on Faculty Identity Development during Doctoral Study	*Studies in Higher Education*	155
2011	**The Role of Relationships in the Transition from Doctoral Student to Independent Scholar	*Studies in Continuing Education*	81
2012	Why Employees Do Bad Things: Moral Disengagement and Transgressive Organizational Behavior	*Personnel Psychology*	318

Figure 3.2 Citation count organizational tool

professor in the humanities (doctoral university, higher research activity), includes appointment history, educational background, teaching experience, and research and other scholarly/creative activities. She included subheadings for journal articles and book chapters, books, journal editorship, research monographs and reports (e.g., invited reviews and encyclopedia entries), and other publications accepted and publications submitted. In addition to citing the publication, she noted coauthors' contribution by percentage (e.g., 30 percent of authorship), and she noted "by invitation" requests as relevant to a given publication and publication status (e.g., in print or forthcoming). Additional subsections included "List significant citations and reviews of publications or creative works" (prepopulated on the form) and "citations relevant to editorship of [journal]," which the faculty member added, given that it aligned with her scholarly efforts and contribution to the field.

TO DO

1 Decide on an organizing framework (e.g., Excel, literally writing out details in a Word document)

2 Collect/collate/count your publications

3 Record publication-related details (e.g., impact factor, authorship order, contribution)

Regardless of your organizational preference, the details are quantifiable examples that illustrate scholarly excellence via publications, including total number, type, quality (e.g., impact factor), and contribution to the field (e.g., citation counts). Be sure to included details about peer-reviewed/refereed journal articles, book chapters and reviews, refereed conference proceedings, refereed (and nonrefereed) conference presentations, monographs, books, and technical reports. At a minimum, provide detail about the total number and type of publication as well as pre- or posttenure achievement to illustrate a sustained scholarly agenda since earning tenure and promotion.

Grants. Another measure of scholarly productivity that resonates across institutional types is grants. The expectations associated with the kinds of grants and frequency with which grants are secured varies, but external and internal funding is yet another measure of scholarly excellence. The highlights summary shared in figure 3.1 includes an active National Science Foundation grant in which I hold a senior personnel position. In the narrative, I highlight other external grants I have secured as well as internal faculty-development grants secured. For each, I provide details about the amount received and a brief description of the grant (e.g., purpose of the research), my associated responsibilities, and target population. The following examples show how you might communicate grant details, starting with an example of mine from a baccalaureate college: arts and sciences focus (social sciences); followed by doctoral university, highest research activity (social sciences); and doctoral university, higher research activity (humanities).

Example #1
- Principal Investigator, Supporting Midcareer Faculty Members (Spring 2016–Summer 2017). This subproject of the Initiative for Faculty Development in Liberal Arts Colleges focuses specifically on the experiences, challenges and needed supports of midcareer faculty members in the Great Lakes College Association (GLCA). A mixed-methods study involving faculty focus groups at four GLCA sites as well as a survey administration involving the thirteen member institutions focuses on career-stage challenges, institutional supports, leadership aspirations/experiences, promotion and tenure, and work/personal considerations. Supported by the Henry Luce Foundation (New York). Amount: $50,000.

Example #2
- Coinvestigator of a $1.3 million Noyce grant from the National Science Foundation. Role is to employ qualitative methods to better

understand how community college students experience and develop mentoring relationships.

Example #3
- Investigator. National Writing Grants (1996, 1997, 1998). The National Writing Project focuses the knowledge, expertise, and leadership of our nation's educators on sustained efforts to improve writing and learning for all learners. Total amount funded: $51,850.

A woman academic from a community college (junior colleges: mixed transfer/career and technical-mixed traditional/nontraditional) shared the following details about how, and in what ways, scholarship expectations are addressed in her institution's application materials. While scholarly publications were not specifically required, "participation in scholarly activities" and "demonstrated scholarly leadership" were necessary for career advancement. Examples of evidence noted by a full professor candidate (professional field) included attendance and participation in professional conferences (national and regional) as well as conferences focused on community college teaching in her professional field. This woman faculty member also maintains professional certification, which requires eighty hours of continuing-education hours over two years. The candidate noted in her application, "Forty of those hours must be seminars, classes, or self-study. I focus on areas that will help in my classroom subject area."

Scholarly Awards and Recognition. A great number of institutions and professional associations confer awards to recognize scholarly or field (disciplinary) excellence. Such awards should be included in the highlights snapshot, with additional detail provided in narrative form expanding on the purpose and scope of the award. A woman full professor from a comprehensive university (master's colleges and universities: larger programs) illustrated her reputation across the three levels provided in her institutional handbook (state, regional, national) by including details about awards received, such as the early-career scholarship and service award, fellow status achieved in her professional association, "featured member" on a professional association's webpage, and invitations to serve as a research scholar at several institutes. For each of these awards and recognition, she included the year awarded and details about the award.

Teaching

To the masses, the notion of teaching conjures visions of a great orator imparting wisdom and knowledge from the front of the classroom to open and eager future leaders and community engagers. However, those of us in the academy know that this perception is flawed, at best. Teaching has evolved over the years, resulting in "increased pressures on the faculty to rework their pedagogical strategies for learners whose characteristics include the tendencies to comprehend visually, to shift attention easily, and to expect interaction and collaboration in the classroom" (Szybinski and Jordan 2010, 4). With this evolution comes new conceptions about what constitutes "teaching excellence." For some professors, teaching excellence is measured through course or teaching evaluations. For others, a broader definition of teaching is applied that acknowledges the ways and varied locations in which teaching (and learning) occurs.

Similar to scholarship, I recommend including a highlights summary of teaching excellence that incorporates quantifiable measures. The teaching categories and corresponding detail included in figure 3.1 may differ for you, based on institutional and disciplinary expectations. However, I talk about why these categories make sense for me in chapter 4 and why I strongly encourage my clients to broaden the categories in a way that makes sense and aligns with their joys and value-added contributions. The most common measures of evidence of teaching excellence include course or teaching evaluations, advising, course- or program-development activities, and teaching awards.

Teaching evaluations. There is a great debate about the value and reliability of teaching and course evaluations as well as documented gender bias (Bartlett 2015; MacNell, Driscoll, and Hunt 2015). However, this system permeates the academy regardless of institution type and must be

Semester	Course	Professor effectiveness	Value of course
Fall 2017	LA 101—Lessons Learned at the Office	4.7	4.7
	BUS 351—Intl. Entrepreneurial Exchange	4.84	4.7
	E&M 359—Management	4.7	4.74
Summer 2017	E&M 362—International Management	no evals.	no evals.

Figure 3.3 Course evaluation, baccalaureate college: arts and sciences focus

Term	Course name and number	Total enrollment	Mean instructor rating (range: 1–5)	Survey response rate
Fall 2007	ED XXX—Research Methods	25	4.9	76%
Spring 2008	HSA XXX—Administration	14	4.3	93%

Figure 3.4 Teaching evaluation, research university

addressed in a narrative or as part of dossier materials. I recommend the use of a table, organized per semester, per course, and including quantitative metrics as one measure of excellence. For example, see two recent semesters in figure 3.3.

Once promotion and tenure are earned at Albion College, teaching evaluations are collected on a rolling basis by division unless the faculty member opts in, hence the "no evals." designation in figure 3.3.

Bullet points with or without an accompanying table are another way to organize (social scientist, doctoral university, highest research activity). See figure 3.4.

- My nine-year average instructor rating at [prior institution] for 32 courses was 4.7 out of 5.0 (SD = .32). Additionally, I received median instructor scores that were higher than the University median for the three courses that I taught during my first year at [current institution].

Here's an example from a master's college/university: larger programs:

- In each year of merit evaluation since my arrival at [institution], I received ratings of "exceptional" and "very good" in teaching. In addition, during my promotion and tenure review, I received a teaching rating of "exceptional" at every level of internal review.

Returning to the humanities professor whose institution uses a prepopulated form, instructions related to "teaching excellence" might read something like this: "List all courses taught at [institution] during the past five years, indicating enrollment in each. Indicate if courses are team taught and what fraction of each course is taught by the candidate" (example from doctoral university, higher research activity). The full professor candidate included a three-column table using the following headings: semester, course, and enrollment. After the enrollment figure, the candidate noted if the course was team taught and corresponding teaching percentage (e.g., team taught 50/50). From a community college perspective, a prepopulated form might note something like the following: "How have you modeled teaching effectiveness, and how have you performed curriculum and course development?" Information included in an application might address the following: engagement and participation in teaching-center programming; the approach and efforts taken to revise courses on the basis of student feedback and trends in the field; and participation in course-level and departmental programming changes.

In addition to the quantitative measures, I recommend the inclusion of a table with qualitative student comments from the previous two semesters (or some predetermined time frame). Rather than paraphrase or summarize the students' voices, I include all comments. This approach allows me to simply report the "facts" or evidence for my case, using others' voices to speak on behalf of my teaching excellence.

Advising. As a component of teaching, advising is critical to faculty roles and responsibilities. In my highlights snapshot under "teaching excellence," noted previously, I include the total number of advisees I have. In the narrative, I provide details about my advising philosophy, my management approach to support this advisee load (the highest in the college), tracking sheets, and the types of conversations we have (refer to chapter 4). I use the concepts of purpose and scope to guide the information I include and the supplemental narrative I draft to support the quantitative measures noted.

In other institution types, advising can include master's and doctoral students as well as proposal- and dissertation-committee advising responsibilities. Here are some ways in which these details can be quantified (doctoral university, highest research activity):

- I have successfully supervised 8 doctoral students through graduation and have served as a committee member for 13 additional talented and hard-working students, all of whom now hold leadership, policy, or faculty positions across the country. I am particularly proud that five of my students have acquired tenure-track faculty positions at research universities including [list of institutions]. This is notable given these students graduated from an Ed.D. program at a research-aspiring Hispanic-serving institution.
- I currently supervise four Ph.D. and Ed.D. students and serve as a secondary or committee member for 11 students.
- 14 of my publications have been coauthored by doctoral students, all of which were independent of the students' dissertation work.

The following is another way to communicate details about doctoral and master's advisees:

1 *Dissertation Primary for [student name]. Ph.D. student, Cohort XX.
2 Dissertation Primary for [student name]. Ed.D. student, Cohort XX.
3 Dissertation Primary for [student name]. Ed.D. student, Cohort XX.
4 Minor Professor for [student name], Ed.D. student, Cohort XX.

* Presented at a national conference and/or published with student

Name	Major/discipline	Undergraduate	Graduate	Coauthored conference presentation	Publication coauthor	Paid position	Served on master's committee
xxxx	clinical psychology	X	X	X	X		
xxxx	sociology	X	X	X	X (2)	X	
xxxx	psychology		X	X			Chair
xxxx	psychology/ criminology	X		X			
xxxx	psychology	X		X			
xxxx	family therapy	X	X	X		X	
xxxx	psychology/ women's studies	X	X	X	X (4)	X	Chair

Figure 3.5 An example of how to organize advising and mentoring relationship details

I am a big fan of the table organized by a fellow woman full professor from a comprehensive university (master's colleges and universities: larger programs), whose work spans the social sciences and humanities (see figure 3.5). Such a table could be adapted to illustrate the purpose and scope of student advising, mentoring, and collaboration, while leaving an opportunity to expand on these relationships in the narrative.

A woman full professor seeking continuing contract status at a community college (associate's colleges: mixed transfer/career and technical-mixed traditional/nontraditional), shared the following response to a question on a prepopulated form used by her institution: "Please specify how you have participated in individual and/or group advising":

I am an adviser for the [discipline] club at [institution]. I also mentor my students on how to become a [career title] in [state]. Our department has a several-page handout that outlines the educational requirements necessary to become a [career title] in [state] and how students can complete the needed classwork here at [institution] and with our transfer partners to sit for the [certification] exam. I hold a minimum of two hours of office hours daily Monday–Thursday and Friday if needed. I encourage students to drop in or make an appointment to discuss any career or class questions they have concerns about. I advise students on an individual basis regarding any concerns or career goals they may have.

Course-specific details. Course-specific details such as the number of courses taught, developed, and/or substantially revised should be quantified. In the teaching-effectiveness highlights snapshot (figure 3.1), I note the number of new courses I have developed as well as revised during my time at Albion. I was hired specifically to develop the management curriculum. Given this charge, I provide updates in all substantive evaluations on this point. In the narrative, I provide details such as course descriptions, learning goals and objectives, and examples of the project-based, community-based learning that I incorporate into all of my courses each semester to provide insights on the purpose of my courses as connected to my personal teaching mission.

Teaching awards and other recognition. Lastly, provide descriptions of any awards, when they were awarded, and by whom (e.g., student's choice, institutional peers). The internal and external validation is an added bonus in materials. Be sure also to include teaching-focused presentations at regional, national, and international conferences as an area related to teaching performance and contribution.

Service

The final category to address in a dossier or narrative is service. I provide the following example of my service highlights snapshot. Of course, my narrative provides greater details about the purpose and scope of my engagement in these activities.

Institutional Service

- Member—two campus-wide committees: the Institutional Review Board and the Foundation for Undergraduate Research, Scholarship, and Creative Activity (provost-appointed)
- Judge—Distinguished Scholars Program (spring 2017)
- Moderator/panelist—admissions high school guidance counselor visit (spring 2017)
- Panelist—"hands on" session: admitted student visit day (spring 2017)
- Interviewer—candidates for the Philadelphia Center (TPC) recruiter position (summer 2017)

Departmental Service

- Faculty search committee member—tenure-track faculty position in marketing for the Economics and Management Department (review interview files, conduct interviews in San Francisco at professional conference, spring/summer/fall 2017)
- Faculty adviser—Delta Sigma Pi (DSP) business fraternity (spring/fall 2017)
- Coordinator—arranged mock interviews for DSP business fraternity with Albion alumni (17 pairings)
- Departmental representative—two admissions visit days

Community Service

- Developer and deliverer—EmpowHER program called "Learning to Lead"

Other service categories of interest might include institutional, departmental or programmatic, and professional service. Institutional service includes institution-wide faculty committees (e.g., curriculum, personnel, faculty development), strategic planning committees, search committee membership for an executive-level leadership position, and faculty marshal or faculty liaison positions. Departmental service activities include department chair, departmental search committee member and/or chair, admissions representative, and student group advising. Professional service activities include chair or cochair of a preconference workshop, advisory board member and/or chair, task force or ad hoc professional association committee member and/or chair, executive leadership position, and editorial positions.

Community engagement is one type of service that is particularly important for community college faculty members. According to a full professor at a midwestern community college, "Being visible and engaged in community activities beyond the campus is a must. I had to address my involvement in my application for full and was mentored by senior colleagues that the engagement had to be consistent in the years leading up to advancement." In an effort to connect her professional and personal roles and responsibilities, she noted the following in her application: "Having younger children, I have primarily been involved in Girl Scout and Boy Scout activities as well as various school activities and fundraisers. I have volunteered with the Girl Scouts sorting food at the food pantry when the postal workers collected food. Also, I have helped in other activities such as helping clean our local parks. I try to promote [institution name] on a daily basis to anyone I meet. I am so proud to be a member of this exceptional educational institution." Such community engagement may be important in other institutional settings as driven by institutional mission.

Service is an area that can require a great deal of emotional and physical energy yet does not garner the level of recognition that it probably should when it comes to advancement decisions. And, as evinced by scholars, women in general but specifically those from minoritized populations are overburdened with service roles and expectations, which can hinder their career advancement (June 2015). Once promotion and tenure are earned, it becomes imperative to be selective about which service responsibilities are accepted. I do acknowledge, however, that turning down service invitations may be perceived as detrimental to career advancement for women and other underrepresented groups. Make every effort to ensure the service requests accepted are driven by your joy, at least in part, and/or put you in a position to highlight your strengths as a means of gaining greater campus visibility. Try to use service opportunities to enhance strengths and help you develop in other areas of interest.

Administration

An area not addressed formally in one of the three usual categories (scholarship, teaching, service) is administrative roles. Research reveals that once promotion and tenure are achieved, service and administrative roles and responsibilities increase, particularly for women faculty members (Baker, Lunsford, and Pifer 2017; Ward and Wolf-Wendel 2012). At times, this shift in attention can be detrimental to advancing to full professorship (Dow 2014). My clients often ask under which category administrative roles should be addressed. My advice is to create a separate category depending on the type of administrative role occupied. Ward and Wolf-Wendel (2012) share a distinction between service and administration, in which their study participants explain that if the activity garnered some type of monetary payment or compensation (additional salary, course release, stipend), that activity qualifies as administration, whereas uncompensated activities counts as service.

Administrative roles can be a paradox. While such roles can serve as important professional-development opportunities, they often do not contribute substantially to promotion decisions. In fact, as noted earlier, time spent in these roles can detract from career-advancement goals given the shift in professional focus and responsibilities. However, I believe administrative roles can and do support scholarly learning and can be advantageous to crafting a compelling narrative if communicated in an appropriate way.

I provide the following example of an administrative role from a director of composition position at an English department in a research university:

- Mentored and supervised staff of more than 35 graduate teaching assistants and adjunct faculty members responsible for teaching approximately 50 composition and writing intensive courses each semester
- Designed standard curriculum for first-year writing and mentored composition faculty in development of syllabi for sophomore composition and upper-level writing classes

- Handled student complaints and grievances in connection with composition courses
- Planned and facilitated week-long professional development workshop for new graduate teaching assistants and biweekly mentoring luncheons
- Managed $25,000 budget from endowment fund dedicated to enriching the professional lives of writing teachers
- Ensured viability of articulation agreements with regional postsecondary institutions
- Coordinated with supervisor of high school teachers providing dual-credit English courses and organized professional development for high school teachers
- Oversaw the annual publication of student writing, the student journal, and teaching guide to help faculty use student writing effectively in their courses

One of the main takeaways from this example is the focus on purpose and scope. Each core responsibility is identified, described, and quantified, and the primary audience is identified when applicable. Significant emotional, mental, and physical energy goes into serving administrative functions to the highest level. Therefore, the goal is to communicate that performance and contribution in as compelling a way as possible.

Conclusion

Sitting down to prepare a narrative and organizing the corresponding evidence can be (and is) overwhelming. Often my clients struggle with what to include and how to communicate that detail. The goal in this chapter has been to provide you with examples that span institution type and discipline to help minimize the anxiety and uncertainty that accompanies this process. More important, I hope you have been inspired by the organizational approaches used by the women featured in this chapter as they sought to "let the performance speak for itself."

CHAPTER 4

Take Control of Your Narrative

Tara, a woman of color and full professor, said,

> I was doing quite a bit of service work for the college in my associate
> professor years, not only chairing my department but also serving on
> some major committees. My research progressed during this period, but
> my productivity was visible more through external grants awarded and
> invited talks and somewhat less through publications brought to frui-
> tion. My teaching continued, on course, with some new course devel-
> opment but (as is perhaps a bit more typical in a science department)
> primarily continued refinement of existing courses. I'm not sure I had
> any particular strategy associated with the promotion-to-full dossier
> beyond continuing the strategy I laid out in my tenure package. At that
> moment I was very conscious of needing to present my work as part
> of a trajectory, rather than as a list of accomplishments to date. For me
> this was in part because I had started a brand-new research area when I
> started at [institution] and in fact had to shift gears pretty dramatically
> to do so. There were some false starts as well during those early years. So
> although I had a sufficient publication record when I came up for ten-
> ure, my concern was that it wouldn't look sufficiently deeply established.
> So my framing of my work in my tenure package focused a great deal
> on the sense of trajectory and career arc. This is something that I try to

emphasize to all untenured faculty, as it's an easy trap to fall into to think that "checking boxes" is what's important. At the time of promotion to full, I tried to continue that narrative, emphasizing the career trajectory in all aspects of my work, not just on the scholarship front.

Tara is employed at a selective LAC in the natural sciences. Her career has included success in the classroom, in scholarly pursuits, and as an administrator on campus both as department chair and as committee member but also as associate dean of faculty more recently. What I appreciate most about Tara's perspective and advice is her focus on building a rich, well-rounded, and succinct narrative—a narrative that illustrates a trajectory guided by deliberate intentions but that also acknowledges some missteps and redirection along the way.

The aim of this chapter is to help you craft a compelling account of your career trajectory to date, one that connects your contributions and value added across all the areas in which you find joy and that aligns with your institutional expectations. Much as Tara noted, falling into a "check the box" trap to achieve full professorship or continuing contract status can be detrimental to career advancement, given that such an approach is driven by external factors rather than a self-directed, personalized account of your career story. The likely outcome is a narrative driven by generic institutional categories rather than personal strengths and accomplishments that showcase how your unique contributions advance your career and institutional priorities.

Obstacles to Advancement

Refusing to recognize the existence of a gendered power differential means not only denying the sexism women in those institutions experience, but also perpetuating it.

—Peggy O'Donnell (2017)

One need look no further than major higher-education news outlets to gain a glimpse into the experiences and acceptance of women in the academy. Take, for example, the following headlines and taglines: "Female Academics Face Huge Sexist Bias—No Wonder There Are So Few of Them" (Bates 2015); "Study finds female professors experience more work demands and special favor requests, particularly from academically 'entitled' students" (Flaherty 2018); and "Women of Color in Academe Make 67 Cents for Every Dollar Paid to White Men" (Zahneis 2018). As a collective, these stories as well as countless others draw attention to the myriad challenges that women face in the academy and present an unflattering and unwelcoming environment for women academics. Underpaid, underappreciated, and overburdened are just a few of the adjectives that describe the feelings expressed by women in the academy (Baker, Lunsford, and Pifer 2017).

As part of the report *Benchmarking Women's Leadership in the United States*, Tiffani Lennon (2013) urges institutional leaders to review hiring and promotion policies to ensure they are fair, equitable, and unencumbering for women academics and to consider how promotion processes could be reevaluated. Such recommendations are critical for women in the academy. Regardless of institution type, promotion and tenure as well as advancement to full professorship and continuing contract status include an accounting and assessment of excellence across the three areas of scholarship, teaching, and service. For women with multiple marginalized identities, preconceived notions of what constitutes acceptable teaching and scholarship could be detrimental to career advancement given inherent biases.

In chapter 3, I highlight the documented gender biases associated with teaching and course-evaluation systems. As Victor Ray (2018) notes, "using biased evaluations allows colleges and universities to punish those whose identities deviate from white male normativity." Specific associated outcomes of gender-biased teaching evaluations can include a direct negative effect on career progression, a reallocation of resources to the detriment of women faculty members, and a contribution to women's intention to leave academia (Mengel, Sauermann, and Zölitz 2018). Research suggests that teaching is expected to come more naturally to women faculty as compared to their male peers; therefore, accomplishments in this area of professional responsibilities are diminished (Kardia and Wright 2004). In fact, research has revealed that excellence in teaching, particularly for women of color, has the potential to negatively impact career advancement in comparison to their male faculty peers (Griffin, Bennett, and Harris 2013).

I am a member of a Facebook group for academic women with over fourteen thousand members. These members share and request information on a variety of topics related to being a woman in the academy. For example, one member asked peers to share some of the teaching-evaluation comments they have received to prove to a male colleague that women do, in fact, receive inappropriate and unrelated comments on their teaching evaluations at an alarming rate. Within seconds, women academics representing a range of institution types and disciplines shared feedback received related to appearance (e.g., choice of attire, the need to be more physically fit, specific anatomy); personality (e.g., should be more maternal, needs to be less maternal, needs to smile more); and voice (too high pitched, "shrill," or "whiny"), to name a few. Her colleague was dumbfounded by what was noted. Many women expressed their disappointment at how few of the comments received over the years related to course content, course structure, and course practices. Such experiences are frustrating, to say the least, when thinking about how such "evaluations" play into the promotion and career-advancement process. While I have certainly received some inappropriate and unrelated comments over the years, I have been fortunate that such comments have been outliers as opposed to the norm. Many of my women peers at Albion College and prior at Penn State University have not been so fortunate.

Researchers who study the experiences of women in the academy, specifically women of color and other minoritized women faculty populations, have revealed a significantly different academy as a place of employment compared to their white male peers. One issue is the devaluation of scholarly pursuits (Croom 2017; Griffin, Bennett, and Harris 2013), particularly for women of color, that involve the study of marginalized communities. With regularity, questions of validity, rigor, and prestige are raised during evaluation processes, resulting in different standards by which performance and excellence are judged. "Faculty narratives and research on women of color suggest that the interaction of racism and sexism create a unique experience for women of color in the academy" (Griffin, Bennett, and Harris 2013, 491), and that experience is not a positive one, thus contributing to intentions to leave academe (Chambers 2011).

Less research has explored the experiences of lesbian faculty, specifically the challenges they face or the developmental and emotional support they need to navigate the path to full professorship or continuing contract status. In the absence of such research, previous studies have revealed that lesbian and gay faculty experience fear of rejection and must manage the need to conceal their identity. Such experiences are quite complex for lesbian and gay faculty, thus influencing the need to continually renegotiate their surroundings and interactions with colleagues, students, and community members (Dozier 2015). Research by Leah Reinert and Tamara Yakabowski (2017) highlights that some of the experiences shared in their study of lesbian faculty are germane to all women (e.g., seeking balance, negotiating parenthood). Yet "the findings [also] further demonstrate that lesbian academics experience their own set of obstacles and advantages in higher education and therefore need more recognition in the literature" (332).

Overall, these findings point to the need for women faculty to develop clear and deliberate strategies for career management, particularly related to crafting a narrative that represents their career trajectory while simultaneously managing the myriad roles, obstacles, and expectations placed on them. In the absence of the mentorship that is crucial for women in the academy, particularly underrepresented women faculty (Croom 2017; Ward and Wolf-Wendel 2012), my goal in this chapter is to provide the needed support and guidance to help all women faculty manage and minimize the inherent biases to which they are exposed and that account for the small number of women associate professors seeking to advance to full or the number who leave the academy altogether (H. Johnson 2017; Perna 2005). As women, we are unable to control the inherent biases that exist in the academy, and these biases create what can at times appear to be insurmountable obstacles and challenges, particularly for women with multiple marginalized identities. However, I encourage you to take control of what is in your power to manage: your narrative. The career-management strategies described throughout this chapter provide the foundation to craft a compelling narrative as a means of combating the chilly academic environment that defines many women's surroundings, surroundings that fail to recognize the importance of teaching and that devalue the scholarly contributions of women with multiple marginalized identities (Kardia and Wright 2004; Croom 2017).

Building a Strategic Foundation

In my department and university as a whole, there is so much energy and so many resources aimed toward mentoring people through the tenure process and pretty much nothing beyond that.

—associate professor, fine and applied arts, doctoral university, highest research activity

As a means of combating environmental and institutional structures that devalue teaching and scholarly contributions, I encourage all women to employ a more strategic approach to their career management. My disciplinary field provides a useful starting point. As a management professor, I draw a great deal from business and organizational tools aimed at increasing performance at the organizational and individual levels, while being efficient along the way. I teach many organizational tools and frameworks to my students and as part of my consulting workshops with midlevel managers in higher education, but one of the most influential tools I urge everyone to master, or at least to employ at some point, is strategic planning.

Strategic planning is defined as a process employed by an organization to develop a plan for the achievement of long-term organizational goals (Bryson 2018). Engaging in strategic planning is an important organizational process because it provides the individuals engaged in the planning with a sense of direction and outlines measurable goals. Strategic planning also provides much-needed short-term "gut checks" to ensure that progress is moving in the intended direction and helps guide day-to-day decision-making. It also aids in evaluative processes that provide insights into overall progress and offers data-driven evidence should a change in direction be needed. I walk my students and workshop attendees through the basic steps of strategic planning from multiple levels to ensure a well-rounded approach that accounts for individual, departmental (e.g., unit, program), and institutional needs, priorities, and future directions.

The broad aspects of strategic planning involve an understanding of your current position followed by achieving a firm grasp of what is important (e.g., mission statement, vision statement, prioritization of issues). The process of goal setting helps clarify expected objectives and priority issues (see chapter 2), followed by an accounting of organizational resources (e.g., human, physical, financial) to help determine the appropriate allocation of those resources (e.g., who, how, why). Strategic planning requires constant review and assessment to ensure that the process is producing the intended results. If not, it is time to reassess and adjust accordingly.

I have adapted this process to support individual career-management efforts, particularly for midcareer faculty members. In the following section, I walk you through a two-step process to help you (1) to be clear about your contributions and connections across many institutional levels, otherwise referred to as "professional reach," and (2) to connect professional reach to strategic imperatives or priorities of your department and/or institution. Connecting the dots across these considerations helps you to communicate a compelling career trajectory, one that illustrates your evolution as a teacher, scholar, and community contributor and that plays an instrumental role in advancing the strategic priorities of the institution. The aim is to create such a compelling connection between your professional pursuits and institutional priorities that attempts by misinformed colleagues to devalue scholarly and teaching contributions are minimized (and ideally eliminated).

To articulate your value added, you must be clear about your organizational role and your position in the broader disciplinary and scholarly landscape. To gain this clarity, I pose four questions, each followed by examples and tips of how you might answer.

1. What role do I play or position do I occupy in my department?

Depending on the organizational structure at your institution, ask yourself this question at the unit, division, and college levels. For me, my role and position at Albion College are clear. I am the management professor in the Department of Economics and Management (E&M). For those of us at smaller colleges, we may be one of a few or the only person in our department or at our institution who does what we do. I am recognized across campus and by our students as the management professor. In fact, a group of students made me a T-shirt that says, "I am the M, in E&M." Along with this role comes the responsibility of creating, maintaining, and delivering the management-focused curriculum in the department. I have also consistently carried the heaviest advising load in the department, which is another important factor that illustrates my departmental contributions.

2. What role do I play at the institution?

While there is probably some overlap and complementarity between departmental and institutional contributions, distinguish examples across both categories. I teach two gender-category courses (women in business and leadership, human resource management), two global-category courses (international management, international entrepreneurial exchange), and a first-year experience course. These courses are available to and serve a wider student population outside my immediate department and provide an important service to the college.

In addition to teaching contributions at the institutional level, my scholarly focus on the faculty experience and development provides an immediate benefit to the college. I have developed workshops for midcareer faculty in the Great Lakes College Association and for individual member institutions (which increases the visibility of Albion College). I have consulted with the provost, the associate provost, and steering and personnel committees related to faculty-development issues. I have also served as a mentor and invited guest speaker to early-career faculty programming as they work toward promotion and tenure. My expertise provides a significant service to the college and brings visibility at the consortial and national levels.

I am also a member of two committees including IRB (Institutional Review Board) and FURSCA (Foundation for Undergraduate Research, Scholarship, and Creative Activity). In prior years, I have served on other ad hoc committees (assessment, athletics) and faculty-elected committees (curriculum and resources). When answering question 2, be sure to provide examples that span the key areas in which you are expected to perform in your role.

3. What other departments, programs, or units do I most frequently engage?

I am a big advocate for developing and maintaining strategic partnerships outside your departmental domain. These partnerships may include other faculty members, departments, or programs or units or may be an institution-wide effort. Such partnerships enable you to have a broader reach beyond your immediate academic department, to refine existing skills, and to develop complementary skill sets. For example, since arriving at Albion, I have worked very closely with the Gerstacker Institute of Business and Management at Albion. It's a program of distinction in business and one of our premier programs at the college. For eighteen months, I served as interim director (and did so pretenure), and I continue to work with staff members on programming, course offerings including an international partnership, and strategic efforts related to recruitment, professional development, and alumni and advisory-board engagement.

Moving beyond the academic realm, I also work very closely with the Office of Institutional Advancement on campus. Every semester

I host four to six alumni guests in each class. Such relationships with alumni provide the staff a venue in which to engage alumni beyond financial donations. They also help support my pedagogical approach in the classroom and provide students with networking opportunities while exposing them to varied alumni stories spanning career stages, industries, and career trajectories.

As another example, my friend and colleague Karen Erlandson (and the author of chapter 7) has worked closely with the admissions department at Albion, specifically campus tour guides. She helped develop training for tour guides that infused the fundamentals of persuasion, given that part of their job is helping the college to recruit incoming students. Her expertise provides tour guides with a more sophisticated training program as compared to other colleges and universities.

When answering this question, think about the departments, programs, units, or initiatives with which you most frequently engage. What is the purpose and scope of this partnership (see chapter 3)? What do you gain professionally or personally from this partnership? What have you contributed to this partnership (e.g., what are the tangible outcomes or deliverables that you can point to)? Forging and maintaining partnerships outside our immediate department forces us academics out of our disciplinary silos and to think about the ways in which our disciplinary expertise and other professional efforts can add value beyond our immediate surroundings. Note that this can include partnerships outside your institution. For example, one of my colleagues is very connected with her local economic development center, resulting in service-based learning opportunities for her and her students. She and the center's director have even cowritten grants to support redevelopment efforts for her community.

4. Who or what is most affected by my efforts?

Another way to think about this question is, if I fail to do my job, what individuals, departments, units, programs, or initiatives will be negatively impacted? Of course, if we fail to show up for class, lab, or studio, our students suffer. If we do this consistently, our departmental reputation suffers. But I encourage you to think beyond this. For example, the only woman peer in my department is a Chinese economist, who is one of the few women of color faculty members on campus. The large contingent of Chinese students at Albion rely on my colleague a great deal for support. Albion College is in a very rural area of Michigan, which can be a challenging location for international students, given the lack of ethnic diversity in the town or on campus. Her support goes well beyond the classroom and serves Chinese students in all majors, not just economics and management.

TO DO

Determine your professional reach by answering the following questions:

1   What role do I play or position do I occupy in my department?

2   What role do I play at the Institution?

3   What other departments, programs, or units do I most frequently engage?

4   Who or what is most affected by my efforts?

Connecting Professional Reach to Institutional Priorities and Imperatives

Congratulations! By answering these questions, you have achieved the first step of strategic planning: to gain an understanding of your professional reach. In this section, I walk you through two steps to help you connect your professional reach to your institutional (and departmental, if applicable) priorities and imperatives. Such efforts relate to the second step of strategic planning: to gain a firm grasp of what is important, both to you professionally and as aligned with institutional expectations and future directions. Such clarity and well-articulated connections help to overcome inherent institutional and professional obstacles and barriers that characterize the advancement experiences of women in the academy.

Now that you have identified your departmental and institutional contributions as well as strategic partnerships, the next step is to communicate how and in what ways your contributions and partnerships (i.e., professional reach) advance the strategic priorities of your department (if applicable) and your institution. This step is much like an admissions essay, in which prospective students must articulate why they are a strong candidate and worthy of acceptance. A principal part of that story is a clear, communicative understanding about the ways in which the program and community members will provide the needed supports, scaffolding, and professional experience to help them achieve their professional and personal goals. The other part of the admissions essay requires them to illustrate how and in what ways their efforts, knowledge, expertise, and skill sets contribute to the betterment of the program and the individuals involved. When I worked at Harvard Business School (HBS), a member of the admissions staff once quipped, "It's clear why someone would want to come to HBS to earn an MBA. We have thousands of well-qualified, smart individuals apply. The differentiator is when the applicant can thoughtfully make clear how, why, and in what ways their personal and professional life's work to date adds to the diversity of the program and will improve the experiences of others enrolled at the time. And they need to think about how their time at HBS will help them contribute back to the communities of interest."

This approach to crafting a successful admissions essays is the same approach to be used when crafting your faculty narrative. Connections between your professional reach and the strategic priorities of your department and institution are fundamental to articulating how your employment and contributions improve the lives and experiences of those who are enrolled at and employed by the institution.

Step 1: Be Clear about Strategic Priorities

A university invited me to conduct a department-chair workshop. As part of my preparation, I reviewed the institutional website to locate the institution's strategic priorities. I looked in all the logical places and also conducted searches through the institution's search engine. No luck. I emailed my campus point of contact, and he too was unaware of where those might be published and contacted the dean. The dean shared the priorities with the faculty member but informed him that the priorities "weren't widely circulated." My point of contact and I thought that was strange, given that these priorities are what presumably drive decision-making and investments at the institution. As part of my presentation, I included the strategic priorities as a necessary resource in a slide. In fact, these strategic priorities served as the building block for our working time together as part of the department-chair workshop.

I strongly encourage you to review your institutional website and other marketing and admissions materials to get a copy of the institutional strategic priorities, pillars, imperatives, drivers, or whatever term your institution uses. The same applies at the departmental and college levels, if applicable. And if you cannot find them, request the materials from your dean, provost, or steering/governance-committee members. The priorities need to be in clear view while preparing your narrative.

Step 2: Connect Your Professional Reach and Strategic Priorities

The next step involves identifying complementarity between your professional reach and the strategic priorities of the institution. In other words, how are your professional efforts helping to advance the goals of the institution and of your department or program? Faculty-development supports should be situated at the intersection of institutional priorities and individual needs, challenges, and contributions. Such alignment aids the development and maintenance of a more diversified, strategic portfolio of faculty-development supports, which should also account for career-stage supports (Baker, Lunsford, and Pifer 2017). Next, I walk you through the experiences of two faculty members who have implemented these two steps.

TO DO

1 Secure copies of your institutional, departmental, and college-level strategic priorities.

2 Make connections between/among your professional reach and strategic priorities.

Allie's Experience

Allie is an associate professor at a land-grant research university, and her disciplinary field is agriculture. She is also a white woman. I met Allie when she was two years away from submitting her dossier for full, to discuss how to prepare for her submission. She was concerned about what she perceived to be a lack of scholarly evidence. Our first course of action was to work through determining Allie's professional reach by answering questions found in the first to-do list in this chapter. We took great care to include details and corresponding evidence across the areas of teaching, research, and service. We also explored institutional partnerships by thinking through how her work supported other departments and units beyond her immediate department.

In the process of meeting, it became obvious to me that Allie not only was gifted in her agricultural knowledge but was also really adept at the use of technology and innovation to improve learning processes for her students and the farmers who sought her support and guidance, particularly the up-and-coming next generation. She had a treasure trove of "quick tips," public-service announcements, and action steps at her disposal, and she turned these into web-based resources that facilitated dissemination by placing much-needed resources in the hands of intended users. Upon review of her institutional strategic priorities, we were able to connect her efforts on this front to the following institutional strategic initiative: "Enrich community, economic, and family life through research, outreach, engagement, entrepreneurship, innovation, diversity, and inclusiveness."

Her technology-based resources deeply enriched the farming community with which she worked and directly aligned with the land-grant mission of the university. Further, she went on-site to train the farmers on how to access the technology and worked with them on developing strategies to implement the knowledge and tips communicated in the resources. These strategic partnerships with farmers also gave her access to research opportunities. Allie had been previously hesitant to leverage these partnerships, given a bad experience that a farmer had with one of Allie's predecessors; however, this was an opportunity to conduct specific field research. I urged her to pitch the farmer to engage in a research collaboration. At the time of writing this chapter, she had two manuscripts under review, which eased her fears about lack of scholarly evidence. Her reaching out to the farmer and his "yes" response contributed to this outcome.

Allie and I worked to craft examples that clearly articulated purpose, scope, and deliverables for each of the key constituents noted in the strategic imperative (community, economic, and family life). As part of that narrative, she provided specific examples of the impact of her fieldwork and how the use of web-based resources and innovations improved the efficiency and sustainability of the farmers with whom she partnered. The success of the farmers also has economic implications in both the local and regional farming community, as well as for businesses that rely on those farms. Her efforts are directly aligned with and in support of the institutional mission and strategic priorities, and her draft narrative is well on its way to illustrating her professional successes and the ways in which she is helping to advance not only her own career but also the institution on a local, regional, and national level.

Barb's Experience

Barb is an associate professor employed at a liberal arts college in a very rural area on the East Coast. She is a woman of color. She is a social scientist, and her research examines the college experience of first-generation students who come from underrepresented populations.

This topic has personal meaning to Barb, given that she too was a first-generation student. Her assimilation and socialization into the academy was rocky, and that experience has been consistent as a faculty member at her institution. The faculty and student body lack diversity in both gender and ethnicity. As a result, Barb has not been able to find many mentors on campus. Luckily, she has maintained close relationships with her graduate-school adviser and peers and has forged some important new relationships with colleagues in her disciplinary area, whom she connects with at professional conferences.

I met with Barb to help her articulate her professional reach. It was clear that Barb was truly passionate about understanding the experiences of first-generation, minority student populations. Her research identifies the need for both classroom and collegiate supports to ensure that these students are provided the assistance they need to succeed. She describes her classroom as an "incubator to test ideas and interventions" that she has developed as a result of lessons learned through her research. However, Barb has received implicit, and in some cases explicit, messages about the "rigor" of her work. A colleague once described her research as "obvious" and not novel. Others have said her teaching practices "are more aligned with high school" as opposed to the collegiate level. Yet Barb's success in the classroom has garnered teaching awards at the college. She also has had a steady stream of scholarly success in the form of presentations and publications. Overall, she had a very real and valid concern that her work was "not worthy" of promotion to full, on the basis of the impressions of others.

Barb shared with me an institutional partnership with her college's diversity and global initiatives office. Through this partnership, the associated deliverables, and her expertise gained from teaching and scholarship on first-generation minority students, we could connect her contributions back to one of the strategic imperatives of the college: "Build an open, diverse, and inclusive campus community."

In addition, Barb helped to develop and often delivers on-boarding programming and orientation supports to first-generation students to minimize the "at risk" factors associated with this population of students. Barb is one of the first faces these students see on campus and becomes one of their go-to people during their four years, encouraged by her regular engagement through gatherings in their freshman year and beyond. This work is not part of her regular teaching load or other institutional responsibilities; it is her joy. More recently, she has developed cultural and other related training for faculty that is to be delivered in partnership with the college's Center for Teaching and Learning.

I encouraged Barb to use and write about her experience at the college as a best practice on building an institutional model to support this population of students. She did just that, submitting a manuscript about the collaboration between faculty and student support offices to assist first-generation minority students. The publisher suggested that she revise and resubmit, and she featured her institutional efforts as a case study. She is also studying the students' experience longitudinally, which will allow her to have a long-term scholarly pipeline leading to (and beyond) full professorship.

Barb's efforts can be linked to positive outcomes at the student, departmental/programmatic, and institutional levels. Despite the impressions and opinions of a few colleagues about the rigor and quality of her work, the "performance speaks for itself," based on students' accomplishments, the richness and success of the partnerships, and the recognition Barb receives from her disciplinary community. By communicating her professional reach clearly, the associated deliverables, and the ways in which those efforts advance the institution's strategic imperatives, she is crafting a compelling, well-connected narrative rooted in her strengths and joy.

Customizing Your Narrative

If diversity within faculty ranks is valued, then it behooves those of us in academe to reconsider how we value and evaluate faculty generally, and Black women faculty in particular.

—Crystal Renée Chambers (2011, 254)

I am sure it comes as no surprise that I recommend the use of headings as an organizational tool, to highlight the great work you have done using the preceding steps (see chapter 2). And by headings, I do not just mean the headings of scholarship, teaching, and service. Rather, I encourage you to create subheadings under each of these broad categories that align first and foremost with your joy, which I hope drives your professional reach (see chapter 1). Your narrative needs to illustrate the ways in which your engagement across these three areas supports your career trajectory, represents your professional reach comprehensively, and shows how your work advances institutional priorities succinctly and explicitly. In the following sections, I provide examples from dossiers to illustrate how you can and should define what teaching, scholarship, and service mean to you while highlighting your successes.

Teaching

While teaching certainly occurs in the classroom, a great deal of teaching occurs outside the classroom. Teaching takes on many forms and involves a diversity of approaches, partnerships, and innovation. As a result, I suggest first answering the following: What does teaching mean to you? What has informed your teaching? How do you engage in teaching at your institution? Responses to these questions inform the teaching subheadings in your narrative. The first subheading should be an overview of your teaching philosophy, which is consistent regardless of institution type or discipline. The goal is to let the reader know who you are as a teacher, what drives your actions in and out of the classroom, and how and in what ways teaching is a vehicle by which you enhance the lives of your students and your own. After the teaching philosophy overview, the possibilities are endless for how you craft your narrative, taking great care to tell a story that illustrates your career arc/trajectory and evolution as a teacher.

For example, Diane, a professor in the social sciences department at a comprehensive university, has such a teaching narrative. She begins her comments with the following opening statement: "As a first-year graduate student giving my very first lecture on racism and sexism in a psychology course, I knew teaching was one of my passions. I love the challenge of getting students interested in new topics, and I am thrilled to witness the energy they have when discovering something new." She later notes, "My main goal as a teacher is to demonstrate the value of psychology and women's studies in students' lives, emphasizing that learning should be an active, hands-on experience that continues long after the course ends."

I particularly appreciate Diane's use of teaching subheadings that illustrate her teaching pedagogy and approaches, particularly centered on how to engage her students in active-learning processes. Her subheadings under the "teaching" heading are:

1 Fostering understanding of multiple perspectives
2 Encouraging critical questions
3 Creating a comfortable classroom environment
4 Maximizing student interest and active learning
5 Enhancing learning through applied perspectives
6 Practicing pedagogical flexibility (e.g., responding to student needs and responding to unexpected student growth and incorporating instructional technology)

Under each of these categories, she defines the core ideas and how they are enacted. She also offers evidence for each. For example, under "fostering understanding of multiple perspectives," she shares, "I often purposely include readings that argue opposing points on a given issue, such as the underlying causes of gender similarities and differences, and encourage students to weigh the merits and weaknesses of each view or theory." Diane then provides examples of the types of debate, thinking, and reactions that such an exercise elicits from her students and how she supports their critical thinking in the process. When communicating details about "encouraging critical questions," Diane notes, "As an instructor of courses dealing with social issues, prejudice, and controversial topics, I am very aware that students sometimes begin the course with uncertainty and even resistance to the materials. I address their concerns by teaching them critical thinking skills for differentiating between conclusions drawn from research data and popular opinion. 'Who has the power? Who benefits?'" Diane concludes this subheading narrative by stating, "However, it is much more important to me that they incorporate these questions into their analyses of the world around them at the community, regional, national, and global levels."

Diane has done a wonderful job crafting a teaching narrative that highlights her strengths, contributions, and evolution as a teacher. She also connects these approaches back to departmental and institutional priorities to further illustrate the ways in which her teaching reach goes well beyond her classroom and the lives of her students (a priority of her institution's strategic plan).

There is no right or wrong answer with regard to the correct subheadings to use, other than that the subheadings should be relevant and specific to you. I personally rely on five subheadings: classroom, advising, community partnerships, alumni relationships, and notable mentions. Much like Diane, I describe these subheadings by detailing my approach and using corresponding evidence. I then make explicit connections back to Albion's institutional priorities to show how my work advances the goals and aims of the college.

Scholarship

Scholarship occurs in many settings, with different goals and audiences. The notion of scholarship aligns with publications, grants, and presentations. However, scholarship also takes on other forms including creative and artistic works that recognize contributions from our peers in the fine and applied arts and humanities.

One example is from Valerie's body of work to date. She is an associate professor of music at a comprehensive university who is working toward full professorship. Valerie conducts and supports musicians at the collegiate and local high school levels. What I particularly appreciate about Valerie's materials is her use of a personal website that is organized using the following headings: about, CV, teaching, scholarship, service, music and social activism, and tenure/advancement. Nearly every heading includes drop-down subheadings. As part of the career-trajectory storytelling, Valerie not only includes examples of her work across these areas but also has visual evidence both as an instructor and as a performing artist. Under the scholarship tab, she organizes her materials according to refereed publications, invited scholarship, conference presentations, and conducting performances. For the purposes of this chapter, I focus on Valerie's subheading "conducting performances" (for more examples of traditionally defined forms of scholarship, refer to chapters 2 and 3).

Valerie uses this subheading to highlight performances with her institution's philharmonic orchestra. She provides the dates and titles of each performance. For a few of those performances, the titles are hyperlinked to the actual performance program, which provides a visual of the event, including a historical overview of the featured composer and music. She also highlights a list of her orchestral repertoire to illustrate her conducting and performance range.

What is most compelling and engaging related to Valerie's scholarly narrative is her inclusion of actual videos of the performances she lists under the subheading "conducting performances." The talents of Valerie and her students are on full display and illustrate the power of music and art in transforming a community. Those talents have also been recognized externally through state-wide and national competitions, as she has received first place in four separate competitions. Valerie concludes this section with a list of performances in which she was the invited guest conductor, and once again, she includes videos of her performing in this capacity.

Valerie is a talented musician and conductor with immeasurable passion for her students and her craft. That passion and professional reach is on full display and presented so beautifully through her website. I love how the creative nature of her field and life's work is so thoughtfully organized and tells her story, a story that supports her departmental and institutional imperatives.

Service

The term "service" often evokes the notion of faculty governance, which is supported through committee work, whether faculty elected, ad hoc, or provost appointed. Service also includes formal leadership or administrative roles on campus that include department chair, committee chair, or faculty liaison. However, service can also involve program or partnership creation and fundraising efforts that provide scholarships for incoming students.

This latter type of service is what Leah has pursued, which has earned her continuing contract status at the community college in which she is employed. Leah is a faculty member of the Theater and Dance Department, and she is very engaged with her students and in the community supporting local theater efforts. One of her professional priorities is to "infuse the arts throughout the life of the campus and surrounding community." However, given the limited resources at both the community college and local levels, she and her peers have had to rely on the generosity of volunteers and non-guaranteed small grants that support the arts. Frustrated with facing the same funding concerns year after year, she realized that "there is strength in numbers" and pursued and fostered what she called "vital partnerships." Her goal is to improve the educational experience for fine-arts students and to provide much-needed access to the arts for community members.

Leah has organized her service work narrative according to the following subheadings: on-campus partnerships, community partnerships, alumni partnerships, and state-wide partnerships. In her opening remarks, she articulates why partnerships are key to the success and longevity of the fine arts and why partnerships across these levels are most salient to her and the institution. Within each subheading, Leah explains the nature of each partnership as well as the outcomes that have resulted to date. For example, when discussing on-campus partnerships, Leah notes that "given the stronger relationship among theater & dance, arts & communication, and music, [institution] was able to support the delivery of [show title], [show title], and [show title], which would not have been possible prior to." She provides details about her motivation in pursuing this collaboration and the efforts taken to ensure its success. Leah also relies a great deal on alumni (and friends and family of alumni) to help fund future students. Leah notes, "With the support and engagement of alumni and their friends and family, we have nearly doubled the funding available by way of grants and scholarships for incoming undergraduate students in the fine arts at [institution]." Similarly, she articulates her rationale for the importance of alumni relationships and the efforts taken to achieve the acquired funds. Leah is also careful to include brief student profiles highlighting recipients of the generous support of alumni and their family and friends. In her service-narrative summary, she links her efforts back to the institution's motto.

Leah's entrepreneurial spirit and actions have enabled her to advance her career but also have provided a much-needed service to her students, department, institution, and community. By forging strategic partnerships, she has been able to engage in service well beyond traditional faculty governance, to instead expand and enhance the arts and make the arts more visible.

Conclusion

The achievement of full professorship or continuing contract status comes with institutional prestige, recognition of disciplinary contribution and expertise, and influence in institutional decision-making and governance. However, as Natasha Croom (2017) has noted, "advancement at this level is not immune to systems of racism and sexism" (576). The goal of this chapter has been to provide women faculty with a framework to engage in individual strategic planning. Doing so serves as the foundation from which a narrative is produced. The need to prepare and communicate a succinct, developed narrative that represents one's career trajectory, taking special care to highlight professional reach and connection to institutional priorities and imperatives, cannot be overstated. Such a narrative is critical for women in the academy in general but is of particular importance for our minority women faculty peers as a means of pushing against the inherent biases and barriers that exist in the academy.

Additional Resources

For readers interested in learning more about strategic planning, check out the following articles:

Graham, Kenny. 2016. "Strategic Plans Are Less Important than Strategic Planning." *Harvard Business Review*, June 21. https://hbr.org/2016/06/strategic-plans-are-less-important-than-strategic-planning.

Tasler, Nick. 2014. "3 Myths That Kill Strategic Planning." *Harvard Business Review*, May 7. https://hbr.org/2014/05/3-myths-that-kill-strategic-planning.

CHAPTER 5

Smallest Publishable Unit

Smallest publishable unit (SPU), also referred to as least publishable unit (LPU), is an approach to academic publishing in which a particular focus or topical area can be used to generate a publication in a peer-reviewed venue, such as a journal or a conference.

—Wikipedia

I was first introduced to the concept of the smallest publishable unit (SPU) by my minor adviser, Jim, from the business school at Penn State. He was an excellent mentor who urged me to think about how to craft a scholarly agenda (in fact, my entire dissertation committee was helpful both for advice and for modeling behavior). Jim sat me down and talked me through my current and future research agenda and helped me think about data I had in hand and data I would have in hand, with a few critical considerations:

1 Audience (e.g., fellow researchers, practitioners, administrators)
2 Content (e.g., theoretical contribution, empirical contribution, practical contribution)

3 Methods (e.g., quantitative methods, qualitative methods, mixed methods)

4 Process (e.g., scholarly efforts considered to be a "best practice" or adopted and adapted to support programming)

Regardless of the professional effort, I always write down ideas related to these four categories before beginning a research project (including subefforts), so that I can be as strategic and efficient with my time as possible.

The advantages of SPU are many. First, as a career-management strategy, SPU helps women associate professors to view their work more broadly and to increase productivity and work capacity, without requiring nonexistent additional hours. Second, SPU allows women associate professors to focus on an interesting and important aspect of their work, which enables them to highlight each of those key findings or takeaways in separate publishable pieces aimed at varied audiences, increasing readership (i.e., contribution to the field). Third, I firmly believe pursuing such an approach to academic work helps women manage multiple roles successfully while supporting productivity in the process. The concept of SPU can help you to be more selective in your scholarly choices related to these four areas. And finally, SPU provides a framework through which to illustrate and communicate a coherent and all-encompassing career trajectory that supports the achievement of outlined goals (refer to chapters 2 and 4). We can all learn from scholarly efforts that are not just empirically driven but conceptual, theoretical, and practical in focus and intent. It behooves all women—particularly those women seeking to advance to full or continuing contract status who seek to advance in their careers and/ or to contribute to their institutions, fields, and disciplines—to think thoughtfully about all the ways in which they contribute. The SPU framework helps organize those contributions.

In this chapter, I feature the stories of two women associate professors with whom I have worked and their amazing efforts. Taking our joint collaboration as client and coach, I walk you through the SPU concept as applied to their career-management strategy to identify and plan outputs including empirically grounded contributions. First, I offer a conceptual academic model that aligns with and complements the SPU categories I later describe. This framework resonates regardless of institution type, discipline, and career goal, and it provides a foundation for the aims of this chapter.

Boyer's Forms of Scholarship

Your most valuable contribution to science may not come solely, or even primarily, from the work you publish. What really matters may be the great course you teach that inspires dozens of students to pursue careers in science, or that makes a future stockbroker more scientifically conscious and conscientious when he trades shares, votes, or goes to the doctor. It may be the support you give to your institution that helps it maintain or increase the quality of its science program. It may be the support you give to a junior colleague who is struggling, just as you once struggled, to gain a foothold in academe.

—Whitney Owen (2004)

As Ernest Boyer so aptly noted nearly three decades ago in *Scholarship Reconsidered* (1990), "What we urgently need today is a more inclusive view of what it means to be a scholar—a recognition that knowledge is acquired through research, through synthesis, through practice, and through teaching" (24). This model plays an imperative role in the higher-education landscape by drawing attention to the varied ways knowledge is formed across all institution types (Boyer et al. 2015; O'Meara and Rice 2005; Kezar, Maxey, and Halcombe 2015; Rice 2002). Researchers, practitioners, and organizations have relied on this framework to improve undergraduate education and to reassess and reenvision promotion and tenure policies and processes in order to acknowledge the various ways and locations in which scholarship and scholarly learning occurs in and outside the academy (Reinvention Collaborative, n.d.).

KerryAnn O'Meara and R. Eugene Rice (2005) edited a volume in an effort to assess how and in what ways Boyer's call to action in *Scholarship Reconsidered* influenced the higher-education landscape. The publisher explains on the book jacket, "No reform effort in American higher education in the last twenty years has been more important than the attempt to enlarge the dominant understanding of the scholarly work of faculty—what counts as scholarship." The volume editors and contributors shared insights about the pursued actions and outcomes on their respective campuses in response to *Scholarship Reconsidered*, with O'Meara and Rice situating this knowledge in the broader context of national developments. One of the many important takeaways from this volume was the acknowledgment that the four forms of scholarship outlined by Boyer (1990), described later in this chapter, are fundamentally related and should not be viewed as "separate and independent forms of scholarship" (Rice 2005, 307). As Rice (2005) further noted, "It is not an accident that the four forms of scholarly work are incorporated into the mission statements of colleges and universities across all sectors of American higher education" (308). These four forms of scholarship support a more holistic view of today's faculty member—that of complete scholar (O'Meara and Rice 2005).

More recently, two colleagues and I sought to better understand scholarly learning in the contexts of and as influenced by individuals' institutional setting (Baker, Terosky, and Martinez 2017). We were motivated in part by Burton Clark's (1987) acknowledgment of the importance of understanding the faculty experiences of academics in their varied locations, and our aim was to take a look at scholarly learning across institution types so as to dispel myths about the types of scholarly learning that occur and to illustrate that regardless of institution type, faculty members engage in all four forms of scholarship as characterized by Boyer (1990). Such an understanding can and should inform faculty-development supports and practices across all institution types.

The Four Forms of Scholarship Described

Boyer (1990) identified and described four forms of scholarship: discovery, integration, teaching, and engagement. My colleagues and I explain, "It is important to note, like scholarly learning, the scholarships of discovery, integration, teaching and engagement emphasize faculty members' learning and working with their subject matter knowledge" (Baker, Terosky, and Martinez 2017, 27). Context, both discipline and institution type, informs the types of scholarship that faculty members engage in across Boyer's four forms of scholarship. The broader definition of scholarship supports faculty members' scholarly learning.

The scholarship of discovery is what we, in the academy, characterize as traditional research, in which the goal is to create and disseminate knowledge, as well as to test and develop new theories and models. The motivation behind the scholarship of discovery, as noted by Boyer, is knowledge creation for the sake of knowledge creation. The outputs of such efforts include peer-reviewed journal articles, creative works and exhibits, and books and book chapters.

The scholarship of integration is about the synthesis of knowledge across topics within a given discipline and time. The primary goal of the scholarship of integration is to make connections across and among disciplines by pulling knowledge from a variety of resources. The outcome is the identification of trends in knowledge and the creation of new meaning and understanding from those connections. Outputs associated with the scholarship of integration include literature reviews, sharing of interdisciplinary research at conferences, and meta-analyses.

The scholarship of teaching is the study of teaching and learning processes including the development and advancement of pedagogical and curricular practices. Fundamental to the scholarship of teaching is a focus on formats that facilitate public sharing and the opportunity for that sharing to result in application and assessment opportunities by others. Examples of scholarship of teaching include "the study and dissemination of innovative teaching practices, presentations or peer-reviewed publications about the study or implementation of teaching practices . . . and publication of textbooks or teaching materials" (Baker, Terosky, and Martinez 2017, 28).

The scholarship of engagement (formerly referred to as "application") is characterized by the application of disciplinary knowledge and skills to address important social and institutional problems. It aims to connect stakeholder groups, including faculty members along with relevant field experts and other interested parties, to solve real-world problems. Similar to Boyer's other forms, the scholarship of engagement involves peer-review practices as well as dissemination and evaluative components. Examples of the scholarship of engagement include consulting activities that connect faculty members' expertise to community-related activities and sharing subject-matter expertise in media outlets such as podcasts and newspapers.

Despite increased efforts to broaden the definition of scholarship and to incorporate it in faculty handbooks and promotion and tenure language (Baker, Lunsford, and Pifer 2017), the scholarship of discovery is still considered the most prestigious, regardless of institution type (Baker, Terosky, and Martinez 2017; Fairweather 2005; Rice 2005). All four forms of scholarship, however, offer diverse opportunities to contribute to the field and for professional growth.

The SPU Framework

Allow tenure track without so much research focus. Reward great teaching and teaching efforts beyond the classroom. Reward community building as professional development, not just research.

—associate professor, social sciences, baccalaureate college

When engaging in my work, I use the SPU framework along with the four forms of scholarship, given that my work spans these areas. I am fortunate that Albion College does in fact recognize and acknowledge these forms of scholarship, but I still find it important personally and professionally to apply the SPU framework as a means of clearly articulating the purpose and scope of a given scholarly effort or initiative (see chapter 2). I make a deliberate effort to provide clarity about the form of scholarship I am targeting (or engaged in), paying careful attention to articulate the intended audience, content, methods, and process.

The aim of this section is to demonstrate this process as a means of supporting your engagement with the SPU framework across the four forms of scholarship as outlined by Boyer (1990). I provide you with examples of how I and two former clients have used the framework.

My SPU Framework

I begin by examining the big picture of my scholarly agenda before breaking it down into subgoals. My predominant area of research and scholarly interest is understanding the faculty experience. Specifically, my objective is to use the knowledge gleaned from my research to inform faculty-development practices, to help institutional administrators and others tasked with faculty-development responsibilities, and to provide the needed programming and resources to faculty members as they advance and evolve in their careers. Keeping this overarching objective in mind, I identify the subgoals of my scholarly agenda:

1 To contribute new knowledge to the field (scholarship of discovery)

2 To offer new interdisciplinary models and tools to understand better the faculty experience, given my background in both higher education and business (scholarship of integration)

3 To focus on the study of the faculty experience and faculty-development support through the goal of developing and advancing faculty-development practice (scholarship of teaching)

4 To apply the new knowledge garnered to inform the development and delivery of new faculty-development programming and corresponding resources (scholarship of engagement)

Through collaboration with my coauthors, I seek to create more innovative forms of faculty-development supports beyond a one time workshop, models that provide long-term opportunities to take lessons learned in order to adapt and adopt faculty-development practices that are relevant and timely.

To better demonstrate the SPU framework, I will walk you through the four components (audience, content, methods, and process) regarding my scholarship-of-engagement subgoal. I typically identify the SPU framework through a series of questions I ask myself, modeled after Boyer's four forms of scholarship.

Subgoal: To offer new interdisciplinary models and tools to understand better the faculty experience (scholarship of engagement)

Audience question: Who is the primary audience both within and outside higher education and [insert your field here]?

Within higher education, faculty developers, deans or associate provosts of faculty development, center directors, and faculty-development committee members would be interested in such outcomes. Human resource professionals tasked with career development and advancement initiatives outside higher education are a likely secondary audience. I realize that the faculty experience, particularly in institutions with tenure, are quite different from industry and other career fields. However, my overarching goal of supporting and developing engaged, satisfied, and productive employees transcends careers and industries, thus making the interdisciplinary-focused human resources professional a subaudience of this work.

Content question: What is the nature of the deliverables that will be developed?

For this particular subgoal, the content and the intended outcomes are practical in nature. Specifically, the goal is to create developed models and tools that can be adapted, adopted, and implemented for use in the future. Thinking back to the primary and secondary audience, I know that these individuals, given their institutional roles, do not have a great deal of time to re-create or reinvent materials, tools, and resources. They need something that is clear, provides specific direction without being overly prescriptive, and can either enhance or replace existing resources and programs.

Methods question: What kinds of data will help me achieve the subgoal? And what is the best method to obtain the needed data?

Methodologically speaking, given my work in higher education and business, I know the importance of having data driven and informed models and tools. No one is going to buy into a new or adapted approach to faculty development that is grounded in hunches and beliefs. While all of my scholarly efforts to date have been informed first and foremost by the scholarship of discovery, one of my guiding values is that I do not aspire to create or generate knowledge merely for that purpose alone. Rather, I want my research to have an impact and validity, as well as to improve the lives of faculty members.

Process question: Will others benefit from the practice-related knowledge gleaned to support policy and action on their respective campus?

Process is a crucial consideration when applying the SPU framework. While the primary outputs of meeting the noted subgoal are to have data-driven models, tools, and resources to share with the intended audiences, I also look at the process by which the models, tools, and/or resources were developed. I ask myself, Can someone else take this process and the foundational tenets and re-create them on an institutional, departmental, or programmatic basis? Might the process, including the built-in assessment procedures, be of use or provide guidance to others? If yes, I think about how best to communicate and document the process (in publication form) in a way that can be distributed more widely.

Now that I have briefly walked you through the SPU framework, situating it in the context of Boyer's scholarship of engagement, I share the experiences of Fran and Paulina, two amazing women who have benefited from the SPU approach.

Fran's SPU Story

Fran is a STEM faculty member in her tenth year at an LAC and aims to earn full professorship. I met Fran during a campus consulting visit, and I was immediately taken with her energy, enthusiasm, and sense of humor. Fran epitomizes the term "engaged faculty." She supervises and mentors undergraduate research experiences every semester and summer. In fact, with regard to undergraduate research mentorship engagement, she is probably in the top 5 percent of her professor peers on her campus. She remains deeply committed to faculty governance and service, both on campus and in the community. She serves on faculty-elected committees, most notably the personnel committee. Peers hold Fran in high regard and characterize her as honest, trust-worthy, and an asset to the campus and life of the college. Her students from all fields of study adore her, describing Fran as "very caring," "willing to help," "accessible," and "super funny." Fran also has a very strong reputation for doing excellent field work, an aspect of her discipline that is vital to her success in and out of the classroom.

Despite these successes, Fran is concerned about her prospects of earning full professorship due to a lack of publications. It is important to note that Fran does not lack data or results, but the issue lies in ambiguity about how to strategically turn this work into publications and in making schedule adjustments to create the time to do so. Fran's accessibility and engagement with students, her peers, and the campus community leave few hours in the day for her to invest in her own growth, and her health has suffered mightily as a result.

I asked Fran to talk me through her goals, her work, and her greatest frustrations. I also asked her to tell me about her joys and where she finds the most professional pleasure and/or reward. She immediately lit up when talking about the mentoring she does to support undergraduate researchers on her campus, particularly those she is able to engage in the field. She also began to describe a summer field experience in which she has been intimately involved for nearly twenty years beginning as a graduate student and now as a faculty supervisor with the second-longest tenure in the program. The founding faculty member of this field-experience program is phasing out, and Fran, given her position as the next most senior faculty person, feels a deep sense of commitment and responsibility to the program to ensure that the founding values, mission, and quality remain firmly intact.

As part of our conversation, I began to ask Fran about the types of work she engages in as part of the field experience, including data and outputs, as well as partnerships and collaborations that have evolved over the years. This particular field experience has a national reputation as being one of the best programs of its kind. Yet, from our conversation, it appeared that not much has been written about that experience. I felt that this provided an opening to introduce the SPU concept and framework to Fran and to work through it with her so that she could walk away from our time together with a clear plan including timeline, deliverables, and intended outlets.

From my perspective, it was obvious that through her participation and leadership in this field experience, Fran had engaged in all four forms of scholarship (discovery, engagement, integration, and teaching). To touch on the scholarship of discovery, for example, we talked through the data she had in hand or would have in hand as a result of her upcoming participation in the field experience. We talked about the intended audience, the content of that work, the methods, and process, noting that in relation to the scholarship of discovery, the first three components of the SPU framework were most salient. However, during our discussion of the scholarship of engagement, significant opportunity surfaced to "share the story" of this field experience in a very rich, meaningful way. Given that Fran was one of the first individuals involved, she had institutional knowledge and could provide insights into the reason behind the creation of the program, the founding leadership, and the life cycle of the program, including changes in staffing, curriculum, and methodological approaches in response to disciplinary changes in the field over time. Fran could also highlight the importance of industry and university partnerships and the role of foundations and sponsors to supporting the longevity of the program.

Fran realized the amazing opportunity she had to tell others about this experience and to craft a compelling story about this field-experience program that could be used as a model for others to emulate in other areas of the country. As part of this discussion, we searched the internet for possible outlets in which she could publish this work, targeting a few opportunities. We also talked about inviting faculty members who support the field-experience program to engage as coauthors, alleviating some of the time issues that Fran faces.

I also saw a real opportunity for Fran to use her field-experience approach to teaching students who are pursuing her disciplinary field as an intended career. She could produce one or several publications about how field experiences can be used as a pedagogical tool. Given Fran's involvement in this national program, she has been able not only to provide access to the field for students but also to bring those experiences and tools to bear in the classroom when teaching students on her campus. She has tested and perfected many techniques, while learning about the inadequacies of others. Aspiring faculty and scientists in the field can and will benefit from her knowledge, expertise, and experience. We talked about her documenting specific field tests, aspects that were and were not effective, lessons learned, and the application to the advancement of the field. These insights will make an invaluable contribution to the study of teaching and learning. Once again, after mapping out some of this thinking, we searched for discipline-specific pedagogy and teaching journals as well as those focused on publishing "best practices" in undergraduate education, of which field work is an example.

At the end of my time with Fran, we mapped out five solid publications for her to pursue in the coming months as she worked toward full professorship. We chose these publications in part because none of them required new initiatives, data collection, or field experiences to produce. Fran has the needed materials already. Together, we were able to take a step back to look at Fran's body of work, think attentively about the ways in which she engaged in all four forms of scholarship, and talk through each form while applying the SPU framework.

Paulina's SPU Story

Paulina is an associate professor employed at a comprehensive university. She is in her fifteenth year, and her disciplinary field is in the social sciences. Within two years of earning promotion and tenure, she began to engage in administrative work both as department chair and then as assistant dean at her university. A mutual friend and colleague referred Paulina to me, believing that Paulina could use some mentoring and support to help her get "out of her rut." Paulina and I connected via phone, and we made plans to meet during an upcoming professional conference. Our mutual friend shared with me that Paulina aspired to earn full professorship, given her ultimate professional aspirations of becoming dean or provost, but she "let her scholarship lapse" to focus on improving her administrative and leadership skills. Paulina was energized by her administrative work but was "feeling like a failure" because she was "neglecting her scholarly identity and interests" as a result. Paulina is also a mother of two elementary-school-aged children. Both she and her husband, an attorney, have demanding jobs and work to balance child-care duties as best as they can; however, Paulina has more flexibility in her schedule and manages the majority of child-care responsibilities.

Over coffee, Paulina and I chatted about her career trajectory to date. We talked about her scholarly interests and the work she engaged in to earn promotion and tenure, which she considers one of her proudest accomplishments, next to her two children. Paulina planned to pursue administrative opportunities for three to five years posttenure and then return to the faculty life, reengage in her scholarly agenda, and pursue full professorship. However, Paulina noted that those five years passed and then some, and she now finds herself fifteen years into her academic career, enjoying the administrative roles she has pursued but feeling a nagging need to achieve "that last full professor brass ring." Though she feared it was too late, I knew we could still work to achieve her goal with some planning and strategic thinking.

Unlike Fran, Paulina did not have any recent data from which we could draw. It had been years since she had collected data to support her research. And it had been four years since she had published her last empirical manuscript. I realized that the most important goal I had for Paulina was to get her comfortable writing again and thinking in terms of her value added. Paulina has a reputation on campus as a strong administrator, one who is fair, transparent, and inclusive. She is also known for "being a fierce supporter of women" on her campus. Paulina's other talent is to build relationships and partnerships both on campus and in the community. In my mind, these are the two areas in which Paulina had a demonstrated record of success. She felt good about her accomplishments in these areas, and I felt that these successes provided opportunities for Paulina to get back in the habit of writing and to apply the SPU framework.

Paulina began a mentoring program for women faculty on her campus. The program involved the traditional one-on-one dyadic mentoring assignment with a senior woman colleague on campus but also relied on peer mentoring, given the cohort model that Paulina incorporated. In addition, Paulina brings in women alumni to serve as guest speakers with particular expertise in the areas of negotiation, communication, and career counseling and to provide additional mentoring support. She has been managing this program for five years and tracks the professional progress of the women who participate relating to their career advancement and achievement of self-identified career goals.

Given the importance of supporting women faculty in the academy and the success of Paulina's program, I suggested that she prepare a manuscript and/or essay outlining her mentoring program in which she features and explains the various components she has incorporated (scholarship of engagement). As Paulina walked me through this program, she was very thoughtful and deliberate about each component, taking great care to explain why these components were the "right ones" based on her extensive review of the literature as well as lessons learned from previous iterations of the program.

Her mentoring program could certainly be described as a well-oiled machine that produces impressive results and facilitates and supports the agency of the women who participate.

Together, Paulina and I outlined two publications. The first publication is geared toward other administrative peers charged with supporting the advancement of women faculty on their respective campuses (audience). The paper outline included program details such as aims of the program, program components, needed resources, and intended outcomes (content). The paper was organized and written as a how-to guide, in which Paulina details a program roadmap for others to follow and adapt given their personal or institutional needs (process). The second paper features data about the career advancement of the women participants in the mentoring program. The goal of this paper is to share the advancement stories, including opportunities and challenges, for women faculty in comprehensive universities; the stories included individual data on each participant treated as an individual case study (methods). Paulina felt called to tell these women's stories, given the lack of research and resources available to women in the later stages of the professoriate. She thought that other women faculty would benefit from reading about how these women, relying on program support, achieved their career goals on their terms (audience). Paulina also used this paper as an opportunity to follow up with some of the women to reconnect so as to include a "where are they now" update. With additional data in the form of interviews or focus groups with past attendees, Paulina's proposed second paper could certainly be described as the scholarship of discovery.

Given Paulina's hiatus from writing and traditional faculty life, I knew we needed to ease her back into seeing that full professorship was possible but required a reenvisioning of how to get there. I also wanted to help Paulina see how her administrative experiences could be an advantage, not a detriment, toward helping her achieve her career goals, one that could be leveraged to make valuable contributions in the field while also supporting her career-advancement goals. In the bigger picture, I saw these publications as a way to support the knowledge development and learning of others who aspired to or currently occupied a similar role as Paulina. Perhaps most important, Paulina saw a pathway to get back to writing, a pathway that was not overwhelming and that did not require her to conceive of a new study from start to finish. I was certain that once she regained confidence in her ability to produce scholarly contributions, she would be well on her way to achieving her full professorship and administrative career goals.

How to Apply SPU to Your Work

Too many meetings! As a midcareer tenured professor, I should not be in five and a half hours of meetings per week. Our administration uses bullying to pressure faculty to donate time outside the classroom that might otherwise be allocated to research; you sense that no matter how much you do, it's never enough.

—associate professor, natural sciences, comprehensive college

---

This quotation is a not-so-subtle reminder about all the ways in which we are pulled in our jobs. And those conflicting expectations have the tendency to distract us from the activities we need to engage in so we can achieve professional goals. As Fran's and Paulina's stories demonstrate, the SPU framework situated in the context of Boyer's (1990) four forms of scholarship is one tool to guide you to think about those next steps as well as to provide a self-assessment tool of what can support your professional goals now. In this section, I offer thinking points that align with the SPU framework that will help you engage in the work that Fran and Paulina found effective.

Audience

What is the audience that you are seeking to appeal to? Are they scholarly peers in the field who engage in similar work? Practitioners who can benefit from lessons learned from your past experiences? Administrators, campus leaders, or industry experts with whom you can work collaboratively to apply your contributions in their respective environments? Regardless of the audience, know that each audience has specific field-, disciplinary-, and/or industry-specific resources such as peer-reviewed journals, trade journals, magazines, and practitioner-focused resources that they rely on to support their professional efforts and growth. Identifying these resources, familiarizing yourself with them, and targeting them for future contributions is often the first step to applying the SPU framework to your efforts. If you are unsure which ones are most important, identify the leaders in your field and do a quick Google search for their CVs or abbreviated list of their publications to identify where they are publishing and presenting their work. Start a running list. Early in my career, I absolutely did this and found it extremely helpful in guiding my efforts and ensuring that the "right" people (aka audience) were reading my work.

Content

Referring back to the experiences of Fran and Paulina, the goal of the SPU framework is to start in the short term by first determining if data, insights, or resources that you have in hand can be organized and compiled to support the development of outputs (e.g., presentations, publications). I have yet to engage with a client or workshop attendee who has absolutely nothing that she (or he) can draw on to produce one to two deliverables to spark some momentum. Frequently, those future deliverables are the result of some type of collaboration that already occurred, whether it be with students, peers, or other research, teaching, or community partners who can be invited to join as coauthors. If possible, align yourself with individuals who are also seeking to achieve career-advancement goals—similar motivations and peer accountability help to support success.

Once you identify the data, insights, and/or resources that you and possible collaborators have in hand, think about the nature of this material. Is it empirically focused, thus requiring you to outline a more traditional research paper? Is it a new model or framework that is more theoretical in nature? If the answer to the latter question is yes, what fields might benefit from this new, possibly interdisciplinary knowledge? Seek to identify literature from those fields that can serve as the foundation from which to build. Or is the material you have identified something that can support the development of an assessment tool, a new procedure, or an innovative approach to doing the type of work you do? In this instance, think about the critical information, components, and needed information that will help you describe this work in compelling and user-friendly ways.

Method

Knowing what questions you seek to answer will guide the methodological approaches you plan to pursue in your work. Are you traversing a well-documented question in your field but approaching it in a different way with the goal of building on existing work? Or are you asking questions that few have sought to answer? Being clear about what information and understanding is available and the intended goals is a key driver in determining the appropriate methods to pursue.

Early in my career, I pursued questions about the connection between the professional identity development of business doctoral students and their social networks, including individuals both within and outside the academic community. Since not much research at the time explored this question, I did a deep qualitative dive by relying on focus groups and interviews to garner insights into the types of questions I was asking. I followed two cohorts of business doctoral students for the duration of their doctoral programs.

My current interests—the faculty experience and faculty-development trends—are well documented but are lacking in LAC contexts. For this line of work, my colleagues and I have relied on a mixed-methods approach. Existing surveys instruments could be adapted for the liberal arts context. Information gleaned from survey responses have informed the development of our focus group and interview protocols. Our data has been robust and serves to support trustworthiness of the data, given the triangulation of data sources we have pursued.

Process

Process is a consideration and opportunity that seems to be off the radar for the many individuals with whom I have worked. I have not met anyone who wants to work harder, as opposed to smarter. Individuals, regardless of field and institution type, are often looking for ways to enrich and support their work, and they rely on the good work of others who came before (or are working side by side) to support those efforts. Once I move past the traditional scholarship-of-discovery thinking, I always think about how this new knowledge can be used to improve the lives of the individuals whom I seek to support. If you were to look at my complete CV, you would see consistent companion pieces. By this I mean a more traditional (e.g., empirical, theoretical) publication followed up by a more practical publication that is focused on that same topic but takes knowledge gleaned from the traditional scholarly publication and organizes it in more practical terms, including action steps, recommendations, and examples. As I noted earlier, research to action is one of my professional goals, so the process of writing companion pieces is critical to achieving this goal.

Conclusion

I am just not sure if I have done enough in terms of scholarship to earn full professor. And that mind-set is keeping me from organizing my materials.

—associate professor, humanities, comprehensive university

I hear this kind of sentiment most predominantly from women clients and workshop attendees. The unfortunate reality is that there is no metric for understanding what "enough"' means in the context of promotion to full or continuing contract status. Further, an emphasis on "enough" detracts from the goal of crafting a compelling narrative, which tells your career story—a story that is connected to and in support of individual goals and needs and institutional priorities and imperatives (see chapter 4).

The aim of this chapter has been to help you engage in a self-assessment and an inventory of outputs by applying the SPU framework in the context of Boyer's (1990) four forms of scholarship. The scholarship of discovery, integration, teaching, and engagement enable you to understand the ways in which your scholarly efforts contribute to your field, institution, and community in diverse ways beyond the traditional scholarship of discovery. Once the form of scholarship is identified in relation to your scholarly goals and subgoals, the SPU framework of audience, content, methods, and process supports a more strategic career-management approach. Specifically, by answering the questions offered throughout this chapter, you gain clarity about the possible outputs you already have in hand, which allows you to think in broader, more varied terms about how what you have can appeal to and support assorted audiences and their needs. Ideally, this process and framework will help you realize that you have more than enough to chart your path to full.

Additional Resources

If you are interested in reading and learning more about Boyer's forms of scholarship, I suggest the following:

Boyer, Ernest L. 1990. *Scholarship Reconsidered: Priorities of the Professoriate*. Princeton, NJ: Princeton University Press. https://files.eric.ed.gov/fulltext/ED326149.pdf.

———. 1996. "From Scholarship Reconsidered to Scholarship Assessed." *Quest* 48 (2): 129–39. http://boyerarchives.messiah.edu/files/Documents4/1000%200001%2064870cr.pdf.

CHAPTER 6

Mapping Your Mentoring Network

Laura Gail Lunsford

No one ever talked to me about preparing for promotion to full professor.

—associate professor, English department, liberal arts college

---

No one ever talked to me about preparing for promotion to full professor either, which is odd when you think about it. Institutions invest great effort in recruiting and vetting faculty candidates. Then, once hired, these faculty members are left to interpolate what is expected and when, by reading handbooks, attending workshops on promotion (if offered when you can attend), and, if you are lucky, finding a great mentor. Or perhaps Suzanne De Janasz and Sherry Sullivan (2004) are right that it is not so much neglect but rather an assumption that the predictable stages of promotion for faculty members have a built-in mentoring component. This chapter focuses on how to remove chance in favor of intentional engagement with a mentoring network, including how to support a mentoring culture for others.

Recently, my European colleagues told me that I am a "pracademic," which is a practitioner who is also an academic scholar. It is true that I enjoy greatly the applied aspect of my mentoring research. In my pracademic role, I have conversed with faculty members across institutional types, from community colleges to liberal arts colleges and from research extensive to intensive and from research labs to medical residencies. Most everyone asserts that mentoring will just happen and that being more intentional feels, well, distasteful; although usually later in the conversation, they will acknowledge the presence of poor mentors and sometimes even a tormentor. My hope is for this chapter to encourage you, the woman faculty member, to become an advocate and champion of mentoring and to be more deliberate in mentoring for yourself and for others.

When the term "mentoring" is used in this chapter, it refers to a specific type of supportive relationship in which a mentor is one of the relational partners. A mentor is someone who can provide both psychosocial or friend-like support in the form of listening, confidence building, role modeling, and approachability and career support in the form of guidance, sponsorship, and challenge. Peer mentoring is also advocated in this chapter; those relationships are characterized by both parties having an equal status, job title, or relational power. Great mentors are different from the everyday, average mentor in their ability to energize you, share good and bad experiences, connect you with new people and ways of thinking, and come back together with you even after a negative interaction.

My career journey may be instructive in thinking about why you need to think deliberately about mentorship at midcareer. I was an academic administrator for many years before earning my PhD. My adviser helped me to prepare for interviews for my first academic position and, most importantly, to negotiate my offer. I moved thousands of miles to Tucson, Arizona, as a budding mentoring scholar, where I knew no one. Mentors were not jumping out of the shadows to meet me. Thus, I made sure to follow up on introductions and sought face time with fellow faculty to identify who might serve in mentor-like roles for me. Meeting senior scholars at professional conferences was a priority for me, and I stayed in contact with them. These relationships were all important in helping me launch the first stage of my career.

After earning tenure and promotion to associate professor, I did some soul searching and decided it was time to return to the East Coast for family reasons. Here I was at midcareer, with a different set of decisions and goals. This time, almost as an afterthought, I checked in with two peer mentors only when I was negotiating an offer for an administrative position. That offer, which I accepted, came with the promise of working out some type of scholarly appointment. (I hear you groaning now: Promise? Was it in writing? You should have held out for the appointment.) I moved another thousand-plus miles to a place where I loved my position, my colleagues, and where I lived (the beach!); but professionally, the scholarly appointment was slow in coming, and the future opportunities appeared limited. Thus, after two years, I made a move to become professor and chair in psychology at a liberal arts institution. This time I sought advice from mentors before making decisions. These accomplished faculty and university presidents helped me clarify what I wanted for the future and how to move in that direction. With the help of my board of advisers, I negotiated successfully to be appointed as a full professor.

Why was I reluctant to seek advice when moving from Arizona? I was worried what others might think of my decision to move, concerned about being judged for moving down in the rank of universities, and as a result, I failed to leverage my terrific network of mentors. Perhaps I would have still taken the administrative position, but I think consulting my mentors earlier would have saved me some of the winding road I took.

The point is that I know a lot about mentoring and still fail at times to be as intentional as I should be. In part, there is not a strong culture of mentoring for midcareer faculty—much less for women faculty— at most institutions. This chapter offers a roadmap designed to support you in identifying excellent mentorship, as well as how to find it, how to be a great mentor yourself, and how to advocate for a culture of mentoring in your institution. It is a how-to guide to understand better the steps to identify and recruit a variety of mentors who will become your allies and serve on your personal board of advisers.

In both my research and consulting practice across the country, I find that institutions

1 support mentoring of undergraduates;

2 believe that graduate students need mentoring but will ask for it when they need it;

3 believe that faculty members will ask for what they need, and if they don't make it, then they didn't deserve to be here in the first place;

4 focus mentoring support for faculty members on early-career individuals; and

5 need the National Science Foundation ADVANCE grant to consider formal mentoring for women faculty members (and here I exaggerate only slightly).

By the time faculty members are at midcareer, there is a sink-or-swim mentoring philosophy, which needs to be solidly stamped out and on and replaced with greater intention and attention. The academy is warming to women. The numbers show that more women are moving into assistant professor roles, but obstacles remain for women moving into the senior ranks (NCES 2017). This chapter first reviews the landscape for women in senior faculty ranks and then proceeds to describe four steps to intentional mentoring:

1 Assessing the new reality

2 Conducting an environmental scan

3 Building a board of advisers

4 Creating a culture of mentoring

Where Are the Women (and Where Are Their Mentors)?

It is a joke that our college has no women deans, provost, or president. This is 2016!

—associate professor, liberal arts college

This quote illustrates the lack of women in academic leadership positions. Yet there has never been a better time to be a woman in the academy. The landscape is changing, and more women are entering the profession. About seventy-one thousand women faculty members in the United States are at the associate rank at all degree-granting institutions (NCES 2017). It is a good time to be a woman faculty member in science. Clever randomized hiring experiments by Wendy Williams and Stephen Ceci (2015) showed that women in science were twice as likely to be recommended to be hired in assistant professor roles than were men. Ceci and colleagues (2014) analyzed data from the National Science Foundation's Survey of Earned Doctorates. Data from R1 institutions showed no gender differences in who held administrative leadership positions (widely defined, I note), on the basis of representation of men and women at the institution. However, gender differences were found when other institutional types were included. According to Ceci and colleagues, "Women were less likely than men to be deans, directors, or department chairs (12.1% vs. 15.1%; $p < .01$) but were equally likely to be presidents, provosts, and chancellors (1.2% vs. 1.2%)" (Ceci et al. 2014, 83). Thus, it appears at least at R1 institutions, if you manage to obtain a faculty position, you have a fair chance for academic leadership.

Yet, as the academy has diversified, challenges remain in supporting and mentoring women and other underrepresented groups. Informal mentoring is more likely when the group is homogeneous. Women are relatively new to the professoriate and until recently were unrepresented at every rank. Thus, it remains easier for men to connect informally with potential mentors, as there is a richer target environment of senior faculty members who seem similar to them. Women, on the other hand, may be challenged to locate those mentors who are champions or who help them to realize their dreams, as Daniel and Judy Levinson's work on adult development well demonstrated (1996).

The Levinsons (a husband-and-wife team) studied forty-five women in depth, including faculty members. They found that their mentors (who were all male at the time, in the 1970s) provided support to women with the aim of helping them become competent contributors—but not to achieve the top ranks. The Levinsons (1996) observed that a man would probably mentor a woman, with the idea that she was "clearly better off with them than she would have been without them. But the degree of mutuality in the relationship was often limited. Although he liked her and enjoyed being helpful, the male mentor usually found it difficult to regard a woman as becoming like him and perhaps surpassing him in the future" (270).

Indeed, "contradictory" best characterizes the literature on women's underrepresentation in academic science (Ceci et al. 2014, 77) and, I would argue, in the academy writ large. Consider the following less rosy picture. In the United States, only 33 percent of full professors are women; men still outnumber women at the associate rank (NCES 2017). A global view is even gloomier, as outlined in chapter 3.

Where are the women? They are at the assistant professor rank, slowly making inroads to associate professor with far fewer moving into the senior ranks. Many women remain at the associate rank or midcareer level, which limits their future leadership opportunities. When midcareer women take on a front-line leadership role, like a department chair or center director, they are then usually so overwhelmed with administrative work that they are set up to fail in accomplishing the work needed for promotion to full professor. We expect women to take care of the "academic family" more so than we expect of men (Guarino and Borden 2017).

Where (and who) are the mentors of these women? The primary mentor should be the department chair, but often it is not. When I recently became a department chair, I discovered two women faculty members overdue in going up for promotion. They noted that it simply had not been encouraged for them to seek promotion. Yet, even in my short time, I could see that they were valued, contributing faculty members. Perhaps they would have submitted their dossiers had I not arrived, but it is interesting that they both chose to do so after I talked with them.

Most women receive more mentoring from their professional associations at midcareer than they do from their institutions. When provosts and deans are asked about mentoring support for faculty, they agree that it is the role of the department chair. They confirm that this mentorship occurs informally and even suggest that there is disinterest in formal mentoring, noting that once they had to cancel a mentoring scheme due to lack of interest (Baker, Lunsford, and Pifer 2017, 139). In our study on liberal arts colleges, one provost summarized the state of mentoring for associate professors well: "You know, again, in the departments there may or there may not be good mentor[ing] of, say, associate professors" (Baker, Lunsford, and Pifer 2017, 139).

A final reality, especially in smaller universities and colleges, is that department chairs are often associate professors themselves. These front-line roles present leadership opportunities for women. However, it is difficult to learn and manage an administrative role and maintain the productivity in teaching and research that you will need for promotion to full professor. Thus, women can be limited in taking on what seem like great leadership opportunities—because if they accept this role, they are likely to remain stuck there without the time, due to the service burden mentioned earlier, to prepare for promotion to a senior rank. If your department chair is not a full professor (or if you are the department chair), it is even more important that you seek out the dean and full professors for mentoring on your promotion plan to full professor.

Where Are the Mentors?

Discipline matters. A walk through almost any college or university will illustrate, for example, that there are many more women professors in education and psychology and fewer in math. This discrepancy influences both the significance and availability of mentoring. Mentoring is more important in those fields where women are underrepresented, and yet it is often less available. Women are equally represented in non-math-intensive fields, such as the life sciences, psychology, and social sciences, while they are underrepresented in fields such as engineering, economics, mathematics, computer science, and the physical sciences, including chemistry and physics (Ceci et al. 2014). A lack of communality is isolating for some women where there are few women role models.

Further, when we consider supports for women, caution is warranted, as these supports may have unintended negative effects. For example, researchers in economics found that gender-neutral "stop the clock" policies for child rearing resulted in men being more likely to earn tenure. It appeared that men were able to continue to publish when caring for new children, while women were not able to use that stopped-clock time for that purpose (Antecol, Bedard, and Stearns 2016).

It is no wonder that there was a market for an entire book on how men need to mentor women (Johnson and Smith 2016). Women need to develop the skills and confidence to share their achievements with those above them, without it seeming egotistical, and they need to be supported to do so. There need to be clear opportunities for women to share their accomplishments and achievements without feeling like they are being self-serving. Women are more likely to believe that their work will rise on its merits without realizing that relationships matter.

Associate professors and those who have the responsibility of supporting them (full professors, department heads, deans, and provosts) need to be more aware of the science of mentoring. Associate professors need to be more intentional in seeking out mentors and becoming peer mentors themselves. Academic leaders need to be more aware of institutional cultures that support mentoring, formally and informally. Department chairs, deans, and provosts need to actively support women at midcareer to keep moving forward.

Consider if your department chair or dean has asked you the following questions:

1 Have you reviewed the expectations for promotion to the next level or rank?

2 What directions do you plan for your research and teaching to achieve the next level of excellence?

3 How can I help you achieve these goals?

4 Whom do you know who can provide mentoring support and feedback on these goals?

If the answer is no, then take the initiative and schedule an annual or biannual meeting to ask your department chair or dean these questions. Give him or her a copy of this book; maybe bookmark this page. Then document your conversations with a pleasant memo—memory is short, and department chairs and expectations have been known to change.

Conduct an Environmental Scan

An in-depth study at the University of Massachusetts (Misra et al. 2010) found that women faculty members are promoted at a slower rate than men faculty members are and that women faculty members are more burdened with service work. Further, women do not gravitate to the service work; they are asked to do it. For some reason, women faculty fail to develop a mentor network that will help us navigate these departmental expectations well. The first step in navigating is to conduct an environmental scan, on at least a yearly basis.

The possible consequence of failing to conduct an environmental scan is illustrated by a micromentoring session I experienced. I gave a keynote address to orient the faculty members, tenure track and not tenure track, and advisers to support more underrepresented students in science. It was an impressive multidisciplinary team, with people from science and English, that reflected the emphasis on science writing in this program. Afterward, a woman associate professor from the liberal arts sought me out for a micromentoring session. She asked if I knew of resources to help women navigate promotion to full professor. "Tell me more," I said. She was receiving indirect messages from male full professors that concerned her. She felt that the direction of her work, while sufficient for promotion to associate professor, was not going to be supported to advance to full professor. In a heartfelt sigh, she observed that she would be devastated if declined for tenure. Then she said, "No one ever talked to me about preparing for promotion to full professor." How, I wondered, could this incredibly competent person, who just received a big grant, be unsure of herself in this next career stage? Why was she still taking on undervalued service work at the expense of the research she wished to conduct? Why was she still saying yes to her department chair to do work that was not valued by the full professors? She had failed to scan her environment for what matters at promotion time.

Be Future Oriented

Conducting an environmental scan means identifying your access to resources to meet your future goals. At midcareer, it is time to think deeply about what you wish to do. Do you want to take your research in a new direction or develop that set of courses you always dreamed about? Do you want to provide mentoring to others around teaching or take on academic leadership opportunities?

The time to start thinking about your resources and assets is the first year after promotion to associate rank or when you have received that next contract renewal at midcareer. Forget reality for a moment and instead imagine that everything has gone as well as it possibly could in every way, both professionally and personally. You are smiling at the letter you just opened notifying you of your promotion to full professor or to the senior ranks. Consider this set of questions: How do you feel? Whom do you tell first? What achievements do you feel really got you there? How did your colleagues support you? What new friends did you make along the way? Who is on your list to write a note of thanks to for support and colleagueship? Spend a few moments jotting down your answers to these questions. Imagine in detail what this moment is like, along with your reflection on what got you there.

Positive psychology refers to the activity you just completed as a "best possible self" intervention. It has been shown to elevate optimism (Meevissen, Peters, and Alberts 2011) and positive emotions (Sheldon and Lyubomirsky 2006), especially if you engage in this exercise regularly. Your results will direct your environmental scan.

Make a list of all the people you would thank, all the possible funders of your work, all the professional societies or connections that provided you support. Conduct an environmental scan of your resources and assets. Consider these questions:

1 With which professional associations do you affiliate?
2 What other professional associations align with your interests?
3 Who at your own institution holds a position to which you aspire (formally or informally)?
4 Who at another institution has a position to which you aspire (formally or informally)?
5 What do you need to learn to take you to the next level professionally?
6 What strengths are underused at present?
7 What do you really enjoy doing?
8 With whom do (or might) you enjoy collaborating?
9 What self-care do you need to enact to stay refreshed and excited in your career?

Organize your responses into your goals and then two sets of resources. First, list your goals (aspirations). Second, list your personal resources (skills, joyful activity, personal network of support). Third, list is who is accessible to you (at work and through your professional affiliations).

Hold onto this list of assets for when we review how to develop your personal board of advisers. Your aspirations and resources may need some tweaking because "what got you here won't get you there." (Thank you, Marshall Goldsmith.)

What Got You Here Won't Get You There

Marshall Goldsmith (2008), a coach to Fortune 500 CEOs, offers advice that applies to midcareer women faculty members: "What got you here won't get you there." What gets you to midcareer will not get you to the senior ranks. Somehow, we think we know the game by the time we are promoted, without realizing that the game has changed. The challenge of the midcareer period is that we have achieved some measure of success and ways of orienting and working. As Goldsmith's message suggests, successful people need to solicit feedback, reflect on it, and do something about it.

Looking further into the micromentoring session in Texas, the woman faculty member explained that her department chair tapped her for important departmental work around curricular development, which is relevant to her scholarly interests. Yet an offhand comment from a full professor alerted her to the fact that this work would not be valued at promotion time. I asked her if she ever declined a department head's request to revise their curriculum. "I can't say no," she said. "I don't know how." Standing before me was an accomplished, midcareer professional who has published books and articles and has received major grants yet still feels she cannot decline requests that she knows are clearly not valued when it comes to promotion time. I advised her to ask senior colleagues if they would suggest she take on those duties and solicit advice from women colleagues about how they say no.

The challenges presented in this scenario are numerous. First, women may enjoy teaching or doing service work. Since many women find it rewarding, it would not occur to them to decline such an opportunity. Think of your work as existing in boxes labeled "teaching," "service," and "scholarship." If one box is full and especially if the other boxes are not, you need to prioritize and say no—even if you would enjoy the service. Second, women do not wish to do extra service but believe they will displease the asker by declining opportunities. Learning how to replace "no" with "let me think about it" or with the "twenty-four-hour rule" mentioned in chapter 2 or with "that is an intriguing opportunity—let me review my other projects for this semester" seems to work better for these women. Third, academe has unspoken rules or nuances about achieving promotion and tenure. Women need well-placed allies both in and outside their departments to help them navigate the unspoken rules about what is going to be valued at promotion time. In any case, what got this woman to associate professor was not going to get her promoted to full.

The formal rules are usually easy to figure out (when you can find them), but it is the informal interpretation that is challenging. Those rules are different to advance to senior ranks and usually involve some greater reputation demonstrated at the national or international level and promise of leadership in the institution and the profession. Ask colleagues at the senior ranks or full professor how they believe expectations for the next promotion differ from the expectations for your last promotion. Start asking for feedback on your work and sit down with senior faculty for genuine conversations about your contributions. When you do receive feedback, thank people for it even if you think it is wrong. Resist the inclination to defend your actions. What you are receiving is important information about how you are perceived. After reflection, assemble an action plan.

SWOT

Conduct a final scan using the SWOT analysis as described in chapter 2. Strengths and weaknesses are internal to you, while opportunities and threats are external factors. For example, your teaching may be a strength, while prepping for new courses is a weakness as it may limit the time you have to devote to your aspirations (unless, of course, your aspiration is prepping a new course). Opportunities are what you could do—what doors might be open and interesting to walk through? For example, do you want to become the director of the honors program or of a special center on campus? Or might you

Strengths Internal	Weaknesses Internal	Opportunities External	Threats External

Figure 6.1 SWOT

be ready to take on an elected role in your professional association? Threats are factors that might limit your pursuit of opportunities. For example, being asked to take on too many projects might be a threat to pursuing that one great opportunity.

You now have a draft of your aspiration statement, a list of personal and professional resources, and a SWOT analysis. This is all in preparation to review and upgrade your personal board of advisers.

Your Personal Board of Advisers

The mentorship provided to me on negotiating my first academic position is quite different from what I needed when deliberating about moving to a liberal arts college as a full professor. Mentoring has moved beyond a singular one-on-one relationship (Sorcinelli and Yun 2007). The nature of careers today calls for a network of mentors who might provide mentoring support in varying degrees. It is useful to think of your mentoring network as your personal board of advisers.

What Mentoring Is (and Is Not)

What does mentoring look like at midcareer? There is consensus that mentoring involves both psychosocial (friendship) and instrumental (career) support. W. Brad Johnson and David Smith (2016) have written eloquently about what is important in mentoring women. I draw heavily on their work, particularly when describing what you should expect from your mentors and should do for your mentees (see figure 6.2). Their book focuses on men mentoring women, but I find their advice about mentoring helpful even if you are a woman mentor. The goal is to build a network of mentors who can provide psychosocial and career support. Similarly, as you mentor others, consider the extent to which you might engage more frequently in these behaviors.

Psychosocial support does not mean being a best friend or "warm and fuzzy." It means listening and building confidence. Specifically, your mentors need to listen—really listen—to what you are saying and support your decisions. They need to bestow friendship and accept you unconditionally while also imparting honest feedback. You need mentors who will affirm that you belong in the academy.

Some men and women can be uncomfortable with tears, consensus, and collaboration (versus competition). Male mentors may need to check some of their competitive instincts (and not assume that women will make the same choices). Cross-gender mentors need to be aware of perceptions from others about the nature of their relationship. One way to make sure this happens is to establish transparency and boundaries about what the relationship is and is not.

Johnson and Smith (2016) advocate for personal growth support or what is increasingly being referred to as "holistic mentoring" (of the whole person). Personal growth includes helping you to realize your career vision and respect your work-life balance, which may well be shaped by your family and personal priorities. Look for mentors who will both build your confidence and challenge you to be assertive and appropriately promote your accomplishments. Most importantly, expect your mentor to affirm both your professional identity and your sense of self as a woman.

Mentoring can occur spontaneously or naturally, referred to as "informal mentoring," or it may be supported institutionally through a program, referred to as "formal mentoring." Formal mentoring can be as good as informal mentoring when the program is designed well and participants are clear on the expectations and commitments.

Mentoring is not being told what to do or judged for your decisions, and it is not for listening to war stories. It is also the case that

Psychosocial support	Career support	Personal growth
Listen (don't talk so much)	Make sure she gets included	Discern and honor her career vision
Let her decide (don't assume)	Teach her what she needs to know (provide access to hidden politics)	Remember, she (probably) has more work outside of work than you do
Be attuned to outside perceptions and discuss them openly	Challenge her! (and provide the support to go along with it)	Honor her approach to work-life balance
Be honest, direct, and unconditionally accepting	Walk the razor's edge between protection and empowerment	Affirm both her professional identity and her sense of self as a woman
Affirm that she belongs (over and over again)	Open doors and put her name forward	Encourage excellence but challenge perfectionism
Leave competitive instincts at the door	Share power and social capital	Champion her assertiveness
Welcome increasing friendship and collegiality	Brag about her in public, provide correction in private	Take every opportunity to build her confidence
Be transparent, don't be exclusive, discuss your family openly	Help her sharpen her leadership style (don't change it)	Challenge her to take full credit for her accomplishments
In public, treat her like you treat the guys	Be a watchdog for disparities at work	
Prepare for transitions and endings	Help her construct a rich constellation of career helpers	
Be her friend		
Let her cry if she needs to cry		

Figure 6.2 Mentors of women: needed functions and behaviors (adapted from Johnson and Smith 2016)

mentoring can sometimes go off the rails and devolve into a dysfunctional relationship. Scholars find that most instances of dysfunction are due to neglect or mismatch (Eby et al. 2000). Neglect occurs when a mentor seems too busy, answers the phone often in your presence, or fails to connect. However, even good mentors have bad days and less effective relationships. To my horror, I once caught myself engaging in neglectful behaviors, like forgetting when I was to meet with my mentee. After the second time this happened, I addressed it. I realized that my apparent amnesia was in response to feeling that we lacked commonalities, as well as feeling frustrated by her lack of interest in the suggestions I provided. Our time together did not seem valued by her or by me. I discussed with her if someone else might be a better fit; she agreed, while appearing quite relieved.

Mismatch occurs when a mentee needs guidance and support in an area in which the mentor simply does not possess expertise. For example, I was considering how to move into future academic leadership roles. Many of my current (and wonderful) mentors simply had no experience in these areas. Thus, I had to actively look for faculty members who had taken on such roles. Goldsmith's advice applies to mentors too: the mentors who best supported you during your early career may not be the right ones for you at midcareer.

The importance of a well-developed network is clear (Higgins and Kram 2001; Hetty van Emmerik 2004). It is no longer the case for most people that one person can provide all the mentoring you will need. Scholars find that the sources of mentors change over career stages for faculty members (van Eck Peluchette and Jeanquart 2000). For example, early-career faculty members seek mentors in the profession who can help them achieve objective career success. As faculty members move into midcareer, there is a positive, significant relationship between objective career success and having a mentor outside the workplace and having multiple sources of mentors. Interestingly, associate professors who report no mentors also report less productivity. Scholars find that faculty members who have more mentors report a greater sense of intrinsic feelings of success (Hetty van Emmerik 2004).

Gap Analysis

Who should be on your board? Use a gap analysis to evaluate the status of your current mentoring network and identify areas where you need new mentors. Complete a matrix like the example in figure 6.3 using the following instructions:

1 Consider who provides you mentor support now. Write their initials in cells in the first row.
2 Consider the key areas in which you would benefit from mentoring support. Write each area in the cells of the first column.
3 Mark an *X* in the cells of who provides each area of needed support.
4 Circle the initials of the mentor who may be from the same department or organization.

The cells missing an *X* highlight the areas where you might need to add a mentor. If you have a lot of circles around mentors, then your network may not be providing you diverse perspectives, and you may need to add mentors from other departments or areas. In the example,

	Mentor initials					
Areas of needed support	BJ	VB	MP	EK	BB	KN
1 Get a book contract	X					
2 Advice on university service committees				X		X
3 Dealing with my department chair		X	X			
4 Teaching older students						
5 Preparing for future administrative roles				X		
6 An article in an "A" journal						

Figure 6.3 Mentor network analysis: example

I have no mentors around my teaching goal. If there were limited professional-development resources, then that would be a good area in which to look for a new mentor. I may also need to add more than one person to help with key priorities, like preparing to take on the right future administrative roles or getting a book contract.

Bringing New Advisers on Board

I receive many interesting comments and questions when I give seminars on mentoring to faculty members. After one such session in Oregon, a person raised her hand to ask how to find a mentor, as she had tried to no avail. After a few probing questions, it was clear that she was coming on too strong. She would email someone, asking if he or she would consider being her mentor. Whoa! Unless you are in a formal mentoring program, it can be too much to ask someone to mentor you in the first contact. It is like asking someone to marry you during your first date. It may work sometimes, but usually it does not. The mentor may not be sure of making such a commitment or even what that commitment would be.

Recognize that informal mentoring evolves over time. It may be the case that some people might provide micromentoring or engage in single or infrequent interactions. These can be quite meaningful. However, you can and should cultivate mentors intentionally. The steps are to reach out, engage, thank, reconnect, and recycle.

That is, first reach out through email or a phone call to a key person to inquire if he or she will meet with you. Then engage in a meeting, ideally face-to-face but at least by video conference to learn more about what he or she is doing or to ask for the person's feedback for your new ideas. After this initial contact, you thank the person by email or letter and let your potential mentor know about your progress pertaining to the actions suggested in your meeting. Make a note in your calendar to reconnect with this person in a month or two. Then, if this is a useful and mutually beneficial relationship, you recycle by engaging again, expressing gratitude, and reconnecting. Congratulations! You have now added a potential candidate to your personal board of advisers. By the second or third cycle, you may even let the person know that you consider the relationship and his or her advice to be meaningful and that you have a place for him or her on your board of advisers. Remember, you are offering ideas, experiences, and the opportunity for your mentor to show that she or he can develop others. Be sure to connect your mentor with others too.

You can also identify formal mentoring opportunities in which you can participate. These formal mentoring relationships typically have expectations and accountability built into the program. Unfortunately, with a few exceptions, most educational institutions focus on early career for formal mentoring programs (Buch et al. 2011).There are two main sources for formal mentoring. First, department heads should be providing mentoring to associate professors, even though scholars find that they do not often do so (Buch et al. 2011; Baker, Pifer, and Lunsford 2016). Many faculty members tell me that their department chair provides them little to no mentoring. Thus, you might have to create the space for mentoring to occur. Meet at least once a year with your chair and review your plans and goals for promotion. Again, however, many department heads are themselves associate professors and may not feel competent to provide mentoring around promotion. In these cases, peer mentoring might be a good option to engage also with other women associate professors informally in your institution.

Second, you can seek formal mentoring through your professional associations. Serving as a mentor might connect you with other mentors and people who might become candidates for members on your board of advisers. I have found that my involvement in professional conferences on mentoring has connected me with scholars in the field whom I have added to my personal board. I am not sure they all know they are on my board, but they take my calls and emails when I have questions, they are happy to review manuscript drafts or ideas for new scholarship, and they are glad to meet up with me at conferences to reconnect.

The main idea for informal or formal relationships is to collaborate and cultivate the relationship, seek advice, and provide information to your mentor. Check in from time to time and demonstrate accountability through your good follow-up on action items you discussed with this person.

What might you talk about? Kimberly Buch and colleagues suggest six steps to plan your next career stage. Their process provides another framework to think about what you might discuss with your board of advisers and when. For example, get their feedback on your career goals, ask for suggestions on how to develop strengths and limit weaknesses, and review your progress. Engage mentors to provide regular feedback on your plans, ideas, and progress.

Tap into several mentors, not just one. Scholars find that four to five mentors may be an ideal number for faculty members (Thomas, Lunsford, and Rodrigues 2015). The composition to consider is one peer at your institution and one outside your institution (two people); a faculty member who is senior to you at your institution and one outside your institution (two people); and, finally, if there is a demographic characteristic (ethnicity, gender, religion, etc.) that is important to you and your mentors do not share it, then find a fifth person who does.

Anna Neumann, Aimee Terosky, and Julie Schell (2006) also suggest effective strategies for midcareer faculty members that provide good choices for mentoring feedback. The three strategies are integration, containment, and design. My mentors helped me in all of these areas—but only because I asked them for advice. "Integration" refers to selecting what matters to you and focusing your personal, professional, and intellectual effort on that topic. My mentors, when I asked for advice, helped me to select service work that aligned with my mentoring interests. I recall a micromentoring episode in which a senior faculty member also advised me to teach what I love if I have the choice (and thus I taught a course on mentoring that semester). Thus, my interests in mentoring and leadership are reflected in my teaching, research, choice of service activities, and choice of consulting work. It allows me to be more efficient by having a more focused effort. Ask your mentors for advice on how to best integrate your activities.

"Containment" refers to the idea of narrowing your interests so that you can make visible progress and still learn and contribute in that area. In my area of mentoring, for example, I am focused on the psychology of mentoring—how do people get together and what do they do? Therefore, while I might be interested in a variety of populations (e.g., students, employees, faculty members), my focus is always on the psychological aspects. I developed this focus in talking with my mentors, who helped me to put a frame on my research that anyone will understand.

"Design" means being intentional in how you craft your environment to minimize distractions and conserve psychic energy for what matters to you. I struggled, as a new faculty member, to find the best way to organize my time, especially for writing. After talking with some of my peer mentors to learn what worked best for them, I now, for example, have a default time of thirty-minute meetings (which Vicki describes in chapter 2), which is at odds with the sixty-minute standard in most organizations. This strategy saves meeting time to use for writing instead. My writing is best in the mornings, I observed after some prompting from mentors. Therefore, I now protect that time and have meetings in the afternoon when possible. My office-desk placement makes me appear approachable (door is open), but I am not distracted by whoever walks by. Design your physical and mental environment to direct your attention to what matters most. Get advice from mentors about how they design their environments.

Creating a Mentoring Culture

Formal mentoring initiatives are not always fully utilized. At UNC Charlotte (Buch et al. 2011), scholars found that 75 percent of faculty members chose not to participate in a formal initiative, while some of the participants did not fulfill their commitments to participate. When people do not participate, it means that the mentoring does not meet their needs or time constraints. Formal mentoring programs can be effective when they meet the needs of the participants, as the example described in the following subsection demonstrates. Creating a mentoring culture also requires you to engage in supporting and being a great mentor yourself.

High-Visibility Mentoring

Pay more attention to associate professors—particularly women, for whom the path to promotion is often murky and less traveled.

—Kimberly Buch et al. (2011, 39)

Do you aspire to a formal academic leadership role beyond department chair? Then you definitely need to prepare for promotion to full professor. Not so sure? You do not need a formal leadership role to serve as a motivator to move to full professor or the senior ranks. Your options will be broader for informal and formal leadership if you move on to the senior rank. The Modern Language Association's *Associate Professor Survey* (2009) reports that women take one to three and a half years longer than men do to attain promotion to full professor. Senior rank is a pipeline to leadership; without promotion to that rank, you are limiting your options.

Mentoring for women needs to be more intentional, deliberate, and visible. We might wish that more academic leaders would recognize the importance of mentoring; however, you have agency in creating mentoring opportunities at midcareer. Women's centers or committees on the status of women faculty provide a good place to identify allies in developing high-visibility mentoring opportunities for women. An example from a public, master's-level institution is instructive.

At the University of North Carolina (UNC) at Wilmington, the director of the Women's Studies and Resource Center felt that there was an unmet need for mentorship of women associate professors. No institutional supports existed to start or manage that activity. Many administrators agreed to the importance of mentoring, but it simply was not high enough on the priority list for attention. The director approached me with several good ideas about how to do more to support women faculty members. After a spirited discussion, I suggested she select one of her several good ideas to pilot. She chose mentoring of associate professors. She applied and received a $5,000 grant from the American Association of University Women to support a pilot mentoring program. We adapted practices that had been shown to be successful at the University of Arizona through its National Science Foundation ADVANCE work (Thomas, Lunsford, and Rodrigues 2015).

The program lasted for one semester and targeted associate professors who planned to go up for promotion to full professor in the next two years. Three workshops were offered; monthly meetings between mentees and mentors were expected; and a celebratory reception honoring women who were promoted concluded the program (see figure 6.4).

Month	Workshops and events	Additional meetings
February	Workshop 1: Building a Culture of Mentoring and Supporting Women The workshop purpose was to reflect on mentoring, compare participants' understanding of mentoring to scholarly research on definitions, stages, and high-quality mentoring. About twenty-five minutes were allocated for the groups to meet together and discuss successful collaborations and their goals for the mentorship.	Mentoring Meeting
March	Workshop 2: Preparing Great Dossiers The workshop purpose was to provide information about the content of the dossier. Discussion about formal and informal requirements was facilitated by a representative of the provost's office.	Mentoring Meeting
April	Workshop 3: Mechanics of Submitting a Great Dossier The workshop purpose was to demonstrate how promotion dossiers need to be submitted through the online portal. Dr. Diane Ashe facilitated this workshop.	Mentoring Meeting
May	Promotion Celebration and Reception (provost and deans invited)	

Figure 6.4 UNC Wilmington women faculty mentoring program elements (spring semester)

The program evaluation showed that participants viewed it as valuable and relevant. The faculty members found the peer mentoring, the opportunity to meet other women faculty, and the chance to be part of a community who want success for women to be extremely useful. The mentees met with their mentors at least twice during the semester, and many met monthly.

Most of the mentees felt that their dean and department head knew of their participation in the mentoring program, but they all did not feel so. With one exception, they all reported high-quality relationships with their mentor. They overwhelmingly would recommend the program to other women. Over half reported they were on track with their dossier submission plans, with one person ahead of schedule and two behind their planned schedule.

What this example demonstrates is that you can begin to build a culture of mentoring on your campus. Be sure to conduct your activities in a way that builds support and provides data for future support. I attended most of the workshops and conducted the evaluation. The women professors were grateful to have the opportunity to meet and support one another. The evaluation gave the director evidence to advocate effectively for this program to continue. She was able to get the attention of academic leaders, who agreed to move it on the priority list. The evaluation was shared with the provost, who agreed to provide ongoing support for food for the workshops, a graduate student to handle the evaluation aspects, and a stipend for an external speaker on mentoring. It was important to engage the provost and deans to create visibility for the women associate professors and for the importance of mentoring them.

There are external high-visibility leadership opportunities that provide mentoring. If your institution is part of a system or a member of an association, consider if it supports leadership or mentoring programs. For example, the UNC system supports the BRIDGES program for women faculty members. There are national programs like the American Council of Education Fellows Program (ACE, n.d.). The Higher Education Leadership Program for Women is another such example (HERS, n.d.).

How to Be a Great Mentor

We need more academic leaders to be great mentors, and the hope is that you will be one too.

Being a great mentor means actively looking out for men and women to support informally. It means formally advocating for and adding to the conversation about creating structured supports. Individuals tasked with faculty development, promotion and tenure, and supporting faculty need to more visibly support women midcareer faculty. There are three top areas for attention to create infrastructure that supports mentoring:

1 Make data public about promotion rates and time in rank. This action increases awareness about the need for mentorship of mid-career women faculty members.

2 Create workshops and opportunities for faculty members to learn about promotion via the written and unwritten rules. This activity makes privileged knowledge accessible to men and to women.

3 Provide mentoring support to help women identify goals and stay on track in pursuing them. This might mean protecting one's time, taking on fewer service obligations, and learning how to say no gracefully. Create spaces in your professional life for mentoring, and ask others to do the same.

Transition points are excellent times to seek mentoring. Seek full professorship and intentionally develop your board of advisers with the ideas suggested here. Add to the mentoring culture on your campus by mentoring others and sharing what has worked for you. Then, remember to thank your mentors and seek others to mentor.

CHAPTER 7

Developing Your Persuasive Voice

Karen Erlandson

Making your way on the path to full professor or continuing contract status often means being persuasive in multiple contexts. As a woman trying to be persuasive, however, you are likely to encounter obstacles along this path that men do not face. Most of the obstacles women face in the ability to persuade others are a result of stereotypes and expectations (Carli 2004.) Overcoming these stereotypes and expectations requires being strategic and using empirically tested methods for persuasion.

The goal of this chapter is to share persuasive principles that you can incorporate into all phases of your academic experience, with a particular emphasis on service and administrative roles, which increase for women upon earning promotion and tenure. The six principles of persuasion presented here will increase the likelihood of getting positive responses to your requests, regardless of gender. I use examples from academia to demonstrate how you can implement each principle to your advantage. Because you may still experience gender bias, I will also discuss some of the more common biases and offer excellent resources for dealing with them. I end this chapter by introducing some activities for finding your persuasive voice.

Why Persuasion Matters

The only real power available to the leader is the power of persuasion.

—Lyndon B. Johnson

At my institution, teaching, research, and campus/community service guide decisions on promotion and tenure. Since teaching is my passion, I spend hours preparing just the right lecture with just the right examples and just the right timing to make sure my students learn (and maybe have fun in the process). As a scholar, I spend an equal amount of time crafting my results and discussion in a way that will convince editors that my work is meaningful and will make a contribution. As academics, I think we all understand the importance of preparation and strategy when it comes to teaching and research. Yet, in my experience, very rarely do we spend the same time and energy strategizing for weekly meetings and day-to-day encounters, despite the fact that we need to be effective and persuasive to achieve our goals in these settings as well. Whether you are in the first year of your tenure-track career or your last, the strategies presented in this chapter will help you be more persuasive and provide the tools to help you get there.

For women, crafting persuasive skills is especially important since you may be fighting gender stereotypes and bias when engaging with peers and students. The good news is that people judge men and women equally in many ways. For example, while both men and women are rated as effective leaders (Carless 1998), women are more likely to lead through collaboration and to use transformational leadership styles, which are rated as most effective (Hater and Bass 1988). The bad news is that because women are expected to collaborate and cooperate in leadership roles, they are judged negatively when they do otherwise (Matheson 1991). If a woman violates this expectation and acts competitively, she will be judged more harshly than a man will

(Kulik and Olekalns 2012). This bias shows up in numerous contexts that effect your academic career. For example, women only suffer in their evaluations as leaders when they adopt autocratic, or masculine, ways of leading (Carnes et al. 2015). Student evaluations demonstrate that students expect women faculty to provide more interpersonal support than they expect of men (Bennett 1982). Women, particularly from underrepresented populations, are sometimes viewed as less credible to their students, which increases the need to defend their grades and handle more complaints (Denker 2009). Study findings have revealed that underrepresented women have lower compliance ratings from students than white women or Black men do when using the same forms of power (Elias and Loomis 2004). For women, expressing anger during group deliberation can decrease influence, but for men, anger can increase influence (Salerno and Peter-Hagene 2015). This inequality means that creating a good persuasive message is essential for women.

Let me share a personal example to illustrate this point. I served on our faculty steering committee for three years, with my final year as the chair. Each year this committee is responsible for holding elections to fill vacant committee slots. Convincing faculty to volunteer for a committee assignment that offers no compensation and loads of extra work is a hard sell. Faculty meetings where elections take place are notoriously long, and it is always difficult to get enough nominations to fill all the ballots in order to take a vote. As it was my job to do this, I strategized the best ways to solicit nominations before the meeting.

At the time, national concerns were raised about the diminishing role of faculty governance at higher learning institutions, and similar discussions were held at our college. We agreed on the vital role of faculty governance at a healthy LAC. We affirmed our commitment to the American Association of University Professors' 1966 "Statement on Government of Colleges and Universities," which details best practices for shared governance, and we all believed that the committee system was important to maintaining an active and meaningful pipeline of communication between the administration and the faculty

(AAUP 2018). I decided to use this common goal and my training in persuasion to carefully craft the following email to the faculty, containing three of the persuasive tactics I will share in this chapter, identified in brackets:

> Greetings, Faculty and Librarians:
>
> It is that time of year again where the Faculty Steering Committee needs to start considering filling positions for the standing committees that are becoming vacant. Shared governance is one of the best ways to maintain open and effective communication between all parts of the college. Most of us strongly align with the principles in the AAUP 1966 "Statement on Government of College and Universities" that detail best practices for shared governance [*liking-cooperation, social proof*]. We would defend against efforts to minimize our role in the college's shared governance system [*consistency/commitment*]. Yet each year when FSC makes requests to fill positions in our committee system, volunteers are hard to come by. The system won't continue to work if there is no one willing to be part of it [*consistency/commitment*].
>
> I therefore issue a call for nominations for the following standing committee openings and encourage those who are eligible (especially those who have not served in a while) to stand for committee election.
>
> If you are willing to stand for election, please email me with your self-nominations.
>
> Thank you on behalf of FSC,
> Karen [*liking-similarity*]

After one reminder, we had filled all but one of the ballots by the time we had our faculty meeting. This was unusual, and while this was not a controlled experiment, I like to think the use of a thoughtful, ethical, persuasive strategy in the emails I sent was a key to the success of filling committee ballots this particular year. Why did this work? What was it about the message that increased the likelihood that people would volunteer? More importantly, how can you learn to craft more strategic messages in your academic encounters?

Six Principles to Improve Your Personal Persuasive Power

Decades of social science research on persuasion reveal principles that tend to increase the likelihood that people will say yes to a request. Robert Cialdini (2009) has suggested that there are six such universal principles of persuasion: social proof, liking, reciprocity, consistency and commitment, scarcity, and authority. What all six principles have in common is that they are heuristic cues—what we respond to automatically without engaging our logical or critical brain. Think about a deer in headlights, for example. When a deer feels afraid, its response is to freeze. The deer does this automatically and without thinking. As humans, we like to think we are more logical in our responses, but if we had to stop and critically examine every decision we made all day every day, we would never get anything done (see the section on habits in chapter 2).

These heuristics (or shortcuts) are an adaptive behavior that enable us to survive our hectic lives. For example, if I am in a hurry to get to a dinner party and want to buy a nice bottle of wine for my hosts and I know nothing about wine, I will most likely get a bottle that is a little bit expensive. Expensive equals good, right? This heuristic will be correct much of the time, but not always. Unfortunately, these shortcuts can make us vulnerable to abuse, given that criminals, con artists, and unscrupulous salespeople know very well how to take advantage of people according to their trust in heuristic judgments.

Alternatively, people can miss good opportunities to use the tools at hand to create win-win situations. Rather than using heuristics unethically to become a "smuggler," you can choose to be a "sleuth" of persuasion (Cialdini 2003b) by using heuristics ethically to educate and inform someone into a decision that is best for all parties. Sleuths strategically use the principles that are naturally available in a given situation to collaborate with targets to create a win-win scenario. Become a sleuth by identifying opportunities for genuine use of strategic principles. This should also help you recognize and protect yourself when others are attempting to influence you for negative purposes.

While cultural and contextual cues have been demonstrated to show tendencies for use of certain principles over others, according to Cialdini (1993), these heuristics are universal and should therefore increase the likelihood of getting a yes.

Social Proof

Social proof, also called "consensus," is the principle that people tend to follow the lead of others (Lun et al. 2007). When we see other people performing a behavior, we tend to view it as correct. Dozens of studies have supported the effectiveness of this strategy in multiple contexts including public littering (Cialdini, Reno, and Kallgren 1990), returning a lost wallet (Hornstein, Fisch, and Holmes 1968), perceiving humor (Platow et al. 2005), and engaging in "safe" versus "unsafe" promiscuous sexual activity (Buunk and Bakker 1995).

Being in step with our peers is a strong drive. Salespeople and marketers have long known about the power of social proof. Consider how Facebook informs you if your friends "like" a specific post, or think of Travelocity searches that tell you how many people are looking at your hotel "right now."

One thing to keep in mind as you consider how to use social proof in your persuasive attempts is that our tendency to rely on social proof is amplified (1) if we are uncertain about how to behave, (2) if we see many people doing it, and (3) if those people are similar to us (Cialdini 2009). I was using social proof in my email when I mentioned that most of us strongly align with the principles in the AAUP's 1966 "Statement on Government of College and Universities."

To demonstrate the concept of social proof further, consider the following scenarios.

Social Proof Scenario 1. You are a department chair. Your department has just completed an external review. On the basis of feedback from students and a review of required texts for a core course, you believe it is time to adopt a new text. You know that several senior members of the department who were responsible for choosing the current text will be resistant to change. However, it is clear from the external review report that this change is vital to keeping current and competitive with similar programs at other colleges and possibly for continued accreditation. What do you do?

First, don't rely exclusively on your own arguments. Persuasion attempts can be more successful when they come from peers. In your role as department chair, specifically use the external review document to find possible peer support. Perhaps some of your departmental colleagues are uncertain about using this text, and the reviewer feedback supports those concerns. When people are uncertain, it is a perfect time to use social proof. You could do some research and see how many programs that are similar to yours use the new text that you are proposing. If many of them are using it, be sure to build that into your pitch. Perhaps you can secure testimonials from multiple faculty members at other institutions who use the book and like it. The more similar the faculty in your testimonials are to the naysayers, the better.

Social Proof Scenario 2. You are a member of a department whose number of majors has been declining. Your department chair asks you to help recruit more majors since you are teaching many of the introductory-level courses. What do you do?

In one study, researchers found that participants viewing a recruitment website with testimonials from similar others (or peers) found the organization more attractive and the information on the site more credible (Walker et al. 2009). This is your cue to engage current students to secure testimonials for your department website as well as on your web-based course platforms like Moodle or Blackboard. Have a senior who was an exceptionally strong (and popular) student come speak to your introductory courses about the great job she got because of her experiences in your department and major. Remember, the more people you have and the more similar those people are to your intended audience, the more impact your social proof will have.

A final note: make sure to avoid negative social proof. People tend to conform to bad behavior as well, so be sure you are not inadvertently reinforcing a behavior that you do not want. For example, when the Petrified Forest National Park wanted to decrease the number of guests stealing pieces of wood from the park, Cialdini (2003a) conducted a study in which three different conditions in the park were tested: (1) the control condition had no sign posted about theft; (2) a posted sign using negative social proof read, "Many past visitors have removed the petrified wood from the park, changing the natural state of the Petrified Forest," accompanied by a picture of several park visitors stealing pieces of wood; (3) a posted sign read, "Please don't remove the petrified wood from the park, in order to preserve the natural state of the Petrified Forest," accompanied by a picture of one person stealing a piece of wood with a prohibition sign indicating "no." The first condition resulted in a theft rate of 2.92 percent; the second condition resulted in a theft rate of 7.9 percent; and the third condition resulted in a theft rate of 1.67 percent. Thus, no sign would have been better than the negative social proof sign.

Liking

I like to praise and reward in a loud voice and to scold in a whisper.

—Catherine the Great

We tend to want to say yes to people we like, and numerous studies support this tendency (see, for example, Cialdini 1993). For example, think about the home-party method of direct sales (e.g., LulaRoe or LipSense). Many of us have attended such parties and left with a purchase (or two). Social bonds at these events are far more predictive of purchases than liking of the actual product (Frenzen and Davis 1990). Liking, as a persuasive principle, includes three factors: (1) similarity, (2) praise, and (3) cooperation (Cialdini 2003b).

We tend to like people more when they are similar to us. Similarities like national and ethnic identification, religious affiliation and background, and similar values and interests all enhance liking (Burger et al. 2004). We are even more persuaded by someone with a name that is similar to ours (Garner 2005). Take the opportunity to discover similarities with others, and use those similarities to create bonds with new hires or old colleagues to enhance the likelihood that those colleagues will respond favorably to your requests. This strategy is especially useful during the first years of your academic career. Tenure reviews include feedback from your colleagues (often in the form of a formal letter of support). You want to make sure that you are building relationships with colleagues who will support you along your path and eventually at the crucial point of tenure (and, later, career advancement to full or continuing contract status). All the strategies in this chapter help develop mutually beneficial relationships.

While it's true that we prefer to help people we like, this is often predicted by whether we think people like us. Therefore, the more you can find things you genuinely like about someone and praise the person for it, the more likely you will be able to count on his or her support or cooperation. To demonstrate the concept of liking further, consider the following scenarios.

Liking Scenario 1. You are tenured, seeking promotion to full in the next two years, and are on a committee with a difficult colleague. Not only is this colleague someone you will be working with for several years, but the person is likely to be part of your promotion-review committee. You really need to establish a good working relationship with this person, but you are having difficulty finding a genuine similarity. What do you do?

You could try asking this person questions or soliciting advice (particularly regarding something the person cares a lot about). This tactic is supported by research that has found that people like us when we ask them questions (Huang et al. 2017), and this works because questions solicit self-disclosure. People enjoy talking about themselves, and they attribute this enjoyment to the question asker, therefore increasing our liking of that person (Huang et al. 2017). Making positive comments about the traits, attitudes, or performance of someone else creates liking and subsequently increases the person's willingness to comply with requests (Berscheid and Walster 1978). You can also try fostering cooperation, given that research reveals that we like people who cooperate with us on common goals (Johnson, Johnson, and Maruyama 1983). Remember that in my email to the faculty, I stressed the common goal of faculty governance, and I reminded the faculty that we were all on the same side.

Liking Scenario 2. You are faculty senate chair and will be meeting with the board of trustees at the end of a weeklong series of meetings to negotiate changes in the faculty handbook. Faculty at your institution have been upset about weak and unclear language regarding faculty governance and general contract language. What do you do to gain support for plans to increase faculty roles in governance and secure clearer language for contract issues?

Take the advice from experts in arbitration and mediation. In this scenario, the principle of liking should begin during the series of meetings, before the faculty handbook changes must be made. Find commonalties and similar interests with the board members during the week and offer genuine praise. This principle is easy to enact. Start your faculty handbook meeting with small talk focusing on shared similarities or common interests and goals that you have discovered over the course of the week. This will increase the likelihood of reaching an agreement (Sankary 2005).

The liking principle, at its core, is about building effective interpersonal relationships prior to any attempted persuasion request. Throughout all phases of your career, invest in spending the time building cohorts and alliances through sharing genuine praise and expressing genuine liking. I offer this advice because it works. Plain and simple, when people like you, they are more apt to agree with your requests. For example, after I sent the faculty email I mentioned previously, my colleague, who is also a friend, agreed to serve on a committee:

Karen—
   I will stand for the hearing and grievance committee.
   Faculty X

   PS—Karen, I wish I didn't like you so much, damn you :)

Reciprocity

The way to achieve your own success is to be willing to help somebody else get it first.

—Iyanla Vanzant

At a most basic level, people feel obligated to return favors. If someone gets you a birthday present, you feel like you need to get the person a birthday present too. In a classic study by Dennis Regan (1971), subjects who received a favor (in the form of a Coke) from a confederate were more likely to return the favor (in the form of purchasing a raffle ticket). Several replications of this study revealed some key concepts of reciprocity as a strategy. First, it did not matter if the participant liked the confederate. Participants still bought more raffle tickets than participants who did not receive a Coke did. Second, the raffle tickets purchased were far more valuable than the Coke. The moral: the urge to reciprocate a favor was stronger than liking, did not necessarily create an even trade, and occurred whether the participant asked for the Coke or not. The takeaway is that three things increase the power of the reciprocity principle: the favor or gift is (1) personalized, (2) meaningful, and (3) unexpected (Cialdini 2009).

Skilled negotiators have learned that starting with an initial position that is just large enough to open the conversation to a series of small, reciprocal concessions often leads to the best outcome (Weingart et al. 1990). Thus, reciprocity can also be induced through concessions. The lesson for you? Always start high and work down in negotiations.

Finally, gifts are not the only things that count as a favor. Sharing information, time, attention, or anything your audience perceives as important also counts as something that induces indebtedness. To demonstrate the concept of reciprocity further, consider the following scenarios.

Reciprocity Scenario 1. Each year, multiple departments on campus host guest speakers. These departments often have difficulty getting enough people to attend the speaking event. There are three speaking events from other departments before your department hosts its own. What do you do?

Be sure to attend other departments' speaking engagements and incentivize your students to do the same. That way, when the time comes to request a guest speaker for your own department, you can count on the reciprocity from those departments that you supported, creating a mutually beneficial long-term relationship.

Reciprocity Scenario 2. You have been put in charge of collecting a survey from department chairs about campus resources. You need to get a good response rate for your report. What do you do?

Sometimes even small touches can be perceived as meaningful and personalized, thereby inducing reciprocity. Send the survey in hard copy, and attach a handwritten plea on a sticky note with a smiley face on the cover letter. One study showed that doing this was more effective than a cover letter alone (Garner 2005).

Consistency and Commitment

Good turns are one reliable way to make people feel obligated to you. Another is to win a public commitment from them.

—Robert Cialdini (2003b)

We feel pressure from multiple sources to behave consistently once we take a stand (Russo, Carlson, and Meloy 2006). A common application of this strategy (called "the foot-in-the-door technique") is when a small request, once accepted, is followed by a larger request (see, for example, Freedman and Fraser 1966). In one study, restaurants managed to reduce the number of no-shows by changing the reservation process. After the customer made the reservation via phone, the host would turn the comment "Please call if you need to cancel" into a question and wait for an affirmative response, such as "Would you please call if you need to cancel?" (Cialdini 2003b). Responding yes and failing to follow through creates dissonance and inconsistency. The goal becomes building small, consistent steps over time, which can be used as a long-term approach to building gradual support for your cause.

To increase the effect of the consistency and commitment principle, you should make commitments (1) active, (2) public, and (3) voluntary (Cialdini 2003b). To demonstrate the concept of consistency and commitment further, consider the following scenarios.

Consistency and Commitment Scenario 1. You are in charge of mentoring students on academic probation. One of your main charges is to help students raise their GPA. What do you do?

Multiple studies in different contexts have demonstrated that goals stated in public are more likely to succeed than private goals are. To support your efforts, have your students set a goal, state it publicly, and put it in writing. Chapter 2 encourages you to write down your goals; encouraging others to do it is a good strategy as well.

Consistency and Commitment Scenario 2. You have a colleague who often says she will accomplish a task when you are in a department meeting. However, she often does not fulfill the obligation. What do you do?

At the next meeting, when the colleague agrees to a task, ask her to summarize the task in writing before the meeting concludes. Writing down the summary herself is more effective than doing it for her. For instance, doctors' offices reduced the number of no-shows by having the client fill out the appointment card themselves (Cialdini 2003b), which serves to facilitate a stronger commitment. Follow this up with an email memo to the department summarizing the meeting, being sure to include the agreements made by your colleague. This public commitment will be harder to ignore, making it more likely that your colleague will complete the task.

Scarcity

It is the prohibition that makes anything precious.

—Mark Twain

We view opportunities as more valuable when they become less available (Pratkanis and Aronson 2000). For example, when my airline tells me there are only two seats left at my price, I admit to feeling a little pressure to buy right away. For your purposes, unique benefits and exclusive information trigger the scarcity principle as well. Scarcity can be enhanced by (1) competing and (2) focusing on potential losses as opposed to gains (Cialdini 2003b). To demonstrate the concept of scarcity further, consider the following scenarios.

Scarcity Scenario 1. Your department is applying for a new tenure-track position, and you need to submit a proposal to your curriculum committee. You know that the committee will rank the position requests and submit those to the board of trustees, which has committed to just three new tenure-track approvals for the coming year. What do you do?

To make your position stand out, be sure to highlight the unique benefits that your position would offer the college and the students. If you can align these with any college-wide implementations or strategic planning initiatives, that is even better. If your strategic plan focuses on community involvement, for example, be sure to mention that the position you are seeking would include courses that use service learning projects to engage students directly with the local community. Also, be sure to frame your arguments in a way that focuses on potential losses. People, in general, are persuaded by what they stand to lose rather than what they stand to gain (Hobofoll 2001). For example, instead of saying, "With this position, we would be able to offer four extra courses per year, serving two hundred more students," try this instead: "Without this position, we will have four fewer courses to offer, leaving two hundred students without a needed course."

Scarcity Scenario 2. You have been put in touch with a potential donor who is considering supporting your department. You want the donor to commit to a scholarship that helps professors and their students present their work at conferences. What do you do?

Focus your pitch on the potential losses. Mention how many students will be missing out without help. Instead of messages like "Let's do it for the students," try "These students can't miss this opportunity." The goal is to create a sense of urgency and to illustrate who and what stands to miss out.

If you are attempting to recruit millennials on campus, I offer an important caveat to using the scarcity principle. One recent study demonstrated that for millennials, the use of scarcity-based messages for recruiting (for example, members-only benefits like awards and scholarships) had a negative impact. Millennials may be more team focused and think everyone should have the same chance (Serviere-Munoz and Counts 2014).

Authority

Expose your expertise; don't assume it's self-evident.

—Robert Cialdini (2001, 77)

The final principle of persuasion is authority. Stanley Milgram's (1974) early studies on obedience demonstrate the power of an authority figure on subject compliance. Authority, it turns out, like the other principles we have been discussing, is a mental shortcut, a heuristic. We tend to defer to experts or people in power, especially when we are uncertain about how to behave (Cialdini 2009). The trappings of authority tend to activate this shortcut in people. For example, people are more likely to take orders from someone in a uniform (Bushman 1988) and follow the orders of physical therapists more when diplomas and awards are displayed on the walls (Cialdini 2001).

Authority cues work best if the communicator is (1) an expert/ knowledgeable and (2) perceived as credible/trustworthy (Cialdini 2003b). To demonstrate the concept of authority further, consider the following scenarios.

Authority Scenario 1. Your department needs to submit curricular changes to the committee. While you have helped develop a good curricular change and solid implementation plan, you believe there is one weakness in the plan. What do you do?

There are a few ways to use the principle of authority to increase the effectiveness of your proposal. Where you can, try to build in experts or credible sources in the proposal. Also, mention the obvious weakness in your plan before delivering the strongest aspects of it. This has been shown to increase your trustworthiness (Sankary 2005). Be sure, though, that you follow up the weak part of the plan with a strong presentation of all the positive aspects of it.

Authority Scenario 2. You are in your third year after gaining tenure and promotion at your college or university, with the goal of pursuing full professorship in the coming years. Your college or university sponsors a faculty lecture series each year, and your department chair has suggested that you give a presentation on your research for the series. You want to make a good impression on your colleagues, and you have heard that many successful promotion candidates presented their research prior to their bid. What do you do?

First, presenting your research can be an excellent way to provide evidence of your authority and expertise. A presentation of your research is also a good way to get to know your colleagues and make sure they know who you are. If you can, have someone introduce you or advocate for you. Perhaps your dean or provost can introduce you and read a statement about your qualifications. It doesn't matter who introduces you as long as the person describes your qualifications and expertise (Cialdini 2003b). After that, it's up to you to give a great talk!

Setting the Context

Every battle is won before it is fought.

—Sun Tzu

In the book *Pre-suasion* (2016), Cialdini outlines several ways we can prime someone to be receptive to our persuasive appeals in the moments before we make a request. For example, Amanda Shantz and Gary Latham (2011) wanted to determine if images could be used to prime students at a call center to solicit more donations. They passed out tip sheets with helpful information regarding making requests and suggested responses to common questions. For half the callers, the tips were on a plain sheet of paper. For the other half, the tips were printed on paper that displayed an image of a runner winning a race. Callers who saw the runner winning the race on the tip sheet made 60 percent more profits. The researchers explain that viewing success (i.e., the image of winning) primed callers to focus on the idea of achievement.

The literature has revealed numerous environmental factors that affect persuasion. For example, you will view someone who has handed you a hot cup of coffee as opposed to a cold soda as warmer and more caring and therefore more persuasive (Williams and Bargh 2008). Sitting in a soft chair makes you a softer negotiator than if you sit in a hard chair (Lobel 2016). Interviewers who held a resume on a heavy clipboard rated the exact same resume as better compared to interviewers who held it on a light clipboard (Ackerman, Nocera, and Bargh 2010). On dating websites, women who put a red background behind their photos were considered more attractive than those with the same picture against a green or black background (Elliot and Niesta 2008). The takeaway: environmental factors matter and can play an important role.

Contrast Effect

According to Cialdini, if you can't find a contrast, you are not working hard enough. Always be on the lookout for your "compared to what" prospect. For example, when students and parents visit my small liberal arts college, they often ask me about cost compared to a large state institution. I counter by asking, "We are expensive compared to what?" First, the sticker price is not what you pay after you consider the discount rate and scholarships. Second, while our students generally graduate in four years, the average student at a large school takes about five years to graduate. So not only are you paying for that fifth year of school, but you are also not getting paid at a job. Our classes are often smaller, and professors, not teaching assistants, teach most classes. There is considerable value to that. So it *is* expensive, but compared to what?

Know Your Audience

"What's in it for me?" This is a question that all people think, and sometimes ask aloud, when approached with a request. Like all communication, persuasion attempts are best when you take your audience's needs into consideration and use these skills of persuasion ethically. For example, I fostered a relationship with an alumna who later approached me, offering to give the department a financial contribution according to her interests. I happened to know (through building a solid interpersonal relationship) that this alumna really desired to make a difference for students who wanted to pursue a graduate degree. We notified the alumna that our department chose to use the donation to support the fees for a student who could not afford to take the Graduate Record Examination (GRE), followed by a handwritten thank-you note from the student and the department.

Dealing with Gender Bias

As I discussed at the beginning of this chapter, there are some biases that work against women when they try to develop their voice. For example, women are judged more harshly than their male counterparts are if they are not perceived as being collaborative (Kulik and Olekalns 2012); they are viewed as less credible by their students (Denker 2009); and they are hindered when they express anger during group deliberation (Salerno and Peter-Hagene 2015). The stereotype persists that women talk more than men do, even though studies that look at word-for-word comparisons across an average day demonstrate that both use about sixteen thousand words a day (Mehl et al. 2007). Studies also show that men tend to dominate conversations at mixed-sex tables, taking up 75 percent of the conversation (Karpowitz and Mendelberg 2014).

The takeaway here is that you will be fighting gender stereotypes and bias when you communicate. Using the persuasion strategies in this chapter will not change some of these perceptions. However, the principles discussed in the chapter increase effectiveness regardless of gender. For example, you will not be perceived as aggressive if you take time to use sources that your audience considers credible, if you have someone else introduce you before a presentation, or if you give a colleague a compliment. But your use of these techniques will increase your persuasiveness.

Bias exists unfortunately and will continue to persist. In the following subsections, I introduce some common problems and direct you to resources that will aid you in dealing with them.

Mansplaining

---

mansplain   *verb*
to explain something to a woman in a condescending way that
assumes she has no knowledge about the topic

—*Merriam-Webster Online*

If you are a woman reading this, I probably do not need to "woman-splain" to you what mansplaining is. This behavior is problematic since it tends to reinforce gender inequality, but know that there are several good resources describing techniques to combat it. For a short read, I recommend the article "5 Ways to Shut Down Mansplaining" in *Forbes* (2018). It gives five useful tips for dealing with mansplaining when it happens, including using humor and redirection. Debra Bednar-Clark, former head of business strategy and growth at Facebook's Creative Shop, discusses how important it is to deal with it as it happens. When you confront the problem head-on, even if it occurs in a group, it sends an important message that the behavior will not be tolerated (Price 2017). She suggests having a plan or even a script ready if it happens. She also reminds us that we can be strong without sacrificing kindness and approachability.

Interrupting

It can be difficult to exercise the persuasive skills found in this chapter if a colleague interrupts you. I suggest having a few tactics at the ready, so you can confidently squash any interruption.

The short article in *Psychology Today* "How to Deal With People Who Interrupt" (2018) gives some helpful quick tips. Some good suggestions from the article include setting up expectations up front by saying, "Please let me finish before asking questions." If you are interrupted, try saying, "Please let me speak." You want to be clear and firm without sounding or becoming angry.

If you need to interrupt someone who has derailed the discussion, George Thompson and Jerry Jenkins (2013) suggest that you use the "sword of insertion" to put a wedge into the conversation. This is a phrase spoken in earnest, such as "hold on a minute" or "wait a second." Immediately after inserting the wedge, you say, "Let me be sure I heard what you just said," and then paraphrase what the person said. This allows you to interrupt while expressing empathy. It should get people to take a moment, and you can get the discussion back on track.

Thompson and Jenkins's book *Verbal Judo* is an excellent resource for dealing with several other types of negative behaviors. As just one example, from my experience in academia, women are told to calm down more often than men are. Thompson and Jenkins (2013) suggest responding with "Look, I'm obviously not calm, and there are reasons for it. Let's talk about them" (41). If that does not work and neither of the parties is calm, you should leave.

Activities

Now that you know what all the persuasive principles are, see how you can use them with the following case studies. I have provided one example for each. See if you can identify other principles of persuasion that you could use to increase the likelihood of getting a positive response.

Activity 1: Scenarios for Case Study

Scenario Case Study 1. You are planning to apply for a large grant and need a letter of support from your departmental colleagues. The grant will provide funding to support student research, and this is a primary goal of the department. One senior colleague has been particularly critical of you, and you are afraid that this might come out in a letter. What are some principles of persuasion and elements of pre-suasion that you can use?

Try asking him or her for a favor. Some people call this the "Ben Franklin effect," as it is a strategy reportedly used by Franklin to win an opponent to his side. According to records, Franklin had a colleague who did not like him, so he asked the man if he could borrow a book from his prized library. The man was flattered by this request and lent Franklin the book. Franklin returned it a week later with a thank-you note, and apparently, the two became and remained friends from that day on (Franklin 2003). Some experts say that this is because if we do a favor for someone, we decide that we must like the person, therefore increasing liking (e.g., Niiya 2015). Others say that it builds on consistency (Goei et al. 2003). No matter what the mechanism is, the strategy works.

Scenario Case Study 2. You are the chair of the faculty committee in charge of assessment. In this role, you need to convince faculty to attend a series of assessment trainings. These are part of the new president's strategic plan. The faculty have been reluctant to engage in assessment, and you have no real power to compel people to attend. What are some principles of persuasion and elements of pre-suasion that you can use?

After the first training session, I suggest asking faculty to write down a few things that they genuinely liked about the session. Use those testimonials as part of your recruitment and advertising for the next session. This could help foster positive feelings about the event and encourage better future attendance. People will think, "If so-and-so attended and said he or she got something out of it, maybe I will too." What are some other possible strategies you could use? Don't forget to consider any pre-suasion steps that you might take to prime people favorably to your request.

Activity 2: Moments of Power

Moment of Power 1: The After Thank You. According to Cialdini, there are a few privileged moments or "moments of power," when if you are acting as a sleuth, you can increase your persuasiveness. One is right after someone expresses gratitude. Many people are tempted to respond to "thank you" with "it was no problem" or something similar. Cialdini (2003b) identifies this as a "bungler's mistake." People want to feel special. "No problem" means you really did not go out of your way for them. Instead of saying, "No problem," Cialdini (2003b) suggests saying, "Sure, glad to help. I know you would do the same for me." The nickname for our college is "the Brits," and my husband uses this strategy when alumni express appreciation, by saying, "Of course, that's what Brits do for each other." Another way to maximize on a thank you is to ask for testimonials if the situation is appropriate. As you are building relationships on your path to full, don't "bungle" these potential moments of power.

Moment of Power 2: After No. The other moment of power is right after someone says no. Recall from our discussion on reciprocity that concessions can be viewed as gifts. Right after someone declines is the best time to make a concession (Cialdini 2003a). Come back with a second, lower offer. Multiple studies show that people are much more likely to say yes to a response if it was preceded by a larger request that was refused (Cialdini 2009). Be prepared with a backup offer every time you are making a request.

Activity 3: Making a Plan

Use a persuasion principles worksheet to strategize the best plan for your persuasive request. Use the completed worksheet in figure 7.1 as a guide. After you complete your own worksheet, construct a plan. The next steps will vary based on your specific issue. The following email is an example of a worksheet in action, in the form of the statement for a contentious meeting:

> Thank you all for coming to the program meeting today. Several people asked that the research funding report be followed up with a program meeting. What's great is that we are all here for the same goal [*setting the context*]. I am proud to be part of a group that is passionately committed

Define the problem: I need to run a program meeting about funding for faculty and student research. The recent poll I sent out shows the faculty is quite divided on two key issues: (1) what the application process should be for students; (2) the types of activities that should get funded.	What are potential obstacles? Polarization of the faculty on the two issues. Might create a stalemate.	What is the potential contrast? Compared to what? For issue (1): Comparison funding programs. For example, is the process too cmplicated? Compared to what? The NSF? For issue (2): Some people think we are funding inappropriate activities. Compared to what? What are other schools doing?
Who is your audience? My faculty	**What do you know about your audience?** They have very strong and polar opinions about this. They value data. They are all committed to student research and fuding faculty development. Some members will only have negative comments.	**Other notes:** Main goal to have productive conversation. Need to start the meeting on a strong positive note or it will get derailed quickly. Be sure to give everyone a chance to talk, but do not start with negative comments. Focus on what I want from the meeting: collaboration.

Which strategies are ethically and naturally available to you?	
Social proof: *People decide what to do by relying on similar others*	We all want the college to be exemplary in terms of student and faculty research.
Liking: *People prefer to say yes to people they like*	Remind them of the similarities we have. Compliment: great groups of dedicated scholars. Cooperation: there are some areas of agreement already (goals and reward system are not aligned; we should fund activites that combine town and gown).
Reciprocity: *People feel obligated to return favors*	
Consistency/commitment: *Once people take a stand, they prefer to act consistently with it*	We are all committed to student and faculty research. Many people on the survey wrote that they wanted alignment and more funding options. This is written down by a majority of faculty.
Scarcity: *People want things more when they are less available*	
Authority: *People rely on others they see as authorities for guidance*	

Figure 7.1 Persuasion principles worksheet

to our students and to faculty development [*social proof, liking, consistency*]. We want to be an exemplary liberal arts college, and we want to be the best faculty we can be [*liking*]. What's also great is that there are many different ways do this, and I hope that we can use these conversations to help each other be the best faculty members we can be [*liking*]. We already have some great systems in place. Because of strategic planning, we are at a point where we can dream big about ways to expand our funding opportunities and make the existing ones even stronger by better aligning resources, rewards, and institutional goals [*consistency—this was a stated goal of many people on the survey*]. Let's work together to find ways to fund the work we each want to get done [*liking*]. As an example, there was a recommendation that faculty-development funds might be considered for projects that involve the community. This is consistent [*consistency*] with all four aspects of the strategic plan. Perhaps we can ask for and get an endowed grant specifically for campus-community collaborations [*liking—almost everyone on the survey agreed that they wanted to fund this type of thing, so I started with an area of known agreement*]. What other ideas do we have to expand our possibilities? What changes can we make to the current systems to better align our resources, rewards, and institutional goals [*social proof, liking—almost everyone agreed that these were not currently aligned, so I was relying on an area of agreement*]?

Implementing these principles of persuasion in my statement resulted in a productive conversation without a lot of unproductive conflict. I wanted to get everyone to focus on the things we had in common and start the conversation from common ground. I had the benefit of a survey with responses, but you can always do some audience analysis. After my statement, I opened the floor to comments and used the time to set the tone again. I called on someone who I knew would have a collaborative comment rather than the person who probably had a complaint. We had a productive meeting where most everybody was focused on building from common ground. In fact, several people commented to me how well the meeting went. I encourage you to use the worksheet to map out a plan the next time you have a persuasive event coming up.

Conclusion

As women seek to advance in their careers, they are faced with many obstacles and barriers that can impede that advancement. As referenced throughout this book, women are tasked with greater service and administrative roles and responsibilities as compared to their male peers. While these roles are critically important to the functioning of their institutions, service and administrative roles can interfere with women's career-advancement aspirations. The goal of this chapter has been to help women develop their persuasive voice while occupying these roles and to view such positions as an opportunity to hone the needed communication and leadership skills to be successful in all career-advancement pursuits.

CHAPTER 8

Looking Ahead

My biggest advice? Believe in yourself. Too many women languish as associates because they don't believe that they are good enough to be full. If your department documents say you need one book from an academic press, [then] you need one book from an academic press. You don't need two books. You don't need one book from the top academic press. You need one book from an academic press. And don't discount the things that you have done [such as] advising students, developing new courses—highlight those things. If students in your research group got a grant, check with senior faculty in your department to see how that gets documented—in some cases, faculty can count that for promotion. Believe in yourself, and just do it!!! You don't have to be Wonder Woman. You don't have to be the best faculty member ever. You just have to have met the requirements for the promotion. Do it!!!!

—full professor, social sciences, doctoral university,
higher research activity

Women in the academy seeking to advance in their careers face a myriad of challenges and biases, as documented throughout this book. However, as noted in the introduction, I also see advancement to full or continuing contract status as an opportunity to take control of your career narrative, letting joy be the driver of your professional (and personal) pursuits, and as a means of achieving the goals you have set out for yourself, not what others' expectations are for you. I greatly appreciate the advice from the woman full professor featured in this chapter's epigraph. Her positivity is evident, and her advice to avoid peer comparison and self-imposed unrealistic expectations is critical to supporting other women in the academy and to believing in ourselves. I also deeply appreciate her focus on gaining clarity about what is required of you by your institution to advance in your career—nothing more and nothing less.

I also felt a twinge of disappointment at her comment, however, about women languishing at the associate rank, which we know to be true via research and anecdotally (Ward and Wolf-Wendel 2012). Look no further than Donna Strickland, recipient of the 2018 Nobel Prize in Physics, who, in her words, "never applied" for full professorship (Jaschik 2018). To be clear, I am not suggesting that she is languishing at associate (clearly, quite the contrary), but I am curious as to why she never applied. Was this decision a personal choice or based on implicit or explicit messages from the academy about readiness or worthiness? In chapter 6, Laura shared the story about two women associate professors in her department who had yet to pursue full professorship despite meeting the requirements. I firmly believe that Laura's encouragement and mentorship played a vital role in her colleagues submitting their dossiers. I also believe that the simple act of asking these women what their goals were was even more powerful for these women and set the tone for the type of department chair and mentor Laura is. I am confident that if either of these women would have told Laura they were not interested in pursuing full professorship, Laura would mentor them to achieve the goals that were of import to them on their academic journey.

I also recently had a conversation with two peers at Albion, one of whom was a man and full professor and the other a woman and associate professor. The woman peer joined the faculty a year earlier than I did and two years earlier than our male colleague did. Yet we were discussing her timing for submitting her long-overdue dossier for consideration for full professorship. This colleague was a tremendous teacher, a well-respected scholar on campus and in her field, and an important campus contributor. The unfortunate reality is, however, that she received poor mentoring from departmental peers about the timing for advancing to full, particularly advice that contradicted process details outlined in our faculty handbook. During her tenure on the college's personnel committee, she realized this disconnect while tasked with reviewing my application for full. To compound the problem, college policy dictates that if someone on the committee chooses to submit for promotion consideration at the time of his or her committee service, all members at the time must recuse, thus requiring the convening of a new committee, consisting of five members, to review the application. Our woman colleague felt that was too burdensome, resulting in her delaying her application submission until her tenure on the committee was complete. Our male colleague responded, "You still should have submitted and let them convene a new committee." I fully agree with his sentiment. I have no doubt that she will be awarded the promotion. Yet this is just one more example of how poor mentoring and cumbersome institutional policies negatively contribute to women seeking career advancement along the path to the professoriate.

The aim of this final chapter is to feature the voices of women who have advanced to full professor or continuing contract status successfully. Throughout this book, I have offered advice and examples of women from a range of institution types and disciplines at the associate stage who either felt stuck or who were preparing their materials for submission. However, providing the perspectives of women who have traversed this process successfully will demonstrate that "doing it," as the full professor urged in the chapter's epigraph, is possible. I also address the "what's next" question, outlining two activities that inform related thinking, and provide a summary of the main takeaways from each chapter.

Why Focus on Women Full Professors?

Despite existing at the highest tier of the professorial ranking system and their arguably influential role in higher education institutions, the rank of professor and the process to gain this rank have been largely forgotten in the literature. . . . At the same time, it is known that gender imbalances are very much present in the rank.

—Rising Tide Center for Gender Equity (2018, 3)

I have been focused on understanding the path to the professoriate for fifteen years, with a particular focus on the faculty experience for a decade. I have studied thousands of doctoral students and faculty across all stages of the professoriate. During that time, I have focused on understanding the faculty experience, especially career-stage nuances, given that each stage is associated with unique challenges and opportunities. This work has allowed me to interact with faculty, men and women alike, to learn more about their needs and goals for their careers. What I have found is that women, in particular, face a specific set of challenges that are exacerbated by a male-dominated academy riddled with antiquated policies and processes. Such an environment fosters hurdles for women that are, at times, insurmountable.

One of the most challenging periods for women faculty is the transition from associate to full professor or continuing contract status (Wolfinger, Mason, and Goulden 2008). Professional and personal roles, responsibilities, and challenges intersect, causing great strain on career advancement for women (Buch et al. 2011). Couple this personal and professional evolution with lack of clarity around institutional expectations and related career-advancement processes to achieve career-advancement goals, and you have the perfect storm of stalled or stagnant careers for women in the academy. My work and the work of others have revealed a need to better understand the challenges that women face along the journey from associate to full

(Baker, Lunsford, and Pifer 2017; Terosky, O'Meara, and Campbell 2014; Ward and Wolf-Wendel 2012). Further, women along this path need specific supports to help them develop more strategic career-management approaches. This book is a resource specific to career stage that can provide the needed guidance for women faculty as they pursue career-advancement goals.

The topics addressed in this book are directly informed by the women associate professors I have worked with and studied over the past decade. Each individual chapter identifies and acknowledges significant, pervasive concerns and comments from women in the academy. I consistently hear that women (1) are unsure of where to focus efforts to achieve career and personal goals; (2) lack clarity or understanding about how to start the process of preparing dossiers and other application materials for promotion; (3) lack confidence when it comes to their professional contributions, often concerned that "it's not enough"; (4) are frustrated by perceived and real inconsistencies in how scholarly contributions are regarded or, worse yet, dismissed by senior colleagues; (5) feel overwhelmed at the thought of needing to embark on new scholarly initiatives to produce the needed scholarship or creative activity to achieve full or continuing contract status; (6) are in search of ways to broaden their networks to support professional growth and hone their own mentoring skills; (7) need guidance and specific strategies to develop their voice to be successful in the myriad roles they occupy; and (8) are in search of other full professor women to lean on for guidance and support and to see that it is, in fact, possible to achieve career-advancement goals while juggling personal and professional responsibilities.

The literature, research, examples, recommendations, and additional resources shared throughout this book will be of use to a diversity of individuals. Most notably, women at or on the path to the associate rank who aspire to full professorship or continuing contract status or women who have set some other professional goal will benefit from the scaffolded approach to managing their path to promotion and goal attainment strategically. Perhaps even more important, learning from others' struggles and realizing that you are not alone in those struggles provides a sense of camaraderie among this diversely talented group of women in the academy. The tools, tips, and strategies will also provide a roadmap and resources to faculty developers and others on campus tasked with faculty-development responsibilities. My hope is that the statistics and stories shared by women about their reasons for not going up for full or continuing contract status will motivate those with faculty-development responsibilities to track time in rank more closely for women and other minority faculty groups on their respective campuses. Such clarity about who is and who is not going up for promotion and the reasons why creates opportunities to evaluate institutional policies and structures that might be contributing negatively to lengthier time in rank. Understanding the experience for these populations of individuals is critical to attracting and retaining a diverse faculty body and to providing the needed developmental supports to ensure that diversity is represented across all stages of the professoriate.

Strategies and Advice from the Other Side

Don't downplay the work that you do. Strongly state your contributions to the discipline and to your institution. Make explicit why you are important to the functioning of the department.

**—full professor, department chair, social sciences,
research university**

To support the writing of this chapter, I administered an online survey to women full professors who are members of a private Facebook group. The purpose of this Facebook group is to create a community of women academics who are also caregivers—seeking advice, support, and peer mentoring on a myriad of issues related to the roles of academic and mother. These academic women represent a diversity of institutions, disciplines, and personal roles and responsibilities. Fifty women responded to the survey and shared their insights, lessons learned, and experiences. In this section, I share the strategies and advice they offer to other women who aspire to achieve full professorship or continuing contract status. First, however, I provide a brief demographic overview of the women whose insights are shared in this chapter. The study was granted human subjects approval by the Albion College Institutional Review Board.

Of the fifty women who responded, five represent community colleges; eight represent four-year, primarily undergraduate colleges or universities (liberal arts college); six are employed at four-year regional comprehensive master's universities; five are employed at four-year research universities, private; and twenty represent four-year research universities, public. The remaining six women preferred not to indicate institution type. Five of the women identified as Black or African American, two as Asian or Asian American, two as Latina, and one as Indian. Twenty of the women identified as white, with the remaining twenty women indicating they "prefer not to respond." Thirty-three of the women are married or in a long-term partnership, five are divorced, and the remaining twelve preferred not to respond. Eleven women represent fields in the social sciences; nine represent the natural sciences; eight represent the humanities; five represent preprofessional fields; and three represent the fine and applied arts. The remaining fourteen women chose not to respond to this question. Seven of the women held (within the past two years) or currently hold the position of department chair, while eight held (within the past two years) or currently hold the position of center or program director. Two women currently hold the position of dean or assistant dean.

Strategies

The full professor women who shared their stories were very thoughtful and articulate in describing the strategies they employed to navigate this stage of their careers. The strategies shared can be organized in four distinct ways: engage in peer accountability, be bold, ask for help, and know the rules of the game.

Engage in peer accountability. Nearly half of the fifty women full professors who shared their strategies discussed the importance of creating a peer support system. For some, this meant participating in writing groups that met regularly. One woman employed at a comprehensive university noted, "I joined a writing group with other women of my rank, interested in similar areas. It changed my life." Similarly, another woman who is employed at a liberal arts college shared that she participates in a "writing group that meets monthly," which she said kept her working. The act of writing with others, holding each other accountable, and keeping these writing opportunities as "sacred on the weekly or monthly calendar" played a vital role in helping these women achieve their career-advancement goals.

To over 30 percent of the respondents, peer support was available via professional networks, which aligns with the strategies and recommendations offered in chapter 6. For example, one woman employed at a liberal arts college expressed the significance of "developing academic networks and coauthor relationships through conference attendance." She elaborated further by noting the importance of "maintaining those relationships through email and Skype." Another woman, employed at a regional comprehensive university, shared her experience: "I made 'friends' and connections across campus in various departments, and those colleagues invited me to join activities (e.g., search for the new Associate Vice President of Undergraduate Studies) or research (e.g., large grant studying women of color in science) that both boosted my resume and provided support and shared work load." Peer accountability and support helped many of these women overcome the institutional biases and challenges associated with the path to promotion.

Be bold. Over 25 percent of the respondents talked about the need to be bold when managing this phase of their career. Sometimes that boldness was needed in response to a challenging work environment; sometimes that boldness meant finding a new institution. One woman employed at a liberal arts college noted, "Major, multiyear workplace harassment definitely hurt my career. The overall toxic antiwoman workplace culture where I was hurt my career. Lack of mentors hurt my career. Finding the right place is [and was] key." Another woman peer shared a similar sentiment: "I left my previous institution due to the toxic environment. Sorry to put that out there, and I hope people can stay where they want to work. But the good news here is that workplace cultures vary widely, and sometimes a move is exactly the right thing."

To others, boldness was about owning your accomplishments and finding ways to make sure those accomplishments are acknowledged and "on the radar" of others at your institution. One woman from a private research university noted, "Seek the advice of allies who know what the promotion committee is looking for. Try to maintain a presence on campus, and do not be shy about having your accomplishments recognized along the way (get those written up in the campus magazine, etc.)."

Boldness also means taking care of yourself and taking action, if needed, when faced with inequities or discrimination. One woman from a public research university suggested, "Seek accommodations if you need them and seek allies throughout the institution, but remember to be your own advocate. Keep a paper trail of all correspondence, take notes after relevant meetings, be ready to document and challenge any inequities that relate to your career, and be ready to take legal action if necessary. . . . Institutions will take advantage of you if you let them, so be ready to challenge them, and don't back down." To these full professor women, boldness means owning your worth and accomplishments, taking the needed steps to ensure that you are employed at an institution in which your safety and well-being are valued, and refusing to shy away from much-deserved recognition.

Ask for help. The path to full professorship or continuing contract status is not for the faint of heart. At one point or another along this career-advancement path, women will need help, guidance, and support in order to find their joy and be successful. Over 30 percent of the women offered simple yet powerful advice: do not be afraid to ask for help. Some respondents encouraged professionally focused help. I share a few of those examples:

- "Seek out senior mentors. Don't be afraid to ask for help. Cite generously, and especially cite other women in your work!"
- "Talk to your chair and your dean about expectations, and get them in writing."
- "Find allies and mentors that will support you and help you navigate the obstacles (some of them should be majority males)."
- "Seek out other women, and talk to a diversity of them."

For others, asking for help means freeing up time and space (physical and mental) in regard to your personal roles and responsibilities. Child-care, elder-care, and home-care needs and support were mentioned by over 25 percent of the women full professors. As one woman shared, "In balancing professional development with raising small children, I have depended heavily on day care and after-school care, my 50-50 partner in parenting (my husband), and hiring someone to clean the house." Another woman offered the following related advice: "Try to surround yourself with people who believe in you—at work and at home. My husband was a huge help in not only being 50-50 with child-care and household duties (sometimes taking on more when I needed him to) but also helping me to see that I was a good candidate for promotion (and he had been on our promotion committee in previous years—I consulted other people, too, though, because, you know, he may be a smidge biased)."

Seeking the support of others is particularly important for those women who are single parents. As one woman, who is employed at a community college, offered, "I am heavily engaged in the community, which is important institutionally. This engagement, however, comes at a cost. Now that my kids are older, I can bring them along a lot of the time. Prior to that, however, I was heavily dependent on others as a single parent. I am so thankful for my village."

A common theme among the women who talked about the importance of seeking help was the acknowledgment that help seeking is a sign of strength, as opposed to a weakness. Yet seeking help and guidance to support career advancement can be challenging, particularly for women (Stevenson and Orr 2017). The path to career advancement can be a lonely space. Therefore, surrounding yourself with those who are aware of your goals, are willing to help free up time and space for you to achieve those goals, and who can help shoulder some of your responsibilities is essential.

Know the rules of the game. As I share throughout this book, knowing your institutional expectations and processes for career advancement is critical (see chapter 2). I cannot stress this point enough. This aspect to successfully navigating the path to promotion was mentioned by over 40 percent of the study participants. As one woman, who is employed at a public research university, noted, "Gaining clarity on what the expectations of the university were, especially with regard to demonstrated prominence in research field, [is necessary for success]." Understanding what is expected and the associated process serves as the foundation from which to build. But perhaps a more important outcome of having a firm grasp on the expectations and processes is that such knowledge helps to debunk the unrealistic expectations that many associate professor women place on themselves or that are implicitly (and explicitly) communicated to them (June 2016).

As suggested in the advice shared in the epigraph to this chapter, many women faculty delay submitting for full professorship or continuing contract status because they believe they are "not ready" or "don't have enough scholarship." Yet the women full professors who shared their experiences and advice strongly encourage other women associate professors not to fall victim to this career-altering thinking. I share related experiences and advice from respondents:

- "The biggest hurdles were being made to feel that I needed more (pubs. or other things) to be promoted when I did not (now that I served twelve years on the tenure and promotion committee, I realize that I was always well above expectations for promotion). My supervisor did not make my male counterpart feel insecure" (full professor, liberal arts college).

- "I think what helped was being organized and having a good understanding of what was expected in terms of research at each stage. Although I had it in mind that I was going to go up for full after my third book, and a male colleague reminded me that I didn't need it, I had enough. I had always known that, but I sort of forgot it for a while" (comprehensive college or university).

- "Read your promotion documents!!! Do not create imaginary requirements. Read your department promotion documents, and do what it says. If it says you need eight publications posttenure and a minimum $10,000 grant, then that's *all* you need" (comprehensive college or university).

- "Always tie your own metrics to what you see being done at the school you aspire to, rather than listen to people promoted decades ago" (research university, private).

What I find so compelling about these statements is the encouragement offered. I very much appreciate the effort displayed by these women to help their women peers in the academy to get out of their own way and instead to be clear about institutional expectations in relation to their existing body of work.

Advice

Embedded in the strategies and ideas just presented is also advice about how to manage the career-advancement process. I personally am grateful for the thoughtfulness and advice I received from dear friends and colleagues who served as friendly reviewers for the chapters in this book. I also benefited from two outside reviewers, who are leaders in the field of higher education, during the development stage of this book. One of the reviewers suggested incorporating advice from women who have achieved full professorship or continuing contract status who also serve, or have served, on their institutional personnel committees. Seven of the women who responded to the survey also served or are currently serving in such a capacity. They offered the following advice:

- "Document all the work that you have accomplished and, as hard as it may seem, boast about your accomplishments. Don't undersell yourself or downplay what you have achieved, and never assume that your record will just speak for itself—be your own best advocate" (comprehensive college or university).
- "Ask for help. Don't let your ego get in the way. Stay grounded, and don't lose yourself in your career" (comprehensive college or university).
- "Be clear about how you have met your goals and requirements. Get trustworthy outside readers. Have a group. Prop each other up. Labor for each other" (comprehensive college or university).
- "Don't wait: No one says, 'Go up now.' You have to decide, and people too often seem to err on the side of not thinking they're ready. I see too many women stay at associate professor level, laboring under the belief they're not ready and don't have what they need. I think this contributes to gender disparities in full professorship—I don't see male professors talking themselves out of asking for promotion as much as women do" (research university, public).
- "If I waited for someone to tell me it was time, pursuing promotion may have never happened. And I am very sure my male colleagues did not wait to get green-lighted by someone" (community college).

Overall, this advice suggests documenting contributions in the key areas that are of importance at your respective institution; crafting a narrative that "connects the dots" among and across the areas that are vital for career advancement while also telling your personal career story; connecting your contributions to your institution and department in very deliberate ways; and seeking the counsel of those whom you trust and value for their professional opinion and assessment. Most essential, I believe, is the need to believe in yourself. You are your own best advocate because you know your work and contributions better than anyone else does. To put it simply, do not get in your own way with negative or misguided thinking in relation to your readiness for promotion.

So What's Next?

I would love to sit back and enjoy this accomplishment [earning full professorship], but the time is just not available to do that. Instead, I think about what is next on the to-do list.

—full professor, humanities, comprehensive university

The academy is one of those environments in which successes are short-lived. I have often lamented with friends and colleagues who are also employed in the academy that we, as academics, rarely have an opportunity to sit back and enjoy our successes because of the continued ratcheting up of expectations, regardless of institution type. Such an environment keeps you in a perpetual state of thinking about and looking ahead to what is next. For example, you earned that tenure-track position? Congratulations! But you need to work toward promotion and tenure. You earned tenure and promotion? Whew! But do not get too comfortable because up next is earning full professorship or continuing contract status. Your first book is in print? Great! Now it is time to think about preparing that next book prospectus. This cycle keeps going and going. Along this path, you keep working to secure more publications, more grants, more collaborators, more community engagement, and more invited talks or showings of your work as evidence of your contribution to the field. In sum, you feel compelled to push for more of just about any professional pursuit you can imagine. I rarely, if ever, have had or have taken the opportunity to sit back to bask in the successes that I have experienced along my career path. I know I am not alone in this experience. I feel like this is one of the unfortunate aspects to this career that seems to be self-perpetuating at the individual and institutional levels.

I wish I could say that earning full professorship has lessened this feeling. In reality, it is still something I struggle with continually. However, experiencing the rapid pace at which my kids are growing (at the time of writing this chapter, five and four years old, respectively) has helped me refocus my efforts and be more empowered with regard to my voice and my time. My mother has reminded me that there will be a day when my kids are engrossed in their own lives, with their friends and activities. All too soon the house will be empty and quiet, providing ample opportunity to write and pursue my professional projects. For me, these two roles, mother and professor, are constantly on the forefront of my thinking about "what's next" given the twenty-plus-year runway I have remaining in my career.

In the following section, I walk you through two activities that I use with students and clients to assess current and future endeavors. These activities serve as a good gut check for me, in order to identify where I currently am and where I want to be.

Five Must Haves and Five Can't Stands

I often have students and clients approach me to talk about life. To my students, life means both as a college student and as an early-career professional upon graduation. To my clients, it is about managing the midcareer stage and looking ahead five to ten years. Many find the task of deciding what they will do in the next phase or stage of their lives daunting, to say the least. When viewed at this level, such a decision can seem so overwhelming and finite. And should that decision not be the "right" one, the feelings of failure can be quite heavy. For those students and clients who are very unsure of where to begin, I have them work through what I call the "Five Must Haves and Five Can't Stands" exercise.

Five Must Haves

First, write down the five things that you would need to have happen with some regularity to be happy. In other words, what are your five must haves? When situated in the professional context, ask yourself what are five aspects of work that need to happen regularly. This same activity can also apply to personal aspects of your life, such as relationships (e.g., partner, collaborator). For the purposes of this chapter, I focus on the work context. The five must haves can be related to opportunities such as traveling to share your research or engage in professional development, the chance to work in teams, the prospect of working autonomously, or the need to work in an industry or for an organization whose values and goals closely align with your own. Write those must haves down and be clear about what each is and why it is so important to you. I remind individuals that every day will not and cannot be filled with the five must haves, but if you can experience them at least three out of the five workdays, you are pretty lucky. I genuinely enjoy getting in my car and driving to work every day at Albion (despite a one-hour commute each way) because of my students, many of my colleagues, and the professional opportunities that I have been afforded. I want others whom I have the responsibility for supporting to feel the same way, and I work with them to consider what opportunities, characteristics, and individuals need to be present to feel that same way in their work environments. I believe this to be one of the more important responsibilities bestowed on me as a professor, coach, and mentor.

Five Can't Stands

After preparing your five must haves, turn your attention to the five can't stands. For this, think about those aspects of your work environment, work tasks, coworkers, institutional or organizational mission, and the like that would be downright draining for you to engage in or to be exposed to. Or, to use the words of Michael Scott from *The Office*, what can't stands would be "a thief of joy" for you if they were the norm. For example, during an initial meeting with a student, I assigned her this activity to be completed prior to our second meeting. In reviewing her five must haves and five can't stands, I noticed that she preferred to "not be crunching numbers every day." I replied,

"You are an accounting major, so this might be a good time to rethink that major." We both chuckled and went about reviewing her five must haves in reference to a major and career path that would allow her to engage in her five must haves more regularly. (Spoiler: she switched majors, earned a marketing position, and is excited about her future.) I firmly believe that life is too short to be continually charged with engaging in an environment in which the work tasks, the people, or the organizational focus are misaligned with where you are presently or hoping to be in the future.

Among my current and former students, I am known for my top-ten list. It is a way for me to communicate my life's lessons succinctly in a humorous yet directed way. Number 2 on my list is "If you are crying at work, it's time to find a new job," and number 1 on my list is "Life is too short." With regularity, I engage in the Five Must Haves and Five Can't Stands activity in both my professional and personal pursuits as a reminder about what is and is not important to me in a given moment in my life. And I can assure you that what I wrote ten or even five years ago as part of my Five Must Haves and Five Can't Stands list looks very different today, much as it will in another five years. I have evolved personally and professionally, and my guess is that you have too. Take the time to honor that evolution and reassess along the way.

Priorities Assessment

On my way home after an advisory-board meeting this past summer, several colleagues and I engaged in a professionally focused conversation. I was asked by the principal investigator of the grant where I saw myself in the next five years. This is a question I have been thinking about a great deal lately. My kids are about to be in school full-time, which certainly frees up some time and space for me to pursue something new, whether it be an extension of existing work or a new path altogether. Given my faculty-development work at the institutional and individual levels, I have been asked on several occasions if I would be interested in pursuing an administrative post related to faculty development, should such an opportunity present itself. And herein lies the tension. I enjoy engaging in faculty-development work and believe this is an area in which I can provide some value added at the individual, programmatic, and institutional levels. However, most administrative posts are typically twelve-month appointments, which is not of interest to me given that I worked hard to have the flexibility and autonomy I have now. Plus, I enjoy the summertime flexibility with my kids, especially given my husband's job as a general manager for a golf course, resulting in an extremely busy eight months out of the year. With that said, I am interested in envisioning the next phase of my faculty-development work, and an administrative post certainly would offer some new ways of engaging in that space. Despite the tension I feel about what's next and how to manage that with my priorities, I see this as an opportunity to think creatively about how to craft this next evolution.

This kind of dilemma is not new, and many individuals face similar dilemmas in their career. Engaging in a "priorities assessment" helps me think through my priorities with clearly defined paths toward achieving and/or engaging in them. Here I outline related action steps to help you conduct a priorities assessment. Write down each step, and deliberate about it with intention.

Step 1: Identify Broad Priority Categories

The first step in any priority assessment is to determine what your priorities are. For me, those categories are family, professional, and personal. Important to this process is defining what each of these categories means to you. Family and professional are relatively straightforward. Personal, for me, is about self-care.

Step 2: Category Goals

Once you have identified your priority categories, the next step is to list your related, specific goals. For example, under "family," I list one of my primary goals: to free up my weekends during the academic year as much possible to spend quality time with my family. I realize that weekends are my only opportunity to have quality time with my children and husband, and I need to be more selective about my professional projects and other work-related responsibilities that may require travel and weekend commitments. For my "personal" category, one of my goals is to schedule and accomplish four workouts per week. That time is so important to my physical and mental well-being that I need to commit to making it happen. The "professional" category includes limiting the number of projects I pursue in a given year. With that said, my goal is to make sure the projects I do pursue are more value added both personally and professionally and to the primary and secondary audiences that I am targeting. The goal is to still produce outcomes on a yearly basis but to have those outcomes be the result of my engagement in more focused, strategic projects as opposed to many smaller, seemingly disparate projects. Relatedly, I want to make sure my scholarly efforts contribute to practice, so I spend a great deal of time thinking about how to make this goal happen and what it will look like.

Step 3: Time Assignment to Goals and Tasks

Now that you have your priority categories and related goals identified, it is time to map out the associated action steps and time commitment. For example, my workouts goal in the "personal" category would require not only making time for the actual workouts but also assigning time to put those workout sessions on my weekly and monthly calendar. I also ensure that I schedule them ahead in two-week increments through the fitness facility's mobile app. This scheduled time is nonnegotiable; I do not give up that time to some other activity, and I share this schedule with my husband to make sure he is home to cover child care. You have to be a fierce protector of your time and ensure that you build in the time to achieve the goals you have laid out for yourself in relation to your priorities. That old saying is true: If something is important to you, you will make the time for it. If it is not important, you will not.

Over the years, my priorities have changed. And I work to ensure that my priorities are accounted for regularly and am deliberate about how to make my priorities fit with each other. At times, this works well. Other times, I find showering and getting the kids to school on time with brushed teeth my big success on that particular day. Regardless, I am clear about what my priorities are, how I need to make sure I account for them regularly, and how they inform (or do not) my "what's next" pursuits.

Take, for example, my "professional" category. At this stage, my priorities assessment looks quite different from when, say, I was in early career. Now I am thinking about the next "big thing." While I enjoy my faculty-development work, I am now thinking about how I can expand on and broaden this work. Fortunately for me, I have a mentor who keeps gently reminding me that I need to take my faculty-development work outside higher education. Given my focus on the midcareer professional, he is encouraging me to spend time in industry studying what midcareer professional development looks like in other fields and to think about how lessons learned across industries can inform and enhance my existing work, and vice versa. I am looking toward to my next sabbatical in two years, and this project is on the forefront of my project list. This same mentor is helpful in that, along with the gentle reminders he passes on, he also facilitates introductions to key individuals, particularly women, in the field who can be sources of support and collaboration on this effort.

A former client engaged in a priorities assessment, and we reviewed it together, along with a list she created of potential future projects. Engaging in this priorities assessment highlighted areas she needed to recalibrate. For example, being a good mother was her primary goal; however, her priorities assessment conflicted with her proposed project list. We spent time narrowing down that list to be more manageable yet more value added in support of her professional priorities and associated goals. The act of engaging in this activity gave her "permission" to be more selective professionally in order to achieve her main priority of being an available and engaged mother.

Key Chapter Takeaways

Writing this book helped me achieve one of my professional goals, which is to pull together a decade of research and consultation into a resource that not only highlights the stories of the amazing women with whom I have been fortunate to work but is also tailored for the very individuals I seek to support. In this section, I provide a summary of the key chapter takeaways.

Let Joy Be the Driver

My sincere hope is that reading this book reinforces the importance of letting joy be the driver in your life's work, and that includes professional, personal, and spiritual pursuits. All too often we fall victim to obligation and moving through a never-ending to-do list. Yes, there are moments in life and tasks that consume those moments that can be downright draining. But this should not be the norm of your narrative. Instead, a focus on joy reminds you that you do have agency over your choices—the type of teacher you hope to be, the type of scholarship you hope to pursue, and the types of activities you choose to participate in that showcase your value added to your institutional and professional communities.

As outlined in chapter 1, you have the power to engage in a variety of activities that let you assume and act on that power. The process of job crafting, for example, allows you to reenvision aspects of your work, whether it be particular tasks, relationships, or the ways in which you view facets of your work. I am a firm believer in not wasting time or energy on aspects of life or others' behaviors that are out of your control (easier said than done, I know). Job crafting allows you to engage in an assessment of the aspects of your work that bring the most joy, so that you can work to minimize the ones that do not.

Career mapping poses a simple yet compelling question: "Think about yourself at midcareer—what does that look like?" Here you are able to create a type of vision board in which you decide what midcareer means to you and the path along that journey. Be clear, specific, and bold. If you aim to be a university or college president, write down those aspirations proudly, and think about the steps you need to take to get there. If your goal is to be the best teacher at your institution, figure out what that means to you and those you aim to support, and work hard to grow into that role.

Organization Is the Building Block

If joy is the foundation, organization is the building block to a successful midcareer journey. As stated in chapter 2, the first step of that journey requires you to be clear about your goals: write them down and look at them often. It is impossible to arrive at your destination if you are not clear where you are headed. Do not be afraid to think and dream big. This is your life and your career; honor it by owning it.

Also important are knowing the rules of the game. The academy, regardless of institution type, is deeply rooted in institutional norms and expectations, some of which are grossly antiquated. You must be very clear about what the expectations are and the categories in which your worth will be measured. For example, I recently facilitated an hour-long session by request of the associate provost with our newly hired, first-year faculty members at Albion College. The focus of the session was on the tenure and promotion process. To prepare, I copied the most relevant handbook language, including the evaluation criteria. I offered examples of what falls under each category and shared organizational tips on how to start preparing now. Not one faculty member in that room had any clue where to find this information or what the evaluation criteria even were. And they had been meeting monthly as a group all year (the meeting was in late March). After the session, I received several emails from attendees telling me that this was the best meeting all year. I firmly believe that those who are tasked with faculty-development responsibilities should be communicating this information regularly. Clearly that does not always happen. Therefore, it is imperative that you seek this information out to be as prepared as possible. From there, you decide what organizational tools and time hacks will get you there. The ones offered in chapter 2, such as the project-tracking Excel sheet and being clear on what tasks (and meetings) are urgent versus important, have been my tried and true tools throughout my academic and professional career. The good news is that they can be adapted and adopted based on your institutional and disciplinary norms.

Let the Performance Speak for Itself

In a world where "mansplaining," gender stereotypes, and biased policies abound, it is challenging for women in the academy to highlight the value of their contributions and to be heard in the process. Women are often criticized if they are too vocal about the quality of their work or value added. In chapter 3, I offered a framework to help you showcase your contributions but without requiring you to boast about your accomplishments, a framework that includes quantitative and qualitative evidence. A focus on *purpose* (the reason behind engaging in a given activity and the associated goal of that activity) and *scope* (the depth and breadth that a given effort spans, including details about the beneficiary) helps you quantify your key contributions in the areas that bring you joy and that are valued by your institution.

Scholarship, teaching, and service are the aspects of the professoriate in which all faculty members are evaluated, to varying degrees based on institutional type. My favorite aspect of chapter 3 is the variety of examples so willingly offered by women across the academy for inclusion in the book. In sharing the examples, I highlight the ways in which purpose and scope were showcased as part of these women's dossier materials. Such examples can serve as a guide to you as you think about the most effective ways to organize your materials and highlight your most valued contributions.

Crafting Your Narrative

Once you have a handle on the areas in which you are expected to showcase your excellence, organized based on purpose and scope, you are faced with the daunting task of crafting your career narrative in a way that resonates with your colleagues and peers across your campus. To say that this is no easy feat is an understatement. Chapter 4 helped you construct that compelling narrative as you connect to the goals and imperatives of your department, unit, college, and/or institution. My goal was to help you illustrate all the ways in which your teaching, scholarship, service, and administrative tasks not only align with but elevate your institutional mission and strategic imperatives. You are an integral member of your department and institution—here's the time to make sure others realize that too.

The term "strategic planning" is often equated at the organizational or institutional levels with projecting out what we, as an organization, will look like in, say, 2025. In chapter 4, I broke down strategic planning into a two-step process, at the individual level, to help you be clear about your contributions and connections across many institutional levels (aka professional reach) and how to connect your professional reach to strategic imperatives or priorities as part of your narrative. Strategic planning affords you the creative license to define what your institutional evaluation criteria mean to you by adding subcategories of those criteria that showcase your most important contributions. Several examples of how this can be achieved, in a variety of institutional settings, were shared. Such an approach helps you minimize the misinformed, misguided efforts of others who seek to devalue your professional contributions.

SPU

Chapter 5 introduced the smallest publishable unit—a concept and practice that I was first introduced to as a graduate student at Penn State and that has continued to serve me well in my career. In brief, SPU requires you to think thoughtfully and strategically about the myriad goals you pursue as part of your work in order to have the widest appeal. To facilitate that thinking, I offered four critical considerations to include: (1) audience (e.g., fellow researchers, practitioners, administrators); (2) content (e.g., theoretical contribution, empirical contribution, practical contribution); (3) methods (e.g., quantitative methods, qualitative methods, mixed methods); and (4) process (e.g., scholarly efforts considered to be a "best practice" or adopted and adapted to support programming). Any time I embark on a project and I think about related outputs and deliverables, I ask myself, "Who is my intended audience? What is the content of my contribution, such as traditional scholarship or to support practitioners in their work? What methodological approach is necessary to appeal to my intended audience? And am I able to take knowledge gleaned from my scholarly pursuit and communicate it in a way that others can adapt and adopt to support their own practice?"

Scholarly productivity has always been the metric by which professional value is measured at research universities. However, as evinced throughout this book, scholarly productivity is growing in prominence across all institution types, given the associated prestige. The thought of consistently envisioning (and pursuing) new scholarly pursuits to advance in one's career is daunting. SPU, coupled with Boyer's forms of scholarship, helps faculty members see that their current efforts, when viewed from a different perspective, are more than sufficient to produce outputs and other deliverables that highlight their scholarly contributions.

Creating Your Mentoring Network

In chapter 6, Laura made a compelling case for why the assumptions about mentoring that permeate the academy are incorrect (e.g., that mentoring will just happen). In fact, given the murkiness of the mid-career stage, mentoring to support those who aspire to advance in their careers is perhaps paramount to ensuring a diverse, well-prepared, and engaged professoriate. The reality of the academy is that women academics receive more mentoring from their professional associations than they do at their own institutions. Therefore, Laura offered advice, tips, and "how-to" action steps for you to take control of your career advancement as you assemble your mentoring board of directors. In particular, the guided questions to facilitate conversations with your department chair or dean will help you lay the groundwork needed to support short- and long-term career planning.

As stated earlier, you cannot control others' behaviors or a lack of institutional resources. You can, however, control your own agency as you seek to be deliberate and strategic in identifying the human resources you need through mentoring to help advance in your career. As you master these skills, be sure to think about how you can support others in their pursuits. To that end, Laura concluded by offering advice and action steps to help you be a great mentor as you seek to support the next generation of women academics.

Developing Your Persuasive Voice

One of the most common needs I have heard over the past ten years from women academics is, "How can I develop a stronger voice at this stage of my career?" In chapter 7, Karen provided the tools and advice to help you do that, with a particular focus on developing a persuasive voice in service and administrative roles. The discussion of Cialdini's six persuasive principles, coupled with specific examples of how to use those principles, is quite powerful. Also informative is the inclusion of miniscenarios faced by women academics with corresponding advice and action steps to take to manage similar situations in the future. As Karen notes, as academics, we spend a great deal of time preparing our classroom lectures and activities as well as our scholarly pursuits. Yet we fail to strategize and prepare at the same level for our communications with colleagues, administrators, and other important campus and community stakeholders. Chapter 7 aimed to help support you in your efforts to develop your voice, by providing you with the tools and framework, as you advance in your career.

Concluding Comments

I feel very fortunate to be an academic and to have the flexibility that accompanies such a position. However, that is not to say that the academy is free from barriers, biases, and institutional roadblocks that impede professional progress, particularly for women and other underrepresented groups. And I have personally experienced these obstacles throughout my path to the professoriate and once firmly entrenched in it. However, my sincere hope in writing this book, along with the contributions from my two amazing women colleagues, is to provide a roadmap for women academics who find themselves trying to manage the nebulous midcareer, associate professor stage by offering some much-needed guidance and examples from those who are also on this same path and who made it to the other side. I had little formal guidance from within my institution to aid me in managing this stage. Instead, I adapted and adopted disciplinary tools from management and organizational studies to help me prepare for and pursue full professorship. And I benefited from exceptional mentoring along the way, from men and women academics and nonacademics. Also, the support of my family has been and continues to be immeasurable.

Pursuing career advancement in the academy requires a great deal of discipline, sacrifice, and understanding from those who love you the most. My goal is to support as many women as possible and to provide the needed scaffolding to be successful because the academy is a better place with all of us in it. Here's to supporting other women as they seek to achieve their goals and dreams and to showing kindness and offering a helping hand if those goals and dreams take a detour. Finally, let's commit to being the change we hope to see in the academy as we develop the next generation of women academics and leaders.

Additional Resources

If you are looking for additional resources to support you along your career journey, I recommend checking out the following:

National Center for Faculty Development & Diversity, https://www.faculty diversity.org/home. There is a variety of resources, programming, and peer community support available through this center.

Another complementary book to add to your library is by Rena Seltzer: *The Coach's Guide for Women Professors Who Want a Successful Career and a Well-Balanced Life* (Sterling, VA: Stylus, 2015). This book contains a wealth of information for women as they manage their careers.

Acknowledgments

This book would not have been possible without the support and encouragement of many individuals. First, thank you again to the amazing midcareer faculty women at the College of Wooster. My time with you inspired me to pursue this endeavor. Your willingness to share your struggles, needs, challenges, and goals so freely is beyond appreciated. I am your biggest fan. And a specific shout-out to Angie Bos and Jen Bowen: I am so grateful that you found your way to our ALI program and for the continued colleagueship and friendship that followed.

A big thank-you to my clients, research participants, academic friends, and colleagues. Your stories and example materials are featured throughout this book and have provided much-needed depth and truth to this stage of the faculty career for women academics.

Thank you to my dear friends and colleagues who served as friendly reviewers on the chapters featured in this book. Kimberly Griffin, Margaret Sallee, Aimee Terosky, and Tenisha Tevis—you are rock-star women academics, and this book is greatly improved because of your insights. Also, a big thank-you to Lisa Wolf-Wendel and Pam Eddy, who served as external reviewers. Your feedback was invaluable and your time greatly appreciated.

Thank you to the editorial team at Rutgers University Press, with a specific mention of Lisa Banning, my wonderful editor. Also important to the creation of this book is my amazing copy editor, Sarah Ashlock—you are a talented woman, and I am so glad to have you on my team.

Thank you to Laura and Karen for your willingness to share your expertise and develop content for this book. I am a better academic because of my friendship and collaboration with you.

To my male mentors—Jim Detert and Jeff Weedman—I am one blessed person to have been so fortunate to have two men support me along my career journey, who are the fiercest advocates for women.

Lastly, to my family—my coauthor in life, my husband, Bryan, and my two children, McKenna and Henley. Thank you for giving me the most amazing and important reasons to be strategic, deliberate, and thoughtful in managing my career and for giving me the most important role of my life: mother. I always hope to make you proud. To my own mother, Mary Ann, you have always supported me and shown me how to manage a family and career. You always made it seem so effortless, and I now know that it is not. And to my grandfather, Dr. Anton J. Brence, I wish you were here to see this. Thank you for preparing me to thrive in a "man's world" and not back down.

References

AAUP. 2018. "Statement on Governance of Colleges and Universities." www.aaup.org/report/statement-government-colleges-and-universities.

AAUW. 2018. *The Simple Truth about the Gender Pay Gap*. Washington, DC: AAUW. www.aauw.org/aauw_check/pdf_download/show_pdf.php?file=The_Simple_Truth.

ACE. n.d. "Fellows Program." Accessed May 22, 2018. www.acenet.edu/leadership/programs/Pages/ACE-Fellows-Program.aspx.

Acker, Joan. 1990. "Hierarchies, Jobs, Bodies: A Theory of Gendered Organizations." *Gender and Society* 4 (2): 139–58.

Ackerman, Joshua M., Christopher C. Nocera, and John A. Bargh. 2010. "Incidental Haptic Sensations Influence Social Judgments and Decisions." *Science* 328 (5986): 1712–15. doi:10.1126/science.1189993.

Antecol, Heather, Kelly Bedard, and Jenna Stearns. 2018. "Equal but Inequitable: Who Benefits from Gender-Neutral Tenure Clock Stopping Policies?" *American Economic Review* 108 (9): 2420–41.

Armenti, Carmen. 2004. "May Babies and Posttenure Babies: Maternal Decisions of Women Professors." *Review of Higher Education* 27 (2): 211–31. doi:10.1353/rhe.2003.0046.

Austin, Ann E. 2010. "Supporting Faculty Members across Their Careers." In *A Guide to Faculty Development*, 2nd ed., edited by Kay J. Gillespie, 363–78. San Francisco: Jossey-Bass.

———. 2002. "Preparing the Next Generation of Faculty: Graduate School as Socialization to the Academic Career." *Journal of Higher Education* 73 (1): 94–122. doi:10.1353/jhe.2002.0001.

Baker, Vicki L., Laura Gail Lunsford, Gretchen Neisler, Meghan J. Pifer, and Aimee LaPointe Terosky, eds. 2019. *Success after Tenure: Supporting Mid-career Faculty*. Sterling, VA: Stylus.

Baker, Vicki L., Laura Gail Lunsford, and Meghan J. Pifer. 2019a. "The Academic Leadership Institute for Mid-career Faculty." In *Success after Tenure: Supporting Mid-career Faculty*, edited by Vicki L. Baker, Laura G. Lunsford, Gretchen Neisler, and Meghan J. Pifer, 35–54. Sterling, VA: Stylus.

———. 2019b. "Where to Patch Up the Leaking Leadership Pipeline? Fostering Mid-career Faculty Succession Management." *Research in Higher Education* 60 (6): 823–43. https://doi.org/10.1007/s11162-018-9528-9.

———. 2017. *Developing Faculty in Liberal Arts Colleges: Aligning Individual Needs and Organizational Goals*. New Brunswick, NJ: Rutgers University Press.

Baker, Vicki L., Meghan J. Pifer, and Laura Gail Lunsford. 2018. "Faculty Development in Liberal Arts Colleges: A Look at Divisional Trends, Preferences, and Needs." *Higher Education Research & Development* 37 (7): 1336–1351. doi:10.1080/07294360.2018.1483901.

———. 2016. "Faculty Challenges across Rank in Liberal Arts Colleges: A Human Resources Perspective." *Journal of Faculty Development* 30 (1): 23–30.

Baker, Vicki L., Aimee LaPointe Terosky, and Edna Martinez. 2017. "Faculty Members' Scholarly Learning across Institutional Types." *ASHE Higher Education Report* 43 (2): 9–138. doi:10.1002/aehe.20118.

Baldwin, Roger G., and Robert T. Blackburn. 1981. "The Academic Career as a Developmental Process: Implications for Higher Education." *Journal of Higher Education* 52 (6): 598–614. doi:10.2307/1981769.

Baldwin, Roger G., and Deborah A. Chang. 2006. "Reinforcing Our Strategies to Support Faculty in the Middle Years of Academic Life." *Liberal Education* 92 (4): 28–35.

Baldwin, Roger G., Christina J. Lunceford, and Kim E. Vanderlinden. 2005. "Faculty in the Middle Years: Illuminating an Overlooked Phase of Academic Life." *Review of Higher Education* 29 (2): 97–118. doi:10.1353/rhe.2005.0055.

Barsh, Joanna, Susie Cranston, and Geoffrey Lewis. 2009. *How Remarkable*

Women Lead: The Breakthrough Model for Work and Life. New York: Crown Business.

Bartlett, Alison. 2015. "Male Professors Are 'Genius.' Female Professors Are 'Nice.'" *New Republic*, February 10. https://newrepublic.com/article/121024/heres-one-way-gender-discrimination-plays-out-academia.

Bates, Laura. 2015. "Female Academics Face Huge Sexist Bias—No Wonder There Are So Few of Them." *The Guardian*, February 13. www.theguardian.com/lifeandstyle/womens-blog/2015/feb/13/female-academics-huge-sexist-bias-students.

Beaubouef, Tamara, and Karla Erickson. 2017. "Rethinking the Mid-career Malaise: New Lessons from Post-Tenure Liberal Arts Faculty." Presentation at the AAC&U Annual Meeting, January 26, San Francisco. www.aacu.org/sites/default/files/files/AM17/Mid-Career Malaise PPT.pdf.

Bennett, Sheila K. 1982. "Student Perceptions of and Expectations for Male and Female Instructors: Evidence Relating to the Question of Gender Bias in Teaching Evaluation." *Journal of Educational Psychology* 74 (2): 170–79. https://doi.org/10.1037/0022-0663.74.2.170.

Berg, Justin M., Jane E. Dutton, and Amy Wrzesniewski. 2013. "Purpose and Meaning in the Workplace." In *Purpose and Meaning in the Workplace*, edited by Bryan J. Dik, Zinta S. Byrne, and Michael F. Steger, 81–104. Washington, DC: American Psychological Association.

Berscheid, Ellen, and Elaine Walster. 1978. *Interpersonal Attraction*. Reading, MA: Addison-Wesley.

Bingham, Teri, and Susan J. Nix. 2010. "Women Faculty in Higher Education: A Case Study on Gender Bias." *Forum on Public Policy* 2010 (2). https://files.eric.ed.gov/fulltext/EJ903580.pdf.

Boyer, Ernest L. 1990. *Scholarship Reconsidered: Priorities of the Professoriate*. New York: Carnegie Foundation for the Advancement of Teaching.

Boyer, Ernest L., Drew Moser, Todd C. Ream, and John M. Braxton. 2015. *Scholarship Reconsidered: Priorities of the Professoriate*. San Francisco: Jossey-Bass.

Britton, Dana M. 2017. "Is There a Chilly Climate for Women Faculty?" *Gender & Society*, January 24. https://gendersociety.wordpress.com/2017/01/18/is-there-a-chilly-climate-for-women-faculty/.

Bryson, John M. 2018. *Strategic Planning for Public and Nonprofit Organizations: A Guide to Strengthening and Sustaining Organizational Achievement*. New York: Wiley.

Buch, Kimberly, Yvette Huet, Audrey Rorrer, and Lynn Roberson. 2011. "Removing the Barriers to Full Professor: A Mentoring Program for Associate Professors." *Change: The Magazine of Higher Learning* 43 (6): 38–45.

Bugeja, Michael. 2009. "Understanding How Tenure Decisions Are Made." *Chronicle of Higher Education*, July 10. www.chronicle.com/article/ Understanding-How-Tenure/46977.

Burger, Jerry M., Nicole Messian, Shebani Patel, Alicia del Prado, and Carmen Anderson. 2004. "What a Coincidence! The Effects of Incidental Similarity on Compliance." *Personality and Social Psychology Bulletin* 30 (1): 35–43.

Bushman, Brad J. 1988. "The Effects of Apparel on Compliance: A Field Experiment with a Female Authority Figure." *Personality and Social Psychology Bulletin* 14 (3): 459–67.

Buunk, Bram P., and Arnold B. Bakker. 1995. "Extradyadic Sex: The Role of Descriptive and Injunctive Norms." *Journal of Sex Research* 32 (4): 313–18. https://doi.org/10.1080/00224499509551804.

Carless, S. A. 1998. "Gender Differences in Transformational Leadership: An Examination of Superior, Leader, and Subordinate Perspectives." *Sex Roles* 39 (11–12): 887–902.

Carli, Linda L. 2004. "Gender Effects on Social Influence." In *Persuasion: Social Influence, and Compliance Gaining*, edited by Robert H. Gass and John S. Seiter, 133–48. Boston: Allyn and Bacon.

Carnes Molly, Christie M. Bartels, Anna Kaatz, and Christine Kolehmainen. 2015. "Why Is John More Likely to Become Department Chair than Jennifer?" *Transactions of the American Clinical and Climatological Association* 126:197–214.

Case, Jean. 2015. "For Women Only: The ABCs of Breaking Through." *Forbes*, March 25. www.forbes.com/sites/jeancase/2015/03/25/for -women-only-the-abcs-of-breaking-through/.

Ceci, Stephen J., Donna K. Ginther, Shulamit Kahn, and Wendy M. Williams. 2014. "Women in Academic Science: A Changing Landscape." *Psychological Science in the Public Interest* 15 (3): 75–141.

Cejda, Brent D., and Nancy Hensel. 2009. *An Overview of Undergraduate Research in Community Colleges*. Washington, DC: Council on Undergraduate Research. http://www.cur.org/urcc.

Center for Positive Organizations. n.d. "About." Accessed May 4, 2019. http://positiveorgs.bus.umich.edu/about/.

Chambers, Crystal Renée. 2011. "Candid Reflections on the Departure of Black Women Faculty from Academe in the United States." *Negro Educational Review* 62 (1–4): 233–60.

Cialdini, Robert. 2016. *Pre-suasion: A Revolutionary Way to Influence and Persuade*. New York: Simon and Schuster.

——. 2009. *Influence: Science and Practice*. Vol. 4. Boston: Pearson Education.

——. 2003a. "Crafting Normative Messages to Protect the Environment." *Current Directions in Psychological Science* 12 (4): 105–9. https://doi .org/10.1111/1467-8721.01242.

——. 2003b. "Principles of Ethical Influence." Influence at Work. www .influenceatwork.com.

——. 2001. "Harnessing the Science of Persuasion." *Harvard Business Review* 79 (9): 72–81.

——. 1993. *The Psychology of Influence*. New York: William Morrow.

Cialdini, Robert B., Raymond R. Reno, and Carl A. Kallgren. 1990. "A Focus Theory of Normative Conduct: Recycling the Concept of Norms to Reduce Littering in Public Places." *Journal of Personality and Social Psychology* 58 (6): 1015–26. https://doi.org/10.1037/0022-3514.58.6.1015.

Clark, Burton R. 1987. *The Academic Life: Small Worlds, Different Worlds*. Princeton, NJ: Carnegie Foundation for the Advancement of Teaching.

Clarke, Marie, Abbey Hyde, and Jonathan Drennan. 2013. "Professional Identity in Higher Education." In *Academic Profession in Europe: New Tasks and New Challenges*, edited by Barbara M. Kehm, 7–21. Dordrecht, Netherlands: Springer.

Covey, Stephen R. 2013. *The 7 Habits of Highly Effective People*. New York: Simon and Schuster.

Croom, Natasha N. 2017. "Promotion beyond Tenure: Unpacking Racism and Sexism in the Experiences of Black Womyn Professors." *Review of Higher Education* 40 (4): 557–83. https://doi.org/10.1353/rhe.2017.0022.

Croom, Natasha, and Lori Patton. 2012. "The Miner's Canary: A Critical Race Perspective on the Representation of Black Women Full Professors." *Negro Education Review* 62–63 (1–4): 13–39.

Curtis, John W. 2011. "Persistent Inequity: Gender and Academic Employment." Paper presented at "New Voices in Pay Equity" event. www.aaup .org/NR/rdonlyres/08E023AB-E6D8-4DBD-99A0-24E5EB73A760/0/ persistent_inequity.pdf.

De Janasz, Suzanne C., and Sherry E. Sullivan. 2004. "Multiple Mentoring in Academe: Developing the Professorial Network." *Journal of Vocational Behavior* 64 (2): 263–83.

Dempsey, Michelle. 2017. "Women and Self-Care: A Critical Call to Action." *Huffington Post*, September 8. www.huffingtonpost.com/michelle -dempsey/women-and-selfcare-a-crit_b_11896758.html.

Denker, Katherine J. 2009. "Doing Gender in the Academy: The Challenges for Women in the Academic Organization." *Women and Language* 32 (1): 103–12.

DeWolf, Mark. 2017. "12 Stats about Working Women." *U.S. Department of Labor Blog*, March 1. https://blog.dol.gov/2017/03/01/12-stats-about -working-women.

DeZure, Deborah, Allyn Shaw, and Julie Rojewski. 2014. "Cultivating the Next Generation of Academic Leaders: Implications for Administrators and Faculty." *Change: The Magazine of Higher Learning* 46 (1): 6–12. https://doi.org/10.1080/00091383.2013.842102.

Dow, Neal. 2014. "Terminal Associate Professors, Past and Present." *Chronicle of Higher Education*, March 26. www.chronicle.com/article/Terminal -Associate-Professors/145537.

Dozier, Raine. 2015. "A View from the Academe: Lesbian and Gay Faculty and Minority Stress." *Psychology of Sexual Orientation and Gender Diversity* 2 (2): 188–98. https://doi.org/10.1037/sgd0000105.

Eby, Lillian T., Stacy E. McManus, Shanna A. Simon, and Joyce E. Russel. 2000. "The Protege's Perspective Regarding Negative Mentoring Experiences: The Development of a Taxonomy." *Journal of Vocational Behavior* 57 (1): 1–21.

Eddy, Pamela L., and Kelly Ward. 2017. "Problematizing Gender in Higher Education: Why *Leaning In* Isn't Enough." In *Critical Approaches to*

Women and Gender in Higher Education, edited by Pamela L. Eddy, Kelly Ward, and Tehmina Khwaja, 13–40. New York: Palgrave.

Elias, Steven M., and Ross J. Loomis. 2004. "The Effect of Instructor Gender and Race/Ethnicity on Gaining Compliance in the Classroom." *Journal of Applied Social Psychology* 34 (5): 937–58. https://doi.org/10.1111/j.1559 -1816.2004.tb02578.x.

Elliot, Andrew J., and Daniela Niesta. 2008. "Romantic Red: Red Enhances Men's Attraction to Women." *Journal of Personality and Social Psychology* 95 (5): 1150–64.

European Commission. 2017. *Interim Evaluation: Gender Equality as a Crosscutting Issue in Horizon 2020*. Brussels: European Commission. https://ec.europa.eu/research/swafs/pdf/pub_gender_equality/interim _evaluation_gender_long_final.pdf.

Fairweather, James S. 2005. "Beyond the Rhetoric: Trends in the Relative Value of Teaching and Research in Faculty Salaries." *Journal of Higher Education* 76 (4): 401–22.

Flaherty, Colleen. 2018. "Dancing Backwards in High Heels." *Inside Higher Ed*, January 10. www.insidehighered.com/news/2018/01/10/study-finds -female-professors-experience-more-work-demands-and-special-favor.

Forbes. 2018. "5 Ways to Shut Down Mansplaining." February 26. www .forbes.com/sites/work-in-progress/2018/02/26/5-ways-to-shut-down -mansplaining/#785c6cce589e.

Franklin, Benjamin. 2003. *The Autobiography of Benjamin Franklin*. New Haven, CT: Yale University Press.

Freedman, Jonathan L., and Scott C. Fraser. 1966. "Compliance without Pressure: The Foot-in-the-Door Technique." *Journal of Personality and Social Psychology* 4 (2): 195–202. https://doi.org/10.1037/h0023552.

Frenzen, Jonathan K., and Harry L. Davis. 1990. "Purchasing Behavior in Embedded Markets." *Journal of Consumer Research* 17 (1): 1–12. https:// doi.org/10.1086/208532.

Garner, Randy. 2005. "Post-It® Note Persuasion: A Sticky Influence." *Journal of Consumer Psychology* 15 (3): 230–37. https://doi.org/10.1207/s15327663 jcp1503_8.

Garza Mitchell, Regina, and Pamela L. Eddy. 2008. "In the Middle: Career Pathways of Midlevel Community College Leaders." *Community*

College Journal of Research and Practice 32 (10): 793–811. https://doi.org/10.1080/10668920802325739.

Goei, Ryan, Lisa L. Massi Lindsey, Franklin J. Boster, Paul D. Skalski, and Jonathan M. Bowman. 2003. "The Mediating Roles of Liking and Obligation on the Relationship between Favors and Compliance." *Communication Research* 30 (2): 178–97. https://doi.org/10.1177/0093650202250877.

Goldsmith, Marshall. 2008. *What Got You Here Won't Get You There: How Successful People Become Even More Successful.* London: Profile Books.

Government of India, Ministry of Human Resource Development. 2017. "Table 22: State and Post-Wise Number of Male and Female Teacher." *All India Survey on Higher Education 2015–16*, T-71–T-72.

Government of Japan, Gender Equality Cabinet Office. 2017. "Education and Research Fields." In *Women and Men in Japan 2017*, 20–21. Tokyo: Gender Equality Bureau.

Grant-Vallone, Elisa J., and Ellen A. Ensher. 2017. "Re-crafting Careers for Mid-career Faculty: A Qualitative Study." *Journal of Higher Education Theory and Practice* 17 (5): 10–24.

Griffin, Kimberly A., Jessica C. Bennett, and Jessica Harris. 2013. "Marginalizing Merit? Gender Differences in Black Faculty D/discourses on Tenure, Advancement, and Professional Success." *Review of Higher Education* 36 (4): 489–512. https://doi.org/10.1353/rhe.2013.0040.

Guarino, Cassandra M., and Victor M. H. Borden. 2017. "Faculty Service Loads and Gender: Are Women Taking Care of the Academic Family?" *Research in Higher Education* 58 (6): 672–94. https://doi.org/10.1007/s11162-017-9454-2.

Hater, John J., and Bernard M. Bass. 1988. "Superiors' Evaluations and Subordinates' Perceptions of Transformational and Transactional Leadership." *Journal of Applied Psychology* 73 (4): 695–702.

HERS. n.d. "Higher Education Leadership Program for Women." Accessed June 1, 2018. www.hersnetwork.org/programs/overview/.

Hetty van Emmerik, I. J. 2004. "The More You Can Get the Better: Mentoring Constellations and Intrinsic Career Success." *Career Development International* 9 (6): 578–94.

Higgins, Monica C., and Kathy E. Kram. 2001. "Reconceptualizing Mentoring at Work: A Developmental Network Perspective." *Academy of Management Review* 26 (2): 264–88.

Higher Education Research Institute. 2014. *Undergraduate Teaching Faculty: The 2013–2014 HERI Faculty Survey.* Los Angeles: Higher Education Research Institute. www.heri.ucla.edu/monographs/HERI-FAC2014 -monograph-expanded.pdf.

Hobofoll, Stevan E. 2001. "The Influence of Culture, Community, and the Nested-Self in the Stress Process." *Applied Psychology: An International Review* 50:337–421.

Hochschild, Arlie, and Anne Machung. 2012. *The Second Shift: Working Families and the Revolution at Home.* New York: Penguin.

Hornstein, Harvey A., Elisha Fisch, and Michael Holmes. 1968. "Influence of a Models Feeling about His Behavior and His Relevance as a Comparison Other on Observers Helping Behavior." *Journal of Personality and Social Psychology* 10 (3): 222–26. doi:10.1037/h0026568.

Huang, Karen, Michael Yeomans, Alison Wood Brooks, Julia Minson, and Francesca Gino. 2017. "It Doesn't Hurt to Ask: Question-Asking Increases Liking." *Journal of Personality and Social Psychology* 113 (3): 430–52.

Hughes, Alan. 2014. "Earning Tenure at Small Colleges." *Inside HigherEd,* August 11. www.insidehighered.com/advice/2014/08/11/essay-earning -tenure-small-liberal-arts-colleges.

Jaschik, Scott. 2018. "Nobel Winner in Physics 'Never Applied' to Be Full Professor." *Inside Higher Ed,* October 3. www.insidehighered.com/ quicktakes/2018/10/03/nobel-winner-physics-never-applied-be-full -professor.

Johnson, David W., Roger T. Johnson, and Geoffrey Maruyama. 1983. "Interdependence and Interpersonal Attraction among Heterogeneous and Homogeneous Individuals: A Theoretical Formulation and a Meta-Analysis of the Research." *Review of Educational Research* 53 (1): 5–54.

Johnson, Heather L. 2017. *Pipeline, Pathways, and Institutional Leadership: An Update on the Status of Women in Higher Education.* Washington, DC: American Council on Education.

Johnson, W. Brad, and David Smith. 2016. *Athena Rising: How and Why Men Should Mentor Women.* New York: Routledge.

June, Audrey W. 2016. "The Uncertain Path to Full Professor." *Chronicle of Higher Education*, February 14. www.chronicle.com/article/The-Uncertain-Path-to-Full/235304.

———. 2015. "The Invisible Labor of Minority Professors." *Chronicle of Higher Education*, November 8. www.chronicle.com/article/The-Invisible-Labor-of/234098.

Kardia, Diana B., and Mary C. Wright 2004. "Instructor Identity: The Impact of Gender and Race on Faculty Experiences with Teaching." *CRLT Occasional Papers* 19:1–8.

Karpowitz, Christopher F., and Tali Mendelberg. 2014. *The Silent Sex: Gender, Deliberation, and Institutions*. Princeton, NJ: Princeton University Press.

Kezar, Adrianna J., Daniel Maxey, and Elizabeth Holcombe. 2015. "The Professoriate Reconsidered: A Study of New Faculty Models." Pullias Center for Higher Education, University of Southern California.

Klauser, Henriette Anne. 2001. *Write It Down, Make It Happen: Knowing What You Want—and Getting It!* New York: Simon and Schuster.

Krawcheck, Sallie. 2017. *Own It: The Power of Women at Work*. New York: Crown Business.

Kulik, Carol T., and Mara Olekalns. 2012. "Negotiating the Gender Divide." *Journal of Management* 38 (4): 1387–1415. https://doi.org/10.1177/014920 6311431307.

Lennon, Tiffani. 2013. *Benchmarking Women's Leadership in the United States*. Denver: University of Denver Colorado Women's College. https://womenscollege.du.edu/media/documents/BenchmarkingWomens LeadershipintheUS.pdf.

Lester, Jaime. 2015. "Cultures of Work-Life Balance in Higher Education: A Case of Fragmentation." *Journal of Diversity in Higher Education* 8 (3): 139–56.

———. 2008. "Performing Gender in the Workplace." *Community College Review* 35 (4): 277–305. https://doi.org/10.1177/0091552108314756.

Levin, John S., Susan Kater, and Richard L. Wagoner. 2006. *Community College Faculty: At Work in the New Economy*. New York: Springer.

Levinson, Daniel J., and Judy Levinson. 1996. *The Seasons of a Woman's Life: A Fascinating Exploration of the Events, Thoughts, and Life Experiences That All Women Share*. New York: Ballantine Books.

Lobel, Thalma. 2016. *Sensation: The New Science of Physical Intelligence.* New York: Atria Books.

Lun, Janetta, Stacey Sinclair, Erin R. Whitchurch, and Catherine Glenn. 2007. "(Why) Do I Think What You Think? Epistemic Social Tuning and Implicit Prejudice." *Journal of Personality and Social Psychology* 93 (6): 957–72.

MacNell, Lillian, Adam Driscoll, and Andrea N. Hunt. 2015. "What's in a Name: Exposing Gender Bias in Student Ratings of Teaching." *Innovative Higher Education* 40 (4): 291–303. https://doi.org/10.1007/s10755-014-9313-4.

Mason, Mary Ann. 2013. "Should Women Delay Motherhood?" *New York Times*, July 16. www.nytimes.com/roomfordebate/2013/07/08/should-women-delay-motherhood/what-you-need-to-know-if-youre-an-academic-and-want-to-be-a-mom.

Mason, Mary Ann, Nicholas H. Wolfinger, and Marc Goulden. 2013. *Do Babies Matter? Gender and Family in the Ivory Tower.* New Brunswick, NJ: Rutgers University Press.

Matheson, Kimberly. 1991. "Social Cues in Computer-Mediated Negotiations: Gender Makes a Difference." *Computers in Human Behavior* 7 (3): 137–45. https://doi.org/10.1016/0747-5632(91)90003-j.

Mathews, Kiernan, R., 2014. "Perspectives on Mid-career Faculty and Advice for Supporting Them." White paper, COACHE, Harvard Graduate School of Education, Cambridge, MA.

Matthew, Patricia A. 2016. "What Is Faculty Diversity Worth to a University?" *Atlantic*, November 23. www.theatlantic.com/education/archive/2016/11/what-is-faculty-diversity-worth-to-a-university/508334/.

McCracken, Douglas M. 2000. "Winning the Talent War for Women: Sometimes It Takes a Revolution." *Harvard Business Review* 78 (6): 159–67.

Meevissen, Yvo M., Madelon L. Peters, and Hugo J. Alberts. 2011. "Become More Optimistic by Imagining a Best Possible Self: Effects of a Two-Week Intervention." *Journal of Behavior Therapy and Experimental Psychiatry* 42 (3): 371–78.

Mehl, Matthias R., Simine Vazire, Nairán Ramirez-Esparza, Richard B. Slatcher, and James W. Pennebaker. 2007. "Are Women Really More

Talkative than Men?" *Science* 317 (5834): 82. https://doi.org/10.1126/science.1139940.

Mengel, Friederike, Jan Sauermann, and Ulf Zölitz. 2018. "Gender Bias in Teaching Evaluations." *Journal of the European Economic Association*, February 10. https://doi.org/10.1093/jeea/jvx057.

Milgram, Stanley. 1974. *Obedience to Authority*. New York: Harper and Row.

Misra, Joya, and Jennifer Lundquist. 2015a. "Diversity and the Ivory Ceiling." *Inside Higher Ed*, June 26. www.insidehighered.com/advice/2015/06/26/essay-diversity-issues-and-midcareer-faculty-members.

———. 2015b. "Midcareer Melancholy." *Inside Higher Ed*, May 29. www.insidehighered.com/advice/2015/05/29/essay-frustrations-associate-professors.

Misra, Joya, Jennifer Lundquist, Elissa Dahlberg Holmes, and Stephanie Agiomavritis. 2011. "The Ivory Ceiling of Service Work." *Academe* 97:2–6.

———. 2010. *Associate Professors and Gendered Barriers to Advancement*. Boston: University of Massachusetts. https://people.umass.edu/misra/Joya_Misra/work-life_files/Associate%20Professors%20and%20Gendered%20Barriers%20to%20Advancement%20Full%20Report.pdf.

Modern Language Association of America, Committee on the Status of Women in the Profession. 2009. *Standing Still: The Associate Professor Survey*. New York: Modern Language Association. https://apps.mla.org/pdf/cswp_final042909.pdf.

Monaghan, Peter. 2017. "Helping Professors Overcome Midcareer Malaise." *Chronicle of Higher Education*, May 1. www.chronicle.com/article/Helping-Professors-Overcome/240009?cid=cp114.

Murray, Susan. 2011. "Single Motherhood and the Faculty Life." *Antenna*, October 11. http://blog.commarts.wisc.edu/2011/10/11/single-motherhood-and-the-faculty-life/.

NCES (National Center for Education Statistics), IPEDS Data Center. 2017. "Table 315.20: Full-Time Faculty in Degree-Granting Postsecondary Institutions, by Race/Ethnicity, Sex, and Academic Rank: Fall 2013, Fall 2015, and Fall 2016." Digest of Education Statistics. https://nces.ed.gov/programs/digest/d17/tables/dt17_315.20.asp.

———. 2015. "Table 315.20: Full-Time Faculty in Degree-Granting Postsecondary Institutions, by Race/Ethnicity, Sex, and Academic Rank: Fall
2011, Fall 2013, and Fall 2015." Digest of Education Statistics. https://nces
.ed.gov/programs/digest/d16/tables/dt16_315.20.asp.

Neumann, Anna. 2009. *Professing to Learn: Creating Tenured Lives and
Careers in the American Research University*. Baltimore: Johns Hopkins
University Press.

Neumann, Anna, Aimee L. Terosky, and Julie Schell. 2006. "Agents of
Learning: Strategies for Assuming Agency, for Learning, in Tenured
Faculty Careers." In *The Balancing Act: Gendered Perspectives in Faculty
Roles and Work Lives*, edited by S. J. Bracken, J. K. Allen, and D. R. Dean,
91–120. Sterling, VA: Stylus.

Niiya, Yu. 2015. "Does a Favor Request Increase Liking toward the
Requester?" *Journal of Social Psychology* 156 (2): 211–21.

O'Donnell, Peggy. 2017. "The Sexism that Permeates the Academy." *Chronicle of Higher Education*, October 17. www.chronicle.com/article/The
-Sexism-That-Permeates-the/241469.

O'Meara, KerryAnn, and R. Eugene Rice, eds. 2005. *Faculty Priorities
Reconsidered: Rewarding Multiple Forms of Scholarship*. San Francisco:
Jossey-Bass.

O'Meara, KerryAnn, Aimee LaPointe Terosky, and Anna Neumann. 2008.
"Faculty Careers and Work Lives: A Professional Growth Perspective."
ASHE Higher Education Report 34 (3): 1–221.

Ortiz, Anna M., Don Haviland, and Laura Henriques. 2017. "Guidance on
the Process of Gaining Tenure (Essay)." *Inside Higher Ed*, October 26.
www.insidehighered.com/advice/2017/10/26/guidance-process-gaining
-tenure-essay.

Osita, Christian, Idoko Onyebuchi, and Nzekwe Justina. 2014. "Organization's Stability and Productivity: The Role of SWOT Analysis." *International Journal of Innovative and Applied Research* 2 (9): 23–32. http://
journalijiar.com/uploads/2014-10-02_231409_710.pdf.

Owen, Whitney J. 2004. "In Defense of the Least Publishable Unit."
Chronicle of Higher Education, February 9. www.chronicle.com/article/
In-Defense-of-the-Least/44761.

Parker, Kim. 2018. "Women in Majority-Male Workplaces Report Higher

Rates of Gender Discrimination." Pew Research Center, March 7. www
.pewresearch.org/fact-tank/2018/03/07/women-in-majority-male-
workplaces-report-higher-rates-of-gender-discrimination/.

Perna, Laura W. 2005. "Sex Differences in Faculty Tenure and Promotion."
Research in Higher Education 42 (5): 541–67. https://doi.org/10.1007/
s11162-004-1641-2.

Pinder, Craig C. 2014. *Work Motivation in Organizational Behavior*. New
York: Psychology Press.

Platow, Michael J., S. Alexander Haslam, Amanda Both, Ivanne Chew,
Michelle Cuddon, Nahal Goharpey, Jacqui Maurer, Simone Rosini,
Anna Tsekouras, and Diana M. Grace. 2005. "'It's Not Funny If They're
Laughing': Self-Categorization, Social Influence, and Responses to
Canned Laughter." *Journal of Experimental Social Psychology* 41 (5):
542–50. https://doi.org/10.1016/j.jesp.2004.09.005.

Pratkanis, Anthony R., and Elliot Aronson. 2000. *Age of Propaganda: The
Everyday Use and Abuse of Persuasion*. New York: W. H. Freeman.

Price, Emily. 2017. "How to Deal with Mansplaining at Work." *Lifehacker*,
September 10. https://lifehacker.com/how-to-deal-with-mansplaining
-at-work-1803122874.

Psychology Today. 2018. "How to Deal with People Who Interrupt." September 13. www.psychologytoday.com/us/blog/open-gently/201709/
how-deal-people-who-interrupt.

Ray, Victor. 2018. "Is Gender Bias an Intended Feature of Teaching Evaluations?" *Inside Higher Ed*, February 9. www.insidehighered.com/
advice/2018/02/09/teaching-evaluations-are-often-used-confirm-worst
-stereotypes-about-women-faculty.

Regan, Dennis T. 1971. "Effects of a Favor and Liking on Compliance." *Journal of Experimental Social Psychology* 7 (6): 627–39.

Reinert, Leah J., and Tamara Yakaboski. 2017. "Being Out Matters for Lesbian Faculty: Personal Identities Influence Professional Experiences."
NASPA Journal about Women in Higher Education 10 (3): 319–36.

Reinvention Collaborative. n.d. "UVP Network." Accessed September 13,
2019. https://reinventioncollaborative.org/.

Rice, R. Eugene. 2005. "The Future of the Scholarly Work of Faculty." In
Faculty Priorities Reconsidered: Rewarding Multiple Forms of Scholarship,

edited by KerryAnn O'Meara and R. Eugene Rice, 303–12 San Francisco: Jossey-Bass.

———. 2002. "Beyond Scholarship Reconsidered: Toward an Enlarged Vision of the Scholarly Work of Faculty Members." *New Directions for Teaching and Learning* 2002 (90): 7–18.

Rising Tide Center for Gender Equity. 2018. *Study of Experiences in the Process of Promotion to Full Professor at the University of Maine.* Orono: University of Maine. https://umaine.edu/risingtide/wp-content/uploads/sites/239/2018/12/Report-on-Experiences-in-the-Process-of-Promotion-to-Full-P-1.pdf.

Rockquemore, Kerry Ann. 2011. "Mid-career Mentoring." *Inside Higher Ed*, November 28. www.insidehighered.com/advice/2011/11/28/essay-need-tenured-faculty-members-have-mentoring.

Rommel, A., and M. Bailey. 2017. "Extended Length in Rank among Associate Professors: The Problem, Its Implications, and Strategies to Address It." *AdvanceRIT*, September 25. www.rit.edu/nsfadvance/sites/rit.edu.nsfadvance/files/docs/Extended%20Length%20in%20Rank%20Among%20Associate%20Professors.pdf.

Russo, J. Edward, Kurt A. Carlson, and Margaret G. Meloy. 2006. "Choosing an Inferior Alternative." *Psychological Science* 17 (10): 899–904.

Salerno, Jessica M., and Liana Peter-Hagene. 2015. "One Angry Woman: Anger Expression Increases Influence for Men, but Decreases Influence for Women, during Group Deliberation." *Law and Human Behavior* 39 (6): 581–92. http://dx.doi.org/10.1037/lhb0000147.

Sallee, Margaret, Kelly Ward, and Lisa Wolf-Wendel. 2016. "Can Anyone Have It All? Gendered Views on Parenting and Academic Careers." *Innovative Higher Education* 41 (3): 187–202.

Samsel, Haley. 2017. "Most College Students are Female, but College Presidents? Not So Much." *USA Today College*, June 20. http://college.usatoday.com/2017/06/20/most-college-students-are-female-but-college-presidents-not-so-much/.

Sandberg, Sheryl. 2013. *Lean In: Women, Work, and the Will to Lead.* New York: Knopf / Random House.

Sankary, Myer J. 2005. "Keeping Your Cool: The Power of Persuasion in Mediation Applying the Social Science of Influence to the Art of

Negotiation." Paper presented at SCMA's annual Employment Mediation Conference, May 14. http://sankarymediation.com/articles-conferences/the-power-of-persuasion/.

Serra Hagedorn, Linda, and Berta Vigil Laden. 2002. "Exploring the Climate for Women as Community College Faculty." *New Directions for Community Colleges* 2002 (118): 69–78.

Serviere-Munoz, Laura, and R. Wayne Counts. 2014. "Recruiting Millennials into Student Organizations: Exploring Cialdini's Principles of Human Influence." *Journal of Business and Economics* 5:306–15.

Settles, Isis H., Lilia M. Cortina, Janet Malley, and Abigail J. Stewart. 2006. "The Climate for Women in Academic Science: The Good, the Bad, and the Changeable." *Psychology of Women Quarterly* 30 (1): 47–58.

Sexton, Kevin Wayne, Kyle M. Hocking, Eric Wise, Michael J. Osgood, Joyce Cheung-Flynn, Padmini Komalavilas, Karen E. Campbell, Jeffrey B. Dattilo, and Colleen M. Brophy. 2012. "Women in Academic Surgery: The Pipeline Is Busted." *Journal of Surgical Education* 69 (1): 84–90.

Shantz, Amanda, and Gary Latham. 2011. "The Effect of Primed Goals on Employee Performance: Implications for Human Resource Management." *Human Resource Management* 50 (2): 289–99.

Sheldon, Kennon M., and Sonja Lyubomirsky 2006. "How to Increase and Sustain Positive Emotion: The Effects of Expressing Gratitude and Visualizing Best Possible Selves." *Journal of Positive Psychology* 1 (2): 73–82.

Siegel, Vivian. 2016. "Self-Advocacy: Why It's Uncomfortable, Especially for Women, and What to Do about It." *ACSB Newsletter*, November 7. www.ascb.org/newsletter/novemberdecember-2016-newsletter/self-advocacy-why-its-uncomfortable-especially-for-women-and-what-to-do-about-it-november-december-2016-newsletter/.

Smallwood, Scott. 2004. "Doctor Dropout." *Chronicle of Higher Education* 50 (19): A10.

Sorcinelli, Mary D., 2000. "Principles of Good Practice: Supporting Early-Career Faculty. Guidance for Deans, Department Chairs, and Other Academic Leaders." AAHE, Forum on Faculty Roles Rewards, Washington, DC.

Sorcinelli, Mary Deane, and Jung Yun. 2007. "From Mentor to Mentoring

Networks: Mentoring in the New Academy." *Change: The Magazine of Higher Learning* 39 (6): 58–61.

Spreitzer, Gretchen, and Christine Porath. 2012. "Creating Sustainable Performance." *Harvard Business Review* 90 (1): 1–9.

Statistics Canada. 2017. "Number and Salaries of Full-Time Teaching Staff at Canadian Universities." *The Daily*, April 25. www150.statcan.gc.ca/n1/daily-quotidien/170425/dq170425b-eng.htm.

Stevenson, Jane E., and Evelyn Orr. 2017. "We Interviewed 57 Female CEOs to Find Out How More Women Can Get to the Top." *Harvard Business Review*, November 8. https://hbr.org/2017/11/we-interviewed-57-female-ceos-to-find-out-how-more-women-can-get-to-the-top.

Strachan, Glenda. 2016. "Women, Careers and Universities: Where To from Here?" *Advocate: Newsletter of the National Tertiary Education Union* 23 (3): 36–38.

Strage, Amy, and Joan Merdinger. 2015. "Professional Growth and Renewal for Mid-career Faculty." *Journal of Faculty Development* 29 (1): 41–50.

Sturm, Susan. 2001. "Second Generation Employment Discrimination: A Structural Approach." *Columbia Law Review* 101:458–568.

Szybinski, Debra, and Trace Jordan. 2010. "Navigating the Future of the Professoriate." *Peer Review* 12 (3): 4–6.

Terosky, Aimee LaPointe, KerryAnn O'Meara, and Corbin M. Campbell. 2014. "Enabling Possibility: Women Associate Professors' Sense of Agency in Career Advancement." *Journal of Diversity in Higher Education* 7 (1): 58–76.

Thomas, J. D., Laura Gail Lunsford, and Helena A. Rodrigues. 2015. "Early Career Academic Staff Support: Evaluating Mentoring Networks." *Journal of Higher Education Policy and Management* 37 (3): 320–29.

Thompson, George J., and Jerry B. Jenkins. 2013. *Verbal Judo: The Gentle Art of Persuasion.* 2nd ed. Grand Rapids, MI: Zondervan.

Tickle, Louise. 2017. "Why Universities Can't See Women as Leaders." *The Guardian*, March 8. www.theguardian.com/higher-education-network/2017/mar/08/why-universities-cant-see-woman-as-leaders.

Turner, Caroline Sotello Viernes. 2002. "Women of Color in Academe: Living with Multiple Marginality." *Journal of Higher Education* 73 (1): 74–93.

US Census Bureau. 2018. "New American Community Survey Statistics for Income, Poverty and Health Insurance Available for States and Local Areas." September 13. www.census.gov/newsroom/press-releases/2018/acs-1year.html.

van Eck Peluchette, Joy, and Sandy Jeanquart. 2000. "Professionals' Use of Different Mentor Sources at Various Career Stages: Implications for Career Success." *Journal of Social Psychology* 140 (5): 549–64.

Vongalis-Macrow, Athena. 2011. "Stopping the Mid-career Crisis." *Harvard Business Review*, September 7. https://hbr.org/2011/09/stopping-the-mid-career-crisis.

Walker, H. Jack, Hubert S. Feild, William F. Giles, Achilles A. Armenakis, and Jeremy B. Bernerth. 2009. "Displaying Employee Testimonials on Recruitment Web Sites: Effects of Communication Media, Employee Race, and Job Seeker Race on Organizational Attraction and Information Credibility." *Journal of Applied Psychology* 94 (5): 1354–64.

Ward, Kelly, and Lisa Wolf-Wendel. 2012. *Academic Motherhood: How Faculty Manage Work and Family*. New Brunswick, NJ: Rutgers University Press.

Weingart, Laurie R., Leigh L. Thompson, Max H. Bazerman, and John S. Carroll. 1990. "Tactical Behavior and Negotiation Outcomes." *International Journal of Conflict Management* 1 (1): 7–31.

Williams, Joan. 2000. *Unbending Gender: Why Work and Family Conflict and What to Do about It*. New York: Oxford University Press.

Williams, Lawrence E., and John A. Bargh. 2008. "Experiencing Physical Warmth Promotes Interpersonal Warmth." *Science* 322 (5901): 606–7.

Williams, Wendy M., and Stephen J. Ceci. 2015. "STEM Faculty Prefer Hiring Women Professors 2:1." *Proceedings of the National Academy of Sciences*, April 13. doi:10.1073/pnas.1418878112.

Wolfinger, Nicholas H., Mary Ann Mason, and Marc Goulden. 2008. "Problems in the Pipeline: Gender, Marriage, and Fertility in the Ivory Tower." *Journal of Higher Education* 79 (4): 388–405.

Wrzesniewski, Amy, and Jane E. Dutton. 2001. "Crafting a Job: Revisioning Employees as Active Crafters of Their Work." *Academy of Management Review* 26 (2): 179–201.

Yun, Jung H., Brian Baldi, and Mary Deane Sorcinelli. 2016. "Mutual Mentoring for Early-Career and Underrepresented Faculty: Model, Research, and Practice." *Innovative Higher Education* 41 (5): 441–51.

Zahneis, Megan. 2018. "Women of Color in Academe Make 67 Cents for Every Dollar Paid to White Men." *Chronicle of Higher Education*, June 11. www .chronicle.com/article/Women-of-Color-in-Academe-Make/243636.

Index

Academic Leadership Institute, 9, 60

academy: experience of women in other countries in, 68; gender differences in positions held in, 67–68, 70; gender pay gap in, 67–68; as men-dominated workplace, 67; negative experiences and intentions to leave, 96; racism and sexism in, 96, 114; women's experiences in, 10, 69, 95–96, 140; women's leadership in, 70, 140; women's progress and positions held in, 67–68

activities for discovering joy, 25, 208; career mapping, 34–35; job crafting, 28–34; questions activity, 25–28

administrative work: as evaluation category in promotion, 90–91; example of list of, 90–91; gender differences in, 140; midcareer stage responsibilities for, 4–5, 23–24; posttenure increase in roles and responsibilities in, 90; women faculty in, 70

administrators: barriers to women's career advancement reviewed by, xi; support in midcareer stage and, 16

ADVANCE program, National Science Foundation, 47, 139, 159

advising, on promotion applications, 85–87

age, and gender pay gap, 67

agency: job crafting and, 29; in midcareer stage, x, 17–18

Albion College, 3, 4, 51, 95; four forms of scholarship at, 121–22; Gerstacker Institute of Business and Management at,

100; international students at, 102; mentoring and institutional policies at, 189–90; Office of Institutional Advancement at, 100–101; professional reach example for, 99–105; promotion and tenure at, 59, 71–73; SPU framework at, 121–22; survey of women full professors at, 193–201; teaching evaluations at, 83

American Association of University Professors (AAUP), 68; "Statement on Government of Colleges and Universities," 164–65, 167

American Association of University Women, 159

American Community Survey, 67

American Council on Education, 67; Fellows Program of, 160

American Educational Research Association, 34

associate professors: decision not to pursue full professorship by, 40; gender differences in number of, 68; gender differences in time spent on service or research by, 24; importance of focusing on transition to full professor from, 191–93; promotion eligibility and length of time as, 43; stalled midcareer stage and, 17

Associate Professor Survey (Modern Language Association), 158

"Atta Girl" folders, 49–51

audience: persuasive voice and, 179–80; in SPU framework, 123, 131–32

Austin, Ann, 16, 34–35
Australia, women in academic positions in, 68
authority, and persuasive power, 176–78
awards and recognition, 81–82, 87

Baker-Pifer Research and Publication Plan, 52–53
Baldwin, Roger, 15, 16
Bednar-Clark, Debra, 181
Benchmarking Women's Leadership in the United States (Lennon), 94
Berg, Justin, 29
bias. *See* gender bias
bisexual faculty. *See* lesbian, gay, bisexual, and transgender (LGBT) faculty
Black women: emotional and physical exhaustion of nonresearch activities of, 48–49; stalled midcareer stage and, 17. *See also* minority women; women of color
boldness, during promotion process, 195–96
Boyer, Ernest, 12, 119; forms of scholarship concept of, 28, 118–19, 120, 121, 122, 123, 135; *Scholarship Reconsidered*, 118, 119
BRIDGES program, University of North Carolina (UNC), 160
Buch, Kimberly, 156, 158

Canada, women in academic positions in, 68
career advancement: advice and suggestions on, from women full professors, 193–201; biases as obstacles to, 94, 96–97; charting your path to full in, 3–4; lack of opportunities for women in, 70; need for strategic approach to, 97; obstacles to, 93–97; organization's importance in, 38; strategies in, 194–99; women faculty's desire to have a family and, 69. *See also* faculty development; promotion process; tenure process
career mapping, 34–35, 208–9
career support, in mentoring, 137, 149–50, 151
Ceci, Stephen, 140

chairs of committees or task forces as service, 89. *See also* department chairs
Chambers, Crystal Renée, 108
Chang, Deborah, 16
child care: gender bias in treatment of faculty parents' need for, 22, 143; policies on, 143; women faculty and, 5, 69, 197
children, gender bias in organization's response to faculty with, 22, 143
Cialdini, Robert, 166, 167, 169, 173, 176, 179, 183–84, 213
Clark, Burton, 119
cognitive crafting, 29, 33–34
collaboration: gender bias in judging, 180; project tracking sheets in, 52–54; women leaders and, 163–64
College of Wooster, 9
commitment, and persuasive power, 173–74
community colleges: challenges to women's advancement in, xii; example of scholarship expectations at, 81; promotion and tenure decisions in, 41
community engagement: focusing on joy in, 27–28; implications of lack of support for, 17; as service, 89
comprehensive universities: challenges to women's advancement in, xii; promotion and tenure decisions in, 41
conferences: meeting senior scholars at, 137–38; project tracking sheets for, 54; publication of presentations at, 54; service at, 88–89; teaching-focused presentations at, 87
consistency, and persuasive power, 173–74
content, in SPU framework, 123–24, 132–33
continuing contract status: criteria for earning, 40, 41–43; process of earning, 40, 42–43
contrast effect, 179
course evaluations, 82
course-specific details, on promotion applications, 87
Covey, Stephen, 46, 47, 48, 52
credibility, and gender bias, 182
criteria catalog, 59–60
Croom, Natasha, 17, 114

culture of institution: mentoring support in, 143, 157–60; thriving environment for midcareer faculty members and, 20

curricula vitae (CVs): focus on clarity of purpose and scope in, 73; headings as guideposts in, 75; highlights snapshot at beginning of, 75–77; promotion and tenure process with, 23

Curtis, John, 68

customization of narratives, 108–14

deans: career-planning support from, 213; gender differences in, 140; institutional strategic priorities from, 104; mentoring support by, 48, 142, 143, 144, 160; as mentors for promotion plan to full professor, 142; presentation of research and, 178

decision-making: role of joy in, 24–25; strategic planning and, 98

De Janasz, Suzanne, 136

department chairs: barriers to women's career advancement reviewed by, xi; career-planning support from, 213; gender differences in, 140; going up early for tenure at Albion College and, 71–73; holding position as limitation to promotion to full professor, 141, 142; lack of mentoring from, 155; mentoring support by, 140, 142; midcareer women as, 141; as primary mentor for promotion to full professor, 141–42; relational crafting and, 31; as service role, 113; strategic priorities and, 103–4; support for midcareer women from, 143–44

departments: professional reach and role or position in, 99; relational crafting for toxic environment in, 31–33; service in, 88; strategic partnerships with, 100–101

development. *See* faculty development

disciplines: reaching out to full professors in, for assistance in promotion process, 42; variation in number of women professors according to, 142–43

discovery, in Boyer's forms of scholarship, 120, 121

early-career stage: formal mentoring programs for, 155; midcareer stage compared with, 14; research and practice focused on, 15, 16

Eddy, Pamela, ix–xii, 34

elder care, 5, 69, 197

engagement, in Boyer's forms of scholarship, 120, 121

environmental factors, and persuasive power, 178–79

environmental scan, 144–45

Erlandson, Karen, 101, 162–87, 213

Europe, women in academic positions in, 68

evaluation categories, 74–75. *See also* scholarship/research; service; teaching

evaluations, gender bias in, 94, 95

external reviewers, 43

Facebook, 95, 167, 181, 193

faculty development: Boyer's four forms of scholarship and, 119; focusing on joy as first step in planning in, 21–22; midcareer supports and, 16, 17; positive organizational scholarship and, 18

faculty members: support in midcareer stage and, 16. *See also* women faculty members

family: career advancement and women's desire for, 69; child-care and elder-care responsibilities in, 5, 69, 197; gender bias in policies on children in, 22, 143

feedback: "Atta Girl" folders of email with, 49–51; gender bias in, 95; for midcareer women faculty, 147, 148

female faculty members. *See* women faculty members

"Five Must Haves and Five Can't Stands" exercise, 202–4

"5 Ways to Shut Down Mansplaining" (*Forbes*), 181

Forbes, 181

Franklin, Ben, 183

full professorships: associate professors' decision not to pursue, 40; criteria for earning, 40, 41–43; department chair position as limitation to seeking, 141,

full professorships (*continued*)
142; focusing on joy as first step in planning for, 21–22; gender differences in number of, 68; go-to strategies for seeking, 49–54; importance of focusing on transition to, 191–93; posttenure increase in roles and responsibilities as detriment to, 90; process of earning, 40, 42–43; queries about how to prepare for, 21; reaching out to, for assistance in promotion process, 42; where and how to begin seeking, 44–49

Gantt charts, 51, 52
gap analysis, 153–54
gay faculty. *See* lesbian, gay, bisexual, and transgender (LGBT) faculty; queer faculty
gender, as dominant factor in workforce experience of women, 66–67
gender bias: as obstacle to career advancement, 94, 96–97; documenting in promotion application, 82, 94; organization's response to faculty with children and, 22, 143; persuasive voice and, 163–64, 180–82; teaching expectations and, 94–95
gender differences: academic leadership and, 70, 140; academic positions held and, 67–68, 70; experiences in the academy and, 69; length of time to attain promotion, 158; pay gap and, 67–68; service and, 24, 144; stalled midcareer stage and, 17; time spent on research or service and, 24
Gerstacker Institute of Business and Management, Albion College, 100
goals: decision not to pursue full professorship and, 40; eliminating distracting tasks and focusing on, 45–46; focus on joy and, 26; future orientation in setting, 145–46; importance of writing down goals, 44, 45; promotion and setting, 38–40, 44–46; specific focus of, 45; SPU framework with, 122, 131; strategic planning with, 98
Goldsmith, Marshall, 147

Google Scholar, 77
go-to strategies, for promotion, 49–54
Goulden, Marc, 22
grants: details included with, 80; examples of listing of, 80–81
Great Lakes Colleges Association (GLCA), 9, 71, 80, 100
Griffin, Kimberly, 48

Harvard Business School (HBS), 46, 103
Haviland, Don, 75
headings and subheadings: in curricula vitae (CVs), 75; in narratives, 109, 111, 112, 113
help seeking, during promotion process, 196–98
Henriques, Laura, 75
higher education: gender differences in positions held in, 67–68; influence of Boyer's forms of scholarship on, 119
Higher Education Leadership Program for Women, 160
Higher Education Research Institute, 17
hiring process: gender differences in, 140; need for review of policies in, 94
"How to Deal with People Who Interrupt" (*Psychology Today*), 181–82

important-versus-urgent exercise, in time management, 60–62
institutional culture: mentoring support in, 143, 157–60; thriving environment for midcareer faculty members and, 20
institutions: clarity about strategic priorities of, 103–4; connecting professional reach to priorities and imperatives of, 102–5; mentoring networks and, 139; professional reach and role at, 99–100
integration, in Boyer's forms of scholarship, 120

Jenkins, Jerry, 182
job crafting, 28–34; cognitive crafting technique in, 29, 33–34; as continual process, 29–30; description of, 28–29; relational crafting technique in, 29, 31–33; task crafting technique in, 29, 30–31

Johnson, Heather, 68
Johnson, Lyndon B., 163
Johnson, W. Brad, 149, 150
joy, 14–37, 208–9; career mapping activity
for, 34–35; day-to-day activities steered
by, 15; decision-making and, 24–25;
definition of, 14; experience of, after
promotion and tenure, 23; focusing on,
as first step in development planning,
21–22; job crafting activity for, 28–34;
midcareer stage refocusing for, 14–15;
positive organizational psychology and,
18–20; questions activity for discovering focus on, 25–28; to-do list for, 35;
women professors' expression of range
of activities in, 23

Klauser, Henriette Anne, 38, 45–46, 52

LACs. See liberal arts colleges (LACs)
Latham, Gary, 178
leadership positions: gender bias and styles
of, 163–64; gender differences in, 70, 140
learning: attraction of future faculty to
professoriate and, 20; individuals' institutional setting and, 119; thriving workplace and, 19
least publishable unit (SMU). See smallest
publishable unit (SMU)
Lennon, Tiffani, 94
lesbian, gay, bisexual, and transgender
(LGBT) faculty: experiences in the
academy of, 69, 96. See also queer faculty
Lester, Jaime, 34
letters of support: dossier in promotion
process with, 43; example of, 72
Levinson, Daniel, 141
Levinson, Judy, 141
LGBT faculty. See lesbian, gay, bisexual,
and transgender (LGBT) faculty
liberal arts colleges (LACs): challenges
to women's advancement in, xii; early-
career faculty socialization in, 3; increasing importance of scholarly productivity
in, 74; relative weight of teaching,
research, and service to promotion in,
41, 74; teaching as priority in, 74

liking principle, and persuasive power,
169–72
Lunceford, Christina, 16
Lunsford, Laura Gail, 52, 60, 62, 136–61,
189, 212, 213

male faculty members. See men faculty
members
mansplaining, 181
mapping, career, 34–35, 208–9
Mason, Mary Ann, 22
Mathews, Kiernan, 16
McCracken, Douglas, 70
meetings: time-management hacks for,
62–63; urgent-versus-important exercise
for, 60–62
men: gender pay gap and, 67–68; women's
experience of workplace related to
number of, 66–67
men faculty members: child-care policies
and, 22, 143; leadership roles of, 70; as
mentors for women, 143; relational crafting for toxic departmental environment
with, 31–33; stalled midcareer stage and,
17. See also gender differences
mentoring, 136–61, 212–13; associate professors and, 143–44; career support in,
137, 149–50, 151; containment in, 156–57;
creating culture for, 157–60; design in,
157; environmental scan for conditions
in, 144–45; example of using during promotion and later moves, 137–38; external
opportunities for, 160; four steps in,
139; future orientation in working with,
145–47; gap analysis in, 153–54; as high-
visibility activity, 158–59; identifying and
seeking opportunities for, 155; importance of, 47; informal versus formal,
150; institutions and, 139; integration in,
156; mentoring defined, 137; midcareer
faculty members and, 139, 147–48; mismatch in, 152; neglectful behavior in,
152; number of mentors useful in, 156; as
personal board of advisers, 149; personal
growth support in, 150, 151; pilot program for, 159–60; pracademic and, 137;
promotion and, 136; psychosocial

mentoring (*continued*)
support in, 137, 149–50, 151; reluctance
to use, 138; strategies in, 156–57; SWOT
analysis during, 148–49; timing for
advancing to full professorship and, 190;
what is (and is not) included in, 149–52
mentors: cultivating new mentors, 154–55;
defined, 137; men as, 143; mismatch with,
152; need for opportunities for women to
develop as, 143; peer mentors, 129, 138,
143, 155, 157, 160, 193; promotion process
and use of, 48, 141; "Quick Start Guide"
for finding, 48, 64; ways to be a good
mentor, 160
method, in SPU framework, 124, 133–34
#MeToo movement, 66
midcareer faculty members: implications of lack of support for, 17; positive
organizational scholarship and, 19–20;
role of joy in balancing academic work
and motherhood by, 24–25; as terminal
associate professors, 16
midcareer stage, 4–6; administrative and
service expectations in, 4–5, 23–24;
agency in, x, 17–18; early-career stage
compared with, 14; examples of feelings about, 5; "Five Must Haves and
Five Can't Stands" exercise for managing, 202–4; lack of clarity about length
of, 15–16; mentoring needs of, 147–48;
mentoring philosophy of, 139; multifaceted approach needed in, 36; overview of, 15–18; positive organizational
scholarship and, 18–20; refocusing and
having joy as part of, 14–15; research
and practice focused on, 15, 34; strategic
approach to career management by, 97;
support needed in, 16, 17; tenure system
and start of, 16; two categories of, 16
midcareer malaise, 16
Milgram, Stanley, 177
minority women: expectations and burdens of, 26–27; experiences in the
academy of, 95–96; narratives of, 115;
promotion challenges for, 24. *See also*
Black women; women of color
Misra, Joya, 24

Modern Language Association, *Associate
Professor Survey*, 158
motherhood: challenges to academic
careers of, 22–23; role of joy in balancing
academic work and, 24–25; scholarship
and, 23
Murray, Susan, 22
"Must Haves and Can't Stands" exercise,
202–4

narratives, 92–115, 210–11; "Atta Girl"
folders of email used in constructing,
50–51; building a strategic foundation
for, 97–102; "check the box" trap in, 93;
connecting professional reach to institutional priorities and imperatives in,
102–5; customizing, 108–14; determining
professional reach in, 98–102; dossier in
promotion process with, 43; example of,
92–93; examples of experiences crafting, 105–8; grants in, 80–81; headings
and subheadings used in, 109, 111, 112,
113; highlights snapshot at beginning
of, 75–77; need for clear and deliberate strategies for crafting, 96; obstacles
to advancement and, 93–97; personnel
committee members as audience for, 42;
publication and creative works in, 77–80;
reaching out to full professor for copy of,
for assistance in promotion process, 42;
scholarly awards and recognition and,
81–82; scholarship on, 111–12; service on,
113–14; teaching on, 109–11
National Center for Education Statistics
(NCES), 7
National Science Foundation, 80, 140;
ADVANCE program, 47, 139, 159; Survey
of Earned Doctorates of, 140
NCES (National Center for Education
Statistics), 7
Neumann, Anna, 156

O'Donnell, Peggy, 93
O'Meara, KerryAnn, x, 119
organizational software tools, 51
organizations: boldness in dealing with,
196; as career building block, 38, 44, 64,

209–10; challenges of motherhood and caregiving and policies of, 22–23; criteria for full professorship or continuing contract status at, 40, 41–43; goal setting and, 38–40; impact of disengaged midcareer faculty members on, 16–17; importance of, in career advancement, 38; knowing rules of the game in, 198–99; midcareer agency and conditions in, 17–18; need for review of hiring and promotion policies in, 94; positive organizational scholarship on positive behaviors in, 18–20; process of earning full professorship or continuing contract status at, 40, 42–43; relational crafting for toxic departmental environment in, 31–33; relative weight of teaching, research, and service in promotion related to type and mission of, 41, 42; strategic partnerships in, 100–101; thriving environment and, 19–20

Ortiz, Ann, 75

Owen, Whitney, 118

parents, women faculty members as: child care and, 5, 69, 197; gender bias in policies on, 22, 143

parents of faculty members, care for, 5, 69, 197

Parker, Kim, 66

pay gap: academy and, 67–68; workforce and, 67

peer mentoring, 129, 138, 143, 155, 157, 160, 193

peer support system, 195

Penn State University, 65, 95, 116

performance, 65–91, 210; clarity of purpose and scope in CV and, 73; diversity of ways of organizing materials on, 74; evaluation categories in, 74–75; going up early for tenure at Albion College and, 71–73; overview of women in the workforce and, 66–70; women's reluctance to talk about their accomplishments in, 65

personal growth support, in mentoring, 150

personnel committee members: as audience for narratives, 42; contacting for insights on promotion process, 42–43

persuasive voice, 162–87, 213; authority and, 176–78; case studies for, 182–87; common problems and ways to deal with them in, 180–82; consistency and commitment and, 173–74; contrast effect in, 179; environmental factors in, 178–79; example of, 164–65; gender bias and, 163–64, 180–82; importance of, 163–64; interruptions and, 180–81; knowing audience in, 179–80; liking and, 169–72; mansplaining and, 181; moments of power in, 183–84; obstacles to, 162; planning and, 184–86; reciprocity and, 172–73; scarcity and, 175–76; setting the context in, 178–79; six principles for improving power of, 166–78; social proof and, 167–69

philosophy of teaching, 109–10

Pifer, Meghan J., 52–53

planning: "Five Must Haves and Five Can't Stands" exercise for, 202–4; for persuasive events, 184–86; priorities assessment in, 204–7

Porath, Christine, 18, 19

positive organizational scholarship, 15, 18–20; description of, 18–19; goal of, 18; job crafting and, 29; midcareer faculty members and, 19–20; thriving workplace concept in, 19

pracademic, 137

practice, in Boyer's forms of scholarship, 118

presidential positions, women in, 70, 140

Pre-suasion (Cialdini), 178

priorities assessment, 204–7

process, in SPU framework, 124, 134

professional reach, 98; connecting institutional priorities and imperatives to, 102–5; questions for determining, 99–102; to-do list for, 102

projects: tracking sheets for, 51–54; twenty-four-hour rule for, 63, 148; urgent-versus-important exercise for, 60–62

project tracking sheets, 51–54

promotion process: administrative work and, 90–91; advice and suggestions on, from women full professors, 193–201; as application process versus award after length of time as associate professor, 43; asking for help during, 196–98; associate professors' decision not to pursue, 40; "Atta Girl" folders of email in, 49–51; boldness needed during, 195–96; Boyer's forms of scholarship and, 118; "check the box" trap in, 93; contacting personnel committee members for insights on, 42–43; crafting narrative in, 41; criteria catalog used during, 59–60; diversity of ways of organizing materials in, 74; documents needed in dossier in, 43; environmental scan for conditions in, 144–45; evaluation categories in, 74–75; finding out about criteria for, 40, 41–43; finding out about details of, 40, 42–43; friendly reviews within and outside your disciplinary area during, 42; gender-biased evaluations in, 94; gender differences in length of time in, 158; goal setting and, 38–40; going up early for, at Albion College, 71–73; go-to strategies for seeking, 49–54; hacks for reclaiming time during, 62–63; importance of focusing on transition to full professor in, 191–93; institution type and mission differences affecting criteria in, 41, 42; knowing rules of the game in, 198–99; lack of explicit metrics and consistency in, 41; mentoring component of, 136; need for review of policies in, 94; organization's importance in, 38; process of earning, 40, 42–43; project tracking sheet in, 51–54; racism and sexism in, 96, 114; reaching out to full professors in your discipline for assistance in, 42; relative weight of teaching, research, and service in, 41–42, 74–75; scholarship/research and, 75–82; service and, 87–89; service and administrative work versus research and scholarly pursuits in, 24; seven-habits approach during, 46–49; strategies in, 194–99; SWOT analysis

during, 55–58; teaching and, 82–87; timing for advancing to full professorship and, 190; to-do lists for, 44, 54; urgent-versus-important exercise on time management for, 60–62; where and how to begin seeking, 44–49
Psychology Today, 181–82
psychosocial support, in mentoring, 137, 149–50, 151
publication metrics, 43
publications: conference presentations turned into, 54; dossier in promotion process with, 43; prepopulated forms for listing, 78; project tracking sheets for, 54; scholarship of teaching and, 120–21; scholarship/research category and organization of, 77–80; to-do list for, 79. *See also* smallest publishable unit (SMU)
purpose: administrative work on promotion applications and, 91; clarity in CV on, 73

queer faculty: experiences in the academy of, 10, 69. *See also* lesbian, gay, bisexual, and transgender (LGBT) faculty
"Quick Start Guide" for finding mentors, 48, 64

racism, 96, 114
Ray, Victor, 94
reciprocity, and persuasive power, 172–73
recognition and awards, 81–82, 87
Regan, Dennis, 172
Reinert, Leah, 96
relational crafting, 29, 31–33
research: Boyer's forms of scholarship with, 118; exhaustion from nonresearch activities preventing, 48–49; gender differences in time spent on, 24; institution type and mission differences affecting promotion criteria with, 41, 42; lack of explicit metrics and consistency in promotion process and, 41; liberal arts colleges' increasing emphasis on, 41; as priority in research universities, 74; project tracking sheets in, 51–54; scholarship

of discovery and, 120, 121. *See also* scholarship/research
research universities: challenges to women's advancement in, xii; promotion and tenure decisions in, 41, 74; research evaluation in, 74
resumes, headings as guideposts in, 75
Rice, R. Eugene, 119
Rising Tide Center for Gender Equity, 191
Ross School of Business, University of Michigan, 18

scarcity principle, and persuasive power, 175–76
schedules: twenty-four-hour rule in, 63, 148; urgent-versus-important exercise with, 60–62
Schell, Julie, 156
scholarly awards and recognition, 81–82
scholarship: Boyer's forms of, 118–21, 122, 123; of discovery, 120, 121; of engagement, 121; of integration, 120; of teaching, 120–21
Scholarship Reconsidered (Boyer), 118, 119
scholarship/research: as evaluation category, 74, 75–82; example of narrative with, 111–12; grants and, 80–81; headings and subheadings in, 112; highlights snapshot of, 75–77; motherhood and, 23; on narratives, 111–12; promotion and relative weight of teaching and service and, 41, 74–75; publication and creative works in, 77–80, 111; range of forms of, 111; scholarly awards and recognition and, 81–82; smallest publishable unit (SMU) advantages for, 117; women of color and devaluation of, 95–96. *See also* research
science professors, and gender differences in hiring, 140
scope: administrative work on promotion applications and, 91; clarity in CV on, 73
service: categories included in, 88–89; community engagement as, 89; as evaluation category, 74, 87–89; example of narrative with, 113–14; expectations of women for, 70, 89, 144; gender differences in time spent on, 24; highlights

snapshot of, 75–77, 87–88; institution type and mission differences affecting promotion criteria with, 41, 42; lack of explicit metrics and consistency in promotion process and, 41; midcareer stage responsibilities for, 4–5, 23–24; on narratives, 113–14; posttenure increase in roles and responsibilities in, 90; promotion and relative weight of teaching and research and, 41, 74, 75, 89; range of forms of, 113; subheadings used in, 113; taking care in accepting, 89
7 Habits of Highly Effective People, The (Covey), 46–49
sexism, 93, 96, 114
Shantz, Amanda, 178
Simple Truth about the Gender Pay Gap, The (AAUW), 67
smallest publishable unit (SMU), 116–35, 211–12; advantages of, 117; applying to your work, 132–34; audience in, 123, 131–32; content in, 123–24, 132–33; definition of, 116; examples of experiences using, 125–31; four components of, 123–24; framework for, 121–25; goals and subgoals in, 122, 131; method in, 124, 133–34; process in, 124, 134
Smith, David, 149, 150
social proof, and persuasive power, 167–69
Spreitzer, Gretchen, 18, 19
Standing Still: The Associate Professor Survey (Modern Language Association), 158
"Statement on Government of Colleges and Universities" (American Association of University Professors), 164–65, 167
STEM fields, 46, 69
strategic approach: career management with, 97; connecting professional reach to institutional priorities and imperatives in, 102–5; determining professional reach in, 98–102; two-step process in, 98
strategic planning: benefits of using, 98; career-management efforts based on, 98; connecting professional reach to institutional priorities and imperatives in, 102–5; definition of, 97–98; process of, 98

strategic priorities: clarifying, 103–4; connecting professional reach to, 104–5; to-do list for, 105
Strickland, Donna, 189
Sullivan, Sherry, 136
Survey of Earned Doctorates, National Science Foundation, 140
SWOT (strengths, weaknesses, opportunities, and threats) analysis, 42, 55–58; description of, 55; questions to ask based on content of, 57–58; steps in using, 56–57
synthesis, in Boyer's forms of scholarship, 118, 120

task crafting, 29, 30–31, 45
teaching: advising and, 85–87; Boyer's forms of scholarship with, 118, 120–21; course-specific details on, 87; as evaluation category, 74, 82–87; evolution of activities included in, 82; example of narrative with, 109–11; focusing on joy in, 30–31; gender bias and expectations in, 94–95; highlights snapshot of, 75–77, 82; institution type and mission differences affecting promotion criteria with, 41, 42; lack of explicit metrics and consistency in promotion process and, 41; on narratives, 109–111; promotion and relative weight of research and service and, 41, 74, 75; range of forms of, 109; subheadings for, 109, 111; teaching awards and other recognition on, 87; teaching evaluations included with, 82–83; teaching excellence section in, 82, 84–85; teaching philosophy overview for, 109–10; ways of organizing information under, 82–84
teaching awards, 87
teaching evaluations: gender bias in, 95; on promotion applications, 82–83
teaching excellence, on promotion applications, 82, 84–85
tenure, midcareer stage start in, 16
tenure process: administrative work and, 90–91; advice and suggestions on, from women full professors, 193–201; as

application process versus award after length of time as associate professor, 43; asking for help during, 196–98; "Atta Girl" folders of email in, 49–51; boldness needed during, 195–96; Boyer's forms of scholarship and, 118; "check the box" trap in, 93; contacting personnel committee members for insights on, 42–43; criteria catalog used during, 59–60; diversity of ways of organizing materials in, 74; documents needed in dossier submitted in, 43; dossier in promotion process with, 43; evaluation categories in, 74–75; finding out about criteria for, 40, 41–43; finding out about details of, 40, 42–43; friendly reviews within and outside your disciplinary area during, 42; gender-biased evaluations in, 94; gender differences in length of time in, 158; going up early for, at Albion College, 71–73; hacks for reclaiming time during, 62–63; importance of focusing on transition to full professor in, 191–93; institution type and mission differences affecting criteria in, 41, 42; knowing rules of the game in, 198–99; lack of explicit metrics and consistency in, 41; number of years as associate professors and eligibility for, 43; project tracking sheet in, 51–54; racism and sexism in, 96, 114; reaching out to full professors in your discipline for assistance in, 42; relative weight of teaching, research, and service in, 41–42, 74–75; scholarship/research and, 75–82; service and, 87–89; service and administrative work versus research and scholarly pursuits in, 24; seven-habits approach during, 46–49; SWOT analysis during, 55–58; teaching and, 82–87; timing for advancing to full professorship and, 190; to-do lists for, 44, 54; urgent-versus-important exercise on time management for, 60–62
Terosky, Aimee LaPointe, 34, 156
Thompson, George, 182
thriving: midcareer faculty members and, 19–20; workplace concept of, 19

time management: hacks for reclaiming time in, 62–63; meetings and, 62–63; twenty-four-hour rule in, 63, 148; urgent-versus-important exercise for, 60–62

to-do lists: for discovering joy, 35; for professional reach, 102; for promotion process, 44, 54; for publications organization, 79; for strategic priorities, 105

transgender faculty. *See* lesbian, gay, bisexual, and transgender (LGBT) faculty

Trello organizational tool, 51

Twain, Mark, 175

twenty-four-hour rule, 63, 148

United States Department of Labor statistics, 66

University of Arizona, 159

University of Massachusetts, 144

University of Michigan, Ross School of Business, 18

University of North Carolina (UNC): BRIDGES program at, 160; at Charlotte, 157; at Wilmington, 158–59

urgent-versus-important exercise, in time management, 60–62

Vanderlinden, Kim, 16

Vanzant, Iyanla, 172

Verbal Judo (Thompson and Jenkins), 182

visualization of goals, 45

vitality, in thriving workplace, 19

Vongalis-Macrow, Athena, 3

Ward, Kelly, xii, 6, 34, 66, 90

Waters, Maxine, 38

Williams, Wendy, 140

Wolfinger, Nicholas, 22

Wolf-Wendel, Lisa, xii, 6, 66, 90

women: gender as dominant factor in workforce experience of, 66–67; gender pay gap and, 67–68; higher education and, 67–68; percentage holding college degrees in the workforce, 66; talking about their accomplishments by, 65; workforce and, 66–67

women associate professors: charting your path to full by, 3–4; expectations and burdens of, 26–27; gender-biased evaluations and feedback and, 94, 95; gender differences in, 140; importance of focusing on transition to full professor from, 191–93; job crafting and agency of, 29; lack of explicit metrics and consistency in promotion process and, 41; mentoring and, 143–44; need for review of hiring and promotion policies and, 94; pay gap and, 67; smallest publishable unit (SMU) advantages for, 117

women faculty members: academic leadership and, 70, 140; child-care and eldercare responsibilities of, 5, 22, 69, 143, 197; child-care policies and, 143; clear and deliberate strategies for crafting narratives by, 96; discipline and variation in number of, 142–43; experiences in the academy of, 69, 140; gender-biased evaluations and feedback and, 94, 95; gender differences in positions held by, 67–68, 70; gender pay gap and, 67–68; importance of focusing on transition to, 191–93; importance of mentorship for, 47; lag in academic positions held by, 67–68; need for review of hiring and promotion policies and, 94; NSF ADVANCE grant for mentoring, 47, 139; peer support system for, 195; role of joy in balancing academic work and motherhood by, 24–25; service expectations of, 70, 89; stalled midcareer stage and, 17; teaching expectations of, 94–95. *See also* gender differences

women full professors: advice and suggestions from, based on survey, 193–201; Albion College survey of, 193–201; department chair position as limitation to seeking, 141, 142; focusing on joy as first step in planning for, 21–22; gender differences in number of, 68; go-to strategies for seeking, 49–54; importance of focusing on transition to, 191–93; queries about how to prepare for, 21; posttenure increase in roles and responsibilities as

women full professors (*continued*)
detriment to, 90; process of earning, 40, 42–43; reaching out to, for assistance in promotion process, 42; strategies used by, 194–99; where and how to begin seeking, 44–49

women of color: devaluation of scholarly pursuits, 95–96; expectations and burdens of, 26–27; experiences in the academy of, 10, 69, 95–96; importance of mentorship for, 47; lack of explicit metrics and consistency in promotion process and, 41; negative experiences and intentions to leave academe by, 96; obstacles to advancement and, 93–97; promotion challenges for, 24; stalled midcareer stage and, 17; teaching excellence and, 95. *See also* Black women; minority women

workplace, gender as dominant factor in women's experience in, 66–67

Wrike organizational tool, 51

Write It Down, Make It Happen (Klauser), 45

Yakabowski, Tamara, 96

About the Author and Contributors

Vicki L. Baker, PhD, is a Fulbright Specialist and an expert in faculty and leadership development. She earned a BS in safety sciences from Indiana University of Pennsylvania, an MBA from Clarion University of Pennsylvania, and an MS in management and organizations and a PhD in higher education from the Pennsylvania State University. She regularly consults with higher-education and industry to help prepare the next generation of leaders, coaches, and mentors. She also serves as a career coach for academics as they seek to reenvision their careers and advance in the academy. Baker has published seventy peer-reviewed journal articles, book chapters, and essays on these topics. She is a professor of economics and management at Albion College and an instructor in business administration at the Pennsylvania State University's World Campus. Before becoming a faculty member, Baker held positions in Harvard Business School's Executive Education Division and worked at AK Steel Corporation. Baker was the principal investigator for a study titled the "Initiative for Faculty Development in Liberal Arts Colleges" and developed the Academic Leadership Institute for midcareer faculty members at the Great Lakes Colleges Association, funded by the Henry Luce Foundation. The National Science Foundation and Chemical Bank have also funded her work. She is lead author of *Developing Faculty in Liberal Arts Colleges: Aligning Individual Needs and Organizational Goals* and lead editor for *Success after Tenure: Supporting Mid-Career Faculty*. She is the cofounder of Lead Mentor Develop, LLC (www.leadmentordevelop.com).

Karen Erlandson, PhD, is a full professor and chair in the Department of Communication Studies at Albion College. After receiving her BA and MA in interpersonal communication from Michigan State University, Erlandson completed her PhD in interpersonal communication at the University of California, Santa Barbara. She started teaching at Albion College in 2002 and is in her tenth year serving as department chair. She has served on her institution's Faculty Steering Committee and Curriculum and Resources Committee, and she chaired the Strategic Planning Committee. Erlandson teaches courses in interpersonal and family communication, persuasion, communicating gender, intercultural communication, small group communication, professional communication, and public speaking. She holds several certifications including Robert Cialdini's "Principles of Persuasion," Paul Ekman's "Facial Action Coding and Micro-expression Recognition," and John Gottman's "Seven Principles" program.

Laura Gail Lunsford, PhD, is an expert in mentoring and leadership development. She earned a BA and PhD from North Carolina State University and an MS from the University of North Carolina–Greensboro. A frequent speaker and consultant on optimal relationships and leadership development, she has authored numerous peer-reviewed papers, chapters, and books on these topics. She is a professor of psychology and a department head at Campbell University. Previously, Lunsford was a tenured associate professor in psychology at the University of Arizona in Tucson. She has served as the director of UNCW's executive education center; founded the park scholarships at North Carolina State University; and served as Duke University's Fuqua School of Business's first alumni-relations director. She has a black belt in Shotokan karate and enjoys cycling and kayaking. As a board member of the International Mentoring Association, Lunsford was recently appointed to a National Academies Consensus Study on the Science of Effective Mentorship and is on the editorial board of the *International Journal of Mentoring and Coaching in Education.*